ALSO BY WIL HAYGOOD

Colorization: One Hundred Years of Black Films in a White World

Tigerland: 1968–1969: A City Divided, a Nation Torn Apart, and a Magical Season of Healing

Showdown: Thurgood Marshall and the Supreme Court Nomination That Changed America

The Butler: A Witness to History

Sweet Thunder: The Life and Times of Sugar Ray Robinson

In Black and White: The Life of Sammy Davis, Jr.

The Haygoods of Columbus: A Family Memoir

King of the Cats: The Life and Times of Adam Clayton Powell, Jr.

Two on the River (photography by Stan Grossfeld)

The War Within a War

The War Within a War

The Black Struggle in Vietnam and at Home

Wil Haygood

Alfred A. Knopf New York 2026

A BORZOI BOOK
FIRST HARDCOVER EDITION PUBLISHED BY ALFRED A. KNOPF 2026

Published by Alfred A. Knopf, a division of Penguin Random House LLC, 1745 Broadway, New York, NY 10019.

Knopf, Borzoi Books, and the colophon are registered trademarks of Penguin Random House LLC.

Library of Congress Cataloging-in-Publication Data
Names: Haygood, Wil, author.
Title: The war within a war : The Black struggle in Vietnam and at home / Wil Haygood.
Description: First hardcover edition. | New York : Alfred A. Knopf, 2026. | Includes bibliographical references and index.
Identifiers: LCCN 2025017002 | ISBN 9780593537695 (hardcover) | ISBN 9780593537701 (ebook)
Subjects: LCSH: Vietnam War, 1961–1975—Participation, African American | African American soldiers—Biography | Vietnam War, 1961–1975—Biography | African Americans—Civil rights—History—20th century | United States—Armed Forces—African Americans—History—20th century | United States—Race relations—History—20th century | LCGFT: Biographies.
Classification: LCC DS559.8.B55 H38 2026 | DDC 959.704/3092 [B]—dc23/eng/20250724
LC record available at https://lccn.loc.gov/2025017002

penguinrandomhouse.com | aaknopf.com

Printed in the United States of America
3rd Printing

The authorized representative in the EU for product safety and compliance is Penguin Random House Ireland, Morrison Chambers, 32 Nassau Street, Dublin D02 YH68, Ireland, https://eu-contact.penguin.ie.

For Gregory P. Crawford, who understood this mission.

And General Dennis L. Via, who opened doors.

We have seen white men betray the flag and fight to kill the Union; but in all that long, dreary war we never saw a traitor in a black skin.

—Presidential candidate James A. Garfield, in an August 6, 1880, address in New York City before thousands, including many Civil War veterans

Long, long before the Americans decided to liberate the Southeast Asians, they decided to liberate me: my ancestors carried these scars to the grave, and so will I. A racist society can't but fight a racist war—this is the bitter truth. The assumptions acted on at home are also acted on abroad, and every American Negro knows this, for he . . . was the first "Vietcong" victim. We were bombed first.

—James Baldwin

Vietnam was the first time this country had witnessed troops led by African Americans. Vietnam was really the beginning.

—Lloyd Austin III, four-star general, and the first Black man to assume the position of secretary of defense, in 2021

Contents

Part Two

INTRODUCTION

At the time—the year was 1967—it hardly registered to me, a little kid, that there were six Black active-duty soldiers serving in Vietnam who lived within thirty yards of my house in Columbus, Ohio. Larry Wilson, Robert Morris, and the Bolden brothers—Charles and Jimmy—were Army; Steve Collins and Skip Dunn were Marines. Skip, one of the best all-around athletes in the neighborhood, lived right across the street from me, and the Bolden brothers nine houses away on my block. Robert, Larry, and Steve lived on the next block over. I could cut through the alley and be on each one of their front porches in less than four minutes. Larry's brother, Mike, and I played a lot of basketball together. I played touch football with Skip's fleet-footed young brothers. Steve's sister, Beverly, would visit my sister Diane and sit on my family's front porch, contemplating the letters she'd write to her brother in Vietnam, telling him about the goings-on in our neighborhood.

Fort Hayes was the induction center near my neighborhood. It was just a forty-minute walk from my house—down to Fifth Avenue, a left up to Cleveland Avenue and a right, then just past the Timken factory—that would take you straight to the fort. I remem-

In the early years of the war, proportionately more Blacks were drafted than whites. Skip Dunn was one of six Black soldier-teenagers who lived within walking distance of the author's home in Columbus, Ohio. All six ended up in Vietnam.

ber peering through the gates as a kid; I recall seeing lots of jeeps and soldiers in green fatigues. The place seemed foreboding to me. The fort had been a military installation since the Civil War. Not every family in my neighborhood had a car. So there would be recruits from my neighborhood literally walking off to war.

The highly unusual number of Vietnam-fighting soldiers from one two-block radius became a kind of echo of Black America's sacrifice during that war: reports would come to reveal that in the early years Blacks were disproportionately being sent to the front of the battle lines in Vietnam when compared with whites. President Lyndon Johnson's Department of Defense came under sharp scrutiny when that fact was exposed. "We were three percent of the population at the time. And about thirteen percent of the troops being sent to the front lines were Black," the former Marine Steve Collins says.

Columbus was a conservative city, and it was segregated, like so much of America at the time. But our particular neighborhood didn't remind anyone of Mississippi or Alabama or all those horrific scenes of Blacks being beaten and water-hosed we were seeing on the nightly news. The Blacks on my street felt so prideful when Skip, the Bolden brothers, Larry, Robert, and Steve were spotted waltzing up and down the street. Skip even visited our junior-high school in his uniform on a day when soldiers who had attended the school and died in Vietnam were being honored. The soldiers in my neighborhood weren't shy about showing off their military dress. No one could tell me and my playmates that these cool cats in their sharp uniforms weren't the greatest generation, because they were the only generation we knew. Kids my age didn't realize the societal forces arrayed around this Black Vietnam generation. Local and national civil rights officials would soon have to sue the Columbus police and fire departments because of its discrimination against Black applicants. Growing up, we rarely saw a Black policeman or Black fireman. By default, war became a necessary career consideration for so many young Black men.

Skip, the Marine, was summoned home from the war because his stepdad had shot his mom in a murder-suicide tragedy. In the weeks after, I stared at their gray-painted house across the street as if there were ghosts inside. Larry reupped for a second tour of duty, just like Steve and Robert did. My friends believed that only badasses reupped for a second tour in a war, but Steve later told me, "It was because of a lack of job opportunities in the outside world. When I finally came home and couldn't find a job, I was ready to go to Australia and train to become a mercenary. But I finally got a job. I became a railroad brakeman for Norfolk & Western." The Bolden brothers hated the war. Both returned home with serious emotional issues. Skip, back home, set about caring for his eight siblings. As for Robert Morris, he didn't come home alive. He was killed in Vietnam.

Everyone on my street became accustomed to hearing the saxophone.

Maynard Brown would sit out on his front porch, diagonally across the street from my house, and wail. Some of the young soldiers back from Vietnam would go sit on his porch and chat and listen to his music. Maynard dispensed sage advice to us kids: Stay out of trouble; don't run in the street, because of the cars. And don't do drugs! Maynard himself became a heroin addict. It wasn't from Vietnam, because he didn't go. His demons were just the Black-man-in-America kind of demons.

One day, an ambulance appeared next door to Maynard's home. He had gone inside that house to visit a friend. The ambulance workers were inside for a long time. My sisters and I stood on our porch, as still as sentries, gazing across the street, wondering what had happened. The emergency workers finally came out carrying a stretcher with Maynard on it. He had died of a heroin overdose, slipping beneath the water in his neighbor's bathtub. A small story about the death appeared in the local newspaper. The county coroner said the marks on Maynard's arm "looked like a needle puncture mark, possibly made by taking some sort of injection."

Somewhere between the winds of history—and even Maynard's saxophone—lie many truths about Blacks who went to Vietnam and how their presence there shook up both America and the war itself. By 1970, my school classmates and I knew something was greatly amiss in our orbit: Ohio State University, just eight blocks from our neighborhood, had shut down for nearly two weeks because of campus demonstrations against the war and racial inequality. It was an eerie sight to traipse the campus and spot National Guard tanks rolling up and down North High Street. We wondered if the tanks might be coming for us.

No one really saw it coming, how this war would erupt and carve a new racial dynamic into the American mindset. Certainly not all those Black Baptist ministers in pulpits around the country. They had been so accustomed to extolling patriotism, to pointing out those in military uniform who were home on leave and sitting in their pews, asking them to stand up. The uniforms—Marine, Navy, Army, Air Force—looked so crisp. As if they'd never been worn before! The applause always was sweet and reverent, reminiscent of similar scenes during World War II and the Korean War inside those very churches. For many in America, the dawn of the sixties was as if the nation were beginning anew. A New Frontier, it was called. But before long, ominous rumblings were being felt. There were funerals inside those Negro churches, soldiers in horizontal positions, breathless. In my neighborhood, we paid respects to the departed—military or otherwise—at Bethany Baptist Church, which hosted an all-Black congregation. At first it was referred to as a foreign engagement. Then it was that walk-softly-and-carry-a-big-stick mumbo-jumbo.

Finally, it was called what it was: war.

The honeymoon for the Kennedy administration ended rather quickly. Black America, emerging from the fifties and still looking for freedom, never had a honeymoon. Demonstrations, from Louisiana to Mississippi, from Alabama to North Carolina and Ohio, had begun erupting. There was something so prideful and even cool about marching to the sounds of anthemlike songs such as Curtis Mayfield's "People Get Ready" or Sam Cooke's "A Change Is Gonna Come." The music was lyrical as well as political, and served up sly warnings to white America. Black-themed cultural TV shows began popping up. *Say Brother* out of Boston began addressing foreign affairs and colonialism. Conversations about Vietnam began floating around the audiences. Black writers had started making noise, catching the energy of the college kids who were marching and sitting at those segregated lunch counters. Even when they were desegregated, there was still quite a bit of anger. There was still disrespect. There were Off-Broadway plays about racism starring Blacks. But amidst this cultural revolution, buses were still bouncing through inner cities taking Black soldiers off to boot camps—and then to war.

Still, few things highlighted—and proved—Black America's love of America as much as their military service. Their grandparents and parents warmly referred to those in uniform as "Black boys," because the average age of Blacks going off to Vietnam was just nineteen. (It was slightly higher for white soldiers.) Many of those Black soldiers were emerging from America's ghettos, inner cities, and de facto segregated rural towns to go to a place they'd barely heard of to save the country, save the world, from the uncoiled snake of communism. And they were doing it full of a new kind of Black pride that America—and certainly the military—had never seen before.

As the months started to rumble by in Vietnam, slowly but surely, the narrative of Black anguish and protest took a sharp turn. By the time the calendar landed squarely on 1965—and as it moved beyond—a full-blown Second Revolution was beginning to grip America. That first Revolution—Abe Lincoln's cannons and his Emancipation Proclamation—was a century gone. Civil War blue was now Army-in-'Nam green, and still, segregation lay upon the land; too many of those Black church mothers were still having a hard time voting. So many Black soldiers on the ground in Southeast Asia were still wondering just how truly free their families were back home.

Not only did the ministers not see it coming—the thundering clash of Black soldiering and overdue freedom—but neither did the hardworking men with a lot of Ivy League degrees inside LBJ's White House. A lot of them had been Kennedy administration holdovers who stayed put following the president's assassination. They were also arrogant and full of hubris: the journalist David Halberstam mockingly referred to them as "the best and the brightest." They were white men sending a lot of Black boys off to war. And one way to get more of them to war came in the form of a deviously designed program called Project 100,000, which before long quadrupled and became Project 400,000. The program came from the numbers-crunching Secretary of Defense Robert McNamara.

The program gave court systems across America leeway to drop charges against those accused of criminal actions provided they'd agree to sign on with Uncle Sam. Nearly half in this targeted and specifically designed program were Black, and almost all were poor. It is little wonder that, proportionately, in the early years of the war, Blacks were the highest number being sent to the front lines.

In Vietnam, soldiers served twelve-month tours of duty, fighting, killing, being killed. Smoking dope, getting thrown into the brig, getting out of the brig, flying back home to riot-scarred cities. Coming back home alive and seeing more blood, more madness. There were earthmovers destroying their neighborhoods, digging up dirt to build freeways to get those white citizens out to the segregated suburbs! It wasn't easy to make sense of it all. Many of the soldiers had nightmarish dreams.

So—turn up James Brown on the stereo! Pass around that latest Malcolm X speech!

Black is beautiful. It was a hip catchphrase that caught on.

—

If you were in America and Black, war seemed like something out of a jittery and dangerous newsreel being shown around the globe. Vietnam, the big mystery of America, had been flooding the airwaves for nearly a decade. And right beside that picture were inner cities, burning, the streets filled with cries for Black freedom. The white farm communities were untouched. The white suburbs were left in peace. But Newark, New Jersey, certainly was not. In the summer of 1967, Newark—to cite just one city—experienced five days of eruption. The cause was police brutality; others would later point to deep-rooted racist practices of the city government, of the nation. Among the victims was twelve-year-old Joe Bass, Jr., a little Black boy frozen in a *Life* magazine photo, having been caught in crossfire, shot in the neck and thigh—"the inadvertent victim of the same shotgun blast that killed [another Negro victim]," according to the magazine. A total of forty-seven hundred police and National Guardsmen—rifles cocked and bayonets ready—were patrolling the streets of Newark. And firing back at snipers. It looked like a war zone, a link between America and Vietnam.

Vietnam was the war that made critics take stock of American society, of what exactly had been done to Black America. This was the war that helped—along with those civil rights marchers—bring so much into mass focus: bad housing, inferior medical care, uneven crime and punishment, corporate America's racial belligerence, not even a semblance of integration among college faculties. Vietnam was but a tentacle of Black America's ongoing war. World War II had no soundtrack flowing from Black radio. Vietnam did: Here's Edwin Starr—himself a Black Vietnam veteran—and a line from his hit song about the war:

It ain't nothing but a heartbreaker
Friend only to the undertaker.

The Vietnam years got dark and edgy and witchy and funky and horrific rather quickly. Too many Black soldiers were returning Stateside and getting zonked out on drugs that they had first taken in Vietnam. Being hauled into prisons. Singing the blues. Blaming

Vietnam, which haunted them. No one seemed able to decipher how deep the gashing would be in the American ideal of freedom and war—and the Black fighting man. The writer James Baldwin had started going around telling friends that every Vietnamese village being bombed was just like another Black neighborhood in America being bombed.

In 1955, Harlem Congressman Adam Clayton Powell, Jr., attended the Bandung Conference in Indonesia. Twenty-nine Asian and African nations, representing more than half of the world's population, sent high-profile leaders. "I'm known throughout Africa," Powell, one of the few Blacks in Congress at the time, reminded the Eisenhower administration as an incentive for them to send him as a representative of the American government. The Eisenhower camp was spooked by the Cold War, by Russia's and China's maneuverings; they would do no such thing. But the cagey Powell secured an invitation from the Indonesian government—along with press credentials from the Black press—and flew off to Indonesia. (Before Powell departed, a CIA operative approached him and handed him a camera, imploring him to take photographs for the American government.) Powell knew American Blacks were keenly interested in the Bandung gathering; they hoped it would address their concerns about imperialism. The novelist Richard Wright was so intrigued about the gathering that he left Paris to attend. Western nations, the movers of capitalism—and vivid proof of millions living as second-class impoverished citizens in their countries—were downright skittish about such events. Among the most well-known leaders in attendance were Jawaharlal Nehru, prime minister of India; Chou En-lai of communist China; and Abdel Nasser of Egypt. (The Russians skipped the event but sent reporters.) Once everyone was assembled at Bandung, queries were lobbed at Congressman Powell about racism and segregation in his country. Powell told the press that America was improving its race relations. There were disbelieving eyes. Whispers were blowing in Bandung about the American political "advisers" already being seen in Vietnam. Four months after Powell returned from Bandung, young Emmett Till was murdered in Mississippi by white men for allegedly whistling at the store clerk Carolyn Bryant, the wife of one of the men. By the late 1960s, though Powell's political fortunes had darkened because of ethical woes, he came out in furious opposition to the Vietnam War, telling his admirers he had sensed all this from the worried noises he heard years earlier in Indonesia. But, weakened by scandal, Powell was no longer taken as a serious voice in American politics.

Here is what those Black boys returning from Vietnam and their twelve-month tours of duty saw through the looking glass of American headlines: Medgar Evers, shot dead in the driveway of his Jackson, Mississippi, home. Malcolm X, gunned down in Harlem. Martin Luther King, Jr., murdered in Memphis. Adam Clayton Powell, Jr., kicked out of Congress by a band of white House members. (They were later rebuked by the U.S. Supreme Court in a ruling that returned Powell to Congress, but without seniority.)

Vietnam was America's first fully integrated war. And the racial convulsions worried military leaders across all branches. More Blacks were eventually drafted into the Vietnam War than in any other war in American history. One of the little unreported facts in the early years of the war was that Black soldiers were also dying at a disproportionately higher rate than white soldiers. Why? Because they were sent to the front lines more often. Right where the Viet Cong were lying in wait.

So much about Vietnam had wrapped itself around Black America.

A lot of Black Southern women had seen it coming, had seen a time when their sons would be exhausted of playing pawns in a faraway war absent their own supposedly guaranteed freedom in America. But Black women so often found themselves on the very bottom rung of gaining respect—or an ear—from white mainstream society. In the 1960s in Mississippi—and many other places—their living conditions still mirrored the peonage-like living conditions of the 1920s. Many still worked on plantations. Now they began linking their struggle to get the vote with their sons' battles in Vietnam. In 1967, the Blacks of Sunflower County, Mississippi, lost another round of elections for their preferred candidates. A community meeting was convened for Black residents. Lela Mae Brooks never missed these meetings. Whites may have dismissed her as an uppity agitator, but she knew she had followers in the Black community. "Now I want ya'll to understand something," she said at the gathering, an edge in her voice. "We did not lose the election, the white folks stole it; like they stole our land, like they steal our commodities every month, like they stealin' our young men every day to go and fight their war in Vietnam, like they stole our great, great grandparents from Africa a long time ago." The "amen"s began swooping up and around her. She went on: "They think they can scare us with them guns in their cars; we not scared of them guns, and we want them to know it. If we were scared of them guns, we wouldn't even register to vote . . . Now, talk about Vietnam, it can be Vietnam right here; in Sunflower; in Mississippi . . ."

It was little wonder that President Kennedy had famously told an aide he feared the repercussions of Vietnam if the looming war were seen as "a white man's war." Military officials had little historical vision regarding the maelstrom they had dropped the Black soldier into in Vietnam. They were taken from one war—on the streets of America—to another, in a faraway land, and their ensuing narrative unfolded unlike any other in American history. White couldn't survive without Black and Black couldn't survive without white in the war; Black freedom could not be paused any longer, either. The struggle for freedom and equality in America had so often been drenched in blood: now war had become a natural cousin to that reality.

This chronicle will follow seven Black soldiers who served in Vietnam, along with a piano player and a reporter who played a part in the war. Each of them hailed from a different region of the nation. There will be cameos and diversions. I hope the combined stories—alongside the racial eruptions in America at the time—will illuminate a potent struggle for freedom that resonates in present-day America. "Negroes better than anyone else," said the Mississippi activist Bob Moses about Vietnam, "are in a position to question the war—not because they understand the war better, but because they better understand the United States."

Part One

CHAPTER ONE

DOC NELSON LANDS IN THE WAR ZONE

Elbert Nelson was happy to be on the campus of Meharry Medical College in 1964. He well knew how proud his parents—father an employee of the Southern Railway Company, mom employed in a dentist's office—were of his ambitions. Like most young Blacks interested in medicine, he had been inspired by the life of Charles Drew. Drew had been a stellar student and football star at Amherst College in the mid-1920s. Black publications wrote of his achievements. After college Drew became interested in medicine, but American medical schools were ignoring Black applicants, no matter how gifted academically. He left America to attend McGill University Medical School in Montreal. A pioneering career of fellowships and teaching stints followed. His breakthrough while studying the preservation of blood plasma—and consequently better shipping of blood—was known to have saved countless lives during World War II. Drew was only forty-five when he died in 1950 in a car accident, leaving many to wonder what other gifts he might have offered to worldwide medicine.

Meharry Medical School had been born from the nation's history of racial segregation. Howard University's medical school in Wash-

Elbert "Doc" Nelson was one of the few Black doctors in Vietnam. The eruption of the Watts rebellion, which took place in Los Angeles, convinced him that Black soldiers in Vietnam would soon be demanding their equal rights.

ington, D.C., and Meharry had trained most of the Black physicians in America. Elbert Nelson looked forward to joining the small fraternity upon graduation. But another dose of reality struck Nelson about the year 1964: "I knew, if I hadn't been in medical school, I would have been in Vietnam." In that time of explosive civil rights activism, even some faculty members from Meharry were joining the busloads of Freedom Riders that traveled into the deep Southern states. Nashville itself was the scene of memorable lunch-counter sit-ins in which a coterie of students challenged all-white eating establishments.

Nelson would not allow himself to miss the early-evening national news broadcasts—with correspondents filing reports from civil rights hot spots. He watched the unfolding events of the clash on the bridge in Selma, Alabama. Then, five months later, in August 1965, he watched as the streets of a South Los Angeles neighborhood, Watts, turned into a weeklong and horrifying emblem of America's racial agony.

While Elbert Nelson was studying the organs and mysteries of the human body, he couldn't shake the imagery of those two events from his mind. Selma had exposed the wanton savagery of white law enforcement, all absent any help from the federal government to anyone—man, woman, or child—in their time of need. In Los Angeles, throngs of Blacks who had never had much—had never fully experienced the American Dream and were still hemmed in by the depths of racism and real-estate segregation—had broken free as if from harnesses, and wrecked deadly havoc in their community, shocking the nation. And beyond those two events, the drumbeat of Vietnam was at America's front door. Elbert Nelson began to worry: Because of the draft, he had no illusion that he would escape the jungles of Southeast Asia. And what he had seen emanating from Selma and Watts—especially Watts—convinced him that Black anger and defiance would be percolating in Vietnam, because whatever had been loosed upon the American landscape could not be put back into any kind of a bottle. "Watts changed everything as far as race and Vietnam" is how he put it.

Here is what happened on a chilly day in Selma that gripped Elbert Nelson, and had begun to haunt his memory:

It all actually began twenty-five miles away, in the small Alabama town of Marion. A young man by the name of Jimmie Lee Jackson had begun to wonder why Blacks so often were denied the right to vote in the state. He had heard many stories about relatives and parents of friends who had fought in military campaigns for America, and yet couldn't vote. By 1965, the meetings at the local Zion United Methodist Church in Marion, where the Lee family lived, paid taxes, and worshipped, had become more intense concerning the issue of voting. On February 18, 1965, one such church gathering took place. Local law enforcement had tired of and been made nervous by these meetings, and had already summoned Alabama state troopers as reinforcements. Church members sketched a plan to leave the sanctuary after this latest gathering and march over to the local jail, to sing civil rights songs in protest of the arrest of James Orange, a civil rights activist who had been arrested for organizing. About a hundred marchers waded into the night air that evening, leaving others at the church to monitor developments as best they could. But shortly into the march, streetlights in the area were flicked off. The dark got darker. (The lights had actually been turned off by law enforcement, but none of the marchers yet imagined that a trap was unfolding.) The police chief, T. O. Harris, yelled through a bullhorn that the marchers would have to leave the area immediately. A minister among the protesters told of his intention to pray first, and knelt on the ground. When he did, a trooper bashed him in the head with a club and quickly arrested him. Then others, blinded by the inky darkness and the goose-stepping troopers, began to scatter and run. "Negroes could be heard screaming and loud whacks rang through the square," stated a later *New York Times* report about the police attack. Troopers eventually cornered Jimmie Lee Jackson and his mother, Viola, inside Mack's Café. Viola's father and Jimmy Lee's grandfather, Cager Lee Jackson, eventually stumbled into the café. Cager Lee was bleeding. When his daughter and grandson leaped to aid him, Viola was assaulted by troopers, and Jimmie Lee, coming to her aid, was shot twice in the stomach by a trooper. Lee—a twenty-six-year-old deacon at the church—stumbled back outside, into the horror-filled night. He died eight days later.

Those in the Alabama civil rights movement decided they must respond to the Marion tragedy and the death of Jimmie Lee Jackson. A march in nearby Selma was planned.

On March 7, two weeks after the events in Marion, there was a gathering at the Edmund Pettus Bridge in Selma, named after a renowned slave owner and Grand Dragon of the Ku Klux Klan. Everyone prepared for a march to Montgomery, the capital. This would surely bring attention to the plight of Blacks who couldn't vote. Not long after everyone had assembled at the edge of the bridge on March 7, they spotted, in the distance, snorting horses mounted by Alabama troopers in gas masks, evoking a scene of trench warfare in World War I. "May we have a word with the major," Hosea Williams, an aide to the Reverend Martin Luther King, Jr., asked one of the Alabama deputies. He was rebuffed, with an admonishment to leave the Edmund Pettus Bridge, but the marchers stood fast. "Troopers, advance," came the Alabama trooper's cry. The attack, and the subsequent bedlam, was swift; blood was sprayed, backs were lashed with batons, screaming was nonstop, tear gas plumed in the air, and schoolchildren fell, then rose like angels to scamper onward with horror in their eyes. Those watching on TV sets in their living rooms—like the medical student Elbert Nelson—found it hard to believe what they were seeing: dozens upon dozens of white state troopers running to stomp those in front of them. "I've never seen anything like it in my life," the young, brave, and bloodied John Lewis said in a phone call to SNCC (Student Nonviolent Coordinating Committee) headquarters in Atlanta. "They are shooting gas, acid. One very old lady I know has a broken arm."

The day and date—March 7, 1965—would be marked in infamy.

On the very next day, the first American soldiers—soldiers in a military force that was fully integrated for the first time in American history—arrived in South Vietnam to wage war.

Here is what happened five months after Selma, on August 11, in Los Angeles: A potent civilian Black force—resembling an ungainly battalion—had, with great spontaneity, unleashed all that mayhem in Watts. White police officers—members of a force that was often accused of brutality—had stopped a Black man, twenty-one-year-old Marquette Frye, at an intersection. The officers arrested him after he failed a sobriety test. Bystanders were now gathered. When young Frye's mother attempted to intervene, she and her son and some bystanders all started yelling. This ignited the swinging of batons, and reports of another example of police brutality swept the neighborhood like a fire gone wild. Calmer heads might have stopped the ensuing outburst, but to Black Angelenos, the time for calm was over. They had long felt aggrieved. Of three thousand California highway patrolmen in 1965, only three were Black. There was not a single Black in the Los Angeles Police Department above the rank of sergeant. The Frye confrontation—against a backdrop of racial apartheid in one of the nation's largest cities—sparked a weeklong spasm of violence and shock: burnt stores, rampant lethal shootings, looting. TV cameras caught a lot of it. One proof of the reality of separatism in so much of American life was that the *Los Angeles Times,* one of the largest newspapers in the country, had not a single Black reporter on its staff. The newspaper quickly corralled Robert Richardson, a member of their advertising sales staff, and gave him a pep talk and the kind of instructions any cub reporter might be given: Go to the scene of the action and get a story! A press pass in hand, Richardson hustled off to Watts. The scenes he came upon both shocked and frightened him. He trembled, but managed to put together a dispatch, which the newspaper thought to be so remarkable—given the circumstances of his presence on the scene—that the editors attached the following note in parentheses to his byline:

> EYEWITNESS ACCOUNT "Get Whitey" Scream Blood-Hungry Mobs BY ROBERT RICHARDSON (Robert Richardson, 24, a Negro, is an advertising salesman for the Times. He witnessed the rioting in South Los Angeles for nearly eight hours Thursday night.) [Editors]

The opening lines of Richardson's page-one story: "It was the most terrifying thing I had ever seen in my life. I went along with the mobs, watching, listening."

The rebellion served to expose the very deep racial fault lines of America, a spasmodic crime wave that the more expansive-minded believed was a call for justice against a system of racial pain. That Watts was on the West Coast reminded many that racial inequality stretched from coast to coast. The tallying of numbers for the Watts uprising was searing: thirty-four dead, more than a thousand injured, and more than thirty-four hundred placed under arrest. The *Los Angeles Times* referred to the Watts saga as "the four ugliest days in our history."

Though the *Times*'s assessment may have been hyperbolic, it was not hard to convince the Elbert Nelsons of the country that Watts had certainly become one of the most televised and horrific events witnessed throughout the nation.

White House phone operators got no rest in the aftermath of Watts. President Johnson knew that beneath the riot lay a multitude of ills. "Let's get busy and let's get into this housing," Johnson told Martin Luther King, Jr., in a phone call. "Let's get into this unemployment. Let's get into this social security situation. Let's get into this education . . . I've spent the biggest part of my life the last four years on civil rights bills, but . . . all of it comes to naught if you have a situation like war in the world or a situation in Los Angeles."

Lyndon Johnson, with an instinctive sense of the ravages of inequality, appointed a commission to study Watts. "We've just got to find some way to wipe out these ghettoes," Johnson told John McCone, a former CIA chief whom he used as a sounding board. "And find some place . . . housing . . . and put them to work. We trained 12,000 last month and found jobs for them." He was talking about inner-city residents—residents of the American ghettos. He was talking about many of the families suddenly depleted by one member—the one who was off to Vietnam.

The renowned evangelist Billy Graham flew over Watts in the days after the riots, along with Mayor Sam Yorty. The burning embers of Watts took his mind in a unique direction: Graham told the mayor he believed the riots were a rehearsal for "sinister and evil forces . . . whose ultimate objective is the overthrow of the American government." Graham had a huge following.

Martin Luther King, Jr., accompanied by his longtime adviser Bayard Rustin, arrived in Los Angeles nine days after the riots had been quelled for a community meeting organized by a neighborhood association. There were catcalls at the meeting, signs of disrespect, sudden evidence of a more militant attitude toward these traditional civil rights leaders. "All we want is jobs," a man cried out to King. "We get jobs, we don't bother nobody. We don't get no jobs, we'll tear up Los Angeles, period." Southern audiences were always more deferential to King and his nonviolent approach than audiences from other areas of the country. He had solidified his reputation at

Southern pulpits. "I'm here," King told the gathering, "because at bottom we are brothers and sisters. We all go up together or we go down together. We are not free in the South, and you are not free in the cities of the North."

Reading the headlines and watching the nightly news, Elbert Nelson knew he wouldn't have control of his future. "The federal government had a lottery program. This meant some medical students, those going into surgery as a specialty, would get deferments. The other half would be sent to active duty. For those like me whose number did not come up, we would be conscripted in." Elbert Nelson's draft notice arrived in the mail in September 1967. The military gave him time to finish school; then, in August 1969, he was bound for boot camp—and Vietnam. He still couldn't shake what he had seen happen in Selma and Watts. For the average Black recruit and soldier, Selma and Watts had become reflecting mirrors on society. They were the portals into the starkly different reactions against inequality: nonviolence (Selma) and violence (Watts).

Elbert Nelson's family worried a lot about him as he set off for the Army. They would have preferred he return to Georgia and set up a nice family medical practice. There were too few Black doctors in Georgia.

In boot camp, Elbert Nelson didn't hear much about inequality back home; instead, he was hearing a lot of talk about the dangers of communism.

In the fall of 1960, the bearded revolutionary hero of Cuba, Fidel Castro, arrived in America for a planned address before the United Nations. Nearly two years earlier, Castro had overthrown Fulgencio Batista, Cuba's American-backed leader. American military and government officials feared Castro's energetic youth and his communist leanings. Once in New York City, Castro vowed to shine a light on America's "race problem." The vow struck a sour note with American officials, who had kept a system of racial segregation in place since the nation's founding. Castro decamped at a swanky hotel in midtown Manhattan, but on the evening of September 19, his retinue had a dispute about money with the hotel management, and he and his aides abruptly left the hotel and moved uptown, to the Hotel Theresa, in Harlem. Suddenly settled in the Negro mecca of America, Castro began drawing wide applause as he offered impromptu asides about American racism and discrimination. Harlem treated the guerrilla fighter like a newfound political star. Not long after his arrival in Harlem, Castro received his initial guest: Malcolm X, the blunt-talking Muslim leader. The Soviet leader, Nikita Khrushchev—also in the city for the UN meetings—met with Castro, too. "Castro will have to gravitate to us like an iron filing to a magnet," the Soviet leader said. On September 20, Castro and Khrushchev were together in Harlem, with a throng of reporters and New Yorkers gawking. Khrushchev expressed his feelings that, "by going to a Negro hotel in a Negro district, we would be making a double demonstration against the discriminatory policies of the United States of America toward Negroes, as well as toward Cuba."

This Castro-Khrushchev interaction happened two months before the 1960 presidential election.

The average American had routinely paid scant attention to foreign affairs. But that changed with the end of the Eisenhower administration and the arrival of the Kennedy administration. Just three months after entering office, Kennedy authorized an invasion of Cuba, sending more than a thousand CIA-trained Cuban exiles to dethrone Fidel Castro. The White House was hellbent on "liberating" Cuba from the influence of communism. This crudely planned and executed invasion—dubbed the Bay of Pigs—was disastrous, with the guerrilla-hardened Castro arresting and jailing many of the invaders. American CIA operatives heightened their attention on the Cuba-Soviet axis.

In October 1962 came intelligence reports that the Soviets were shipping nuclear missiles to Cuba. Further intelligence revealed the sinister planning of the Soviet leader: he was plotting to bomb the U.S. naval base at Guantánamo. The American military answer was swift: more than a hundred thousand troops were prepared to invade

Cuba. "We still have twenty chances out of a hundred to be at war with Russia," Kennedy remarked to a member of his administration. Families across America descended into basements with boxes of food, believing a nuclear Armageddon was at hand. But, rather than risk war, the Soviet leader decided to withdraw the missiles.

The Kennedy-Khrushchev nuclear showdown assured that the words "communism" and "communists" would ratchet even higher as a daily part of the American conversation. But those words held different and slanted histories when it came to Black and white America. For the most part, the tricky communism debate was a question of who would help—or even feign to help—the American Negro.

In the early 1920s, members of the Communist Party began showing up at labor rallies in America, in Black communities. The rallies also drew whites who didn't care to be part of the political mainstream. A. Philip Randolph, a Black labor leader who in 1925 founded the Brotherhood of Sleeping Car Porters, which became a potent union, identified himself as a socialist and found common ground with the communist philosophy. But that very philosophy—viewed as anti-American and unpatriotic—rattled the nerves of mainstream organizations such as the Black church, the NAACP, and, perhaps most worrisome, American law enforcement. The 1931 case of the Scottsboro Boys would come to expose the rather lethal joinery of communism and the burgeoning civil rights movement.

Nine Blacks had been arrested in rural Alabama (not far from Scottsboro), accused of raping two white women aboard a train. Sensational front-page newspaper headlines quickly appeared throughout the country. The trial—with onlookers yelling and tossing vulgar threats at the desperate-looking defendants—got under way in just two weeks. All were quickly found guilty by the kangaroo court. Eight of the nine were sentenced to death. The International Labor Defense (ILD), seen as closely aligned with the Communist Party, took on the case and filed an appeal. Walter White of the NAACP went to Alabama. He was convinced that the legal alliance between the ILD and the NAACP would come to harm Blacks in the future. "In control of the case, the Communists proceeded to publicize and agitate it in every part of the world," White allowed. "Public meetings of the NAACP were particularly the target of the campaign. A favorite device was to announce in such a meeting that one of the Scottsboro mothers was present and demanded the right to speak. If permission was granted, a Communist would make a lengthy introduction expounding the merits of communism." Across the succeeding years, there was mounting public pressure—along with favorable U.S. Supreme Court rulings on behalf of the convicted Scottsboro Boys—to release them, and both white women had also recanted their charges. Still, after a round of final trials in 1937, they were all sentenced to terms ranging from twenty years to life.

Years later, the momentum of the 1960s drive for civil rights attracted investigations from law enforcement. Those in the movement with socialist or communist leanings were forced to realize they were bringing the wrong kind of attention to the movement. Several aides to Martin Luther King, Jr., had appeared at socialist gatherings—among them Stanley Levison and Bayard Rustin—and were sometimes snooped upon by the FBI. Phones were also bugged. King himself was the victim of a smear campaign orchestrated by FBI Director J. Edgar Hoover linking him to communists. Communism was a spidery web. Blacks, long marginalized in the political arena, kept enough of a distance from communists and communism to see it as something both too exotic and worrisome when it came to their immediate concerns. Only risk takers and mavericks dared openly traffic in its orbit.

Elbert Nelson, on his way to Vietnam, was still a bit confused about the overall mission: "All I was told was that we were on our way to Vietnam to fight communism." At boot camp before flying overseas, he was given instructions on what it meant to be a noncombatant: He was "there to heal people," not to engage personally in battle.

Nevertheless, he received a quick lesson on how to use a rifle. "And you were given a Geneva card, to show to the enemy if you were captured, explaining that you were a noncombatant."

Ever since Lyndon Johnson's landslide 1964 victory, the escalation of the war in Vietnam had appeared inevitable. The foe was communism, a thread of intrigue that had split Vietnam north and south, and threaded its way through the political machinations and power grabs executed by leaders in Russia and China. By 1966, there were 184,000 American troops in Vietnam, and every week thousands more were arriving. The foreign foe of the United States consisted of two armies—the NVA, the North Vietnamese Army, and the National Liberation Front, the Viet Cong. One American general remarked that both of these armies had embarked on "a different kind of war in each of South Vietnam's forty-four provinces."

Elbert Nelson had no idea what kind of military environment he was being ushered into in terms of racial matters. But something had happened a year before his arrival in Saigon that caught the attention of every Black soldier in the war zone.

On October 14, 1968, Lavell Merritt, a Black Army officer, strode into the room used for daily press briefings in Saigon. Merritt had a reputation for being quite sharp and studious. The black horn-rimmed glasses, crisp military uniform, and close-cropped hair gave him a severe look. Major Merritt actually had no official duties in the briefing room that day; he was not a military spokesman. But he did have rank, as an officer, and those in the room, confused as they may have been, stepped aside when he positioned himself in front of the gathered reporters. Merritt had something in his hands; he proceeded to hand out what he referred to as his "statement." Those in the room yanked their eyes downward and began reading, though also glancing up at Merritt, who had written, "The American military services are the strongest citadels of racism on the face of the earth." These were the words of a Black military officer who had graduated from Officer Candidate School, a prestigious training ground for future officers. He had received his commission back in 1953 and was seen as a model of military decorum. Now this surprise. His statement went on to proclaim, "The American people have for years been told that the military leads the nation in breaking down and eliminating all vestiges of segregation and discriminatory treatment of minority groups. That is a blatant lie." The newsmen, eyeballing the other military officers in the room as Merritt continued talking, knew they would have to file a story. "Many black officers," he announced, "had been glorying in our pseudo-acceptance by our fellow officers and clinging to the mistaken belief that patience, diligence and professional competence would yield the benefits enjoyed by the majority ethnic groups." He went on to say that Blacks received no such assurances that their diligence would yield the same promotions achieved by white soldiers in similar situations. "The black military officer group is the largest collection of identifiable accommodationists," he added, and proceeded to break that comment down into starker language, implying that his accommodationist tag was but "a synonym for Uncle Tom." But he still wasn't finished. In words that seemed to stun the mostly white press contingent, Merritt said: "I could get a good efficiency report from a racist because I have been a good nigger." Heads swiveled about as eyes kept darting around the room.

The Merritt bombshell went out over international newswires. If the story had been confined to the Black newspapers in America, it might have seemed an aberration, something pounced on by the Black press for its sensational impact. But the moment was potent enough for the story—and brouhaha—to land in the largest of American newspapers. "Negro Major Charges U.S. Army Is Racist," proclaimed the *Los Angeles Times. The New York Times:* "Army Denounced by Negro Major: Equality and Justice Denied to Blacks, He Asserts."

The military, of course, was a place of hierarchy, of rank and rules and regulations. Those who dared to challenge and try to buck the system, who engaged in acts of insubordination, who went around proper channels, would have to face the consequences. Major Lavell Merritt had already been on the Army's radar for making complaints about what he saw as racial discrimination in the ranks. Being passed over for promotion—which he had been more than once—only intensified his brewing disenchantment. The Army launched an investigation of Merritt and his incendiary charges. When they had completed it, the investigators announced their findings: numerous allegations of misconduct, such as making mistakes on an employee's time card; making sexual jokes around other officers; referring to Lieutenant General Benjamin O. Davis, Jr. (also Black), as an "Uncle Tom"; and, finally, releasing his statement about military racism to the press. Merritt laughed the charges off. But nothing about them was funny to the United States Army. Though the Staff Judge Advocate seemed torn, he announced the conclusion of the Merritt inquiry: "Although it hurts me to say this, for the overall good of the command, I recommend . . . that Major Merritt be removed from the command and retired as soon as possible."

Three months after his impromptu press conference and the subsequent investigation into his actions, Major Lavell Merritt—"contrary to desire"—retired from the military. In the days leading up to his retirement, Merritt had another missive he wanted to pen, a letter to President Lyndon Johnson:

> When I publicly accused the Military of harboring Citadels of racism, I knew full well the scope of the battle I was joining. I understood the magnitude of bitterness and animosity that would be heaped upon me for daring to make such an accusation. But I did not know the extent . . . of the fear that permeates the military hierarchy. Fear for loss of position or favor, fear of being identified as one who supports changes toward dignity and just treatment for all humans, fear of admitting that we do have race problems.

Some years after his retirement, Lavell Merritt—who had spent eighteen years in the military—looked back on his rebellious undertaking. "I had been a true-blue American boy," he said. "But around 1966 I came into an awareness that things were terribly wrong in the military."

—

There was little chatter on the airplane between Elbert Nelson and his fellow soldiers during the flight into Saigon. As the plane descended onto the landing strip at Tan Son Nhut Air Base, he peered through his seat window. He saw some metallic items in the distance—"like long silver bullets"—and couldn't quite make out what they were. When he and the other soldiers exited the plane and glided along a walkway, they realized what those long silver bulletlike objects were: caskets of dead soldiers on their way back to America, to the undertaker.

Dr. Elbert Nelson was assigned to the 2nd Battalion, 5th Cavalry Regiment, an infantry battalion. He prepared himself for medical challenges—shrapnel wounds, broken bones, malaria, machine-gun blasts. He picked up a little of the Vietnamese language. It was war, and he had to take inventory of the many medicinal drugs necessary to treat wounds and ailments—dextrose, penicillin, morphine—and the IV equipment. The ambulances had been flown over from America. It was a bit surprising to see air conditioners. But they, too, had arrived from America. Some things raised curiosity: In a land of rice paddies, why was so much rice arriving from America? He learned that it was because napalm had burned through so many rice paddies.

A hospital corpsman by the name of Luther Benton, from Portsmouth, Virginia, was also in Vietnam in the late 1960s. As a Black military man, he found himself growing more and more curious about the political dynamics of the country. He stopped a group of young Vietnamese men one day and asked them why they themselves weren't fighting for the freedom of their country. "We sit and watch and see you win," one of them said to him. "Whoever win is the one we go with. The Americans are the ones that are crazy, 'cause they not gain anything. They lose their lives and their money here."

The infantry unit Dr. Elbert Nelson was assigned to proceeded to go out into the jungle to make a base camp. Christened Fire Base Ike, this camp held about a thousand soldiers. Its creation required tents, supplies, a ring of concertina wire to protect it, weaponry, and a medical facility. There was an elevated guard post. And a large red cross on the outside of Dr. Nelson's tent. The base included everything an Army unit would need to plan and strategize its assaults on the enemy. "There was nothing around but jungle," Nelson recalls. "And that's where you operated from." They were along an area known as the Mustang Trail. "Our mission was to intercept all Viet Cong traveling that trail."

Because he had come from the South and the roiling civil rights movement, Elbert Nelson felt proud of the discipline he had seen in those who marched in Selma. But then, months later, the wanton destruction that took place in the weeklong Watts uprising had simply left him shaken. As he looked around at his base camp, he kept wondering if any of the Black soldiers had been in Selma, or in Watts. Had any of those from the Chicago area clashed with police officers at the 1968 Democratic National Convention, when officers brutally attacked protesters?

The medical staff worked around the clock: bullet wounds, shrapnel wounds, grenade injuries, arms and legs blown off. "The AK-47 did the most damage," Nelson says.

A lot of the fighting beyond the base camp took place at night. There were a good many surprise attacks in the jungle. Because it was known to be a "nonlinear war"—attacks coming from any and every direction—American military officials figured the base-camp model was the best strategy. Elbert Nelson hadn't studied the psychology of war as an undergraduate, but since he was at war, he began to wonder about the soldiers. "I was interested in how people coped with war. I wanted to see what made them tick." He found out that sleep for soldiers was intermittent. And that there was always the possibility of being attacked while on patrol. "When the fight would start at night, it would become like daylight because of the helicopters dropping flares. Other soldiers would come in to support you. The next morning, the fight is over. The Viet Cong would rarely fight during the day." "During daylight," Nelson told me, "the Army is coming in, dropping napalm."

One of the strangest things soldiers—both Blacks and whites—noticed was that, during fighting, in the field, they would be physically close in battle. But later, back at base camp, the old racial confrontations would rear up yet again. Another strange occurrence: A Vietnamese—wearing loose-fitting and ragged clothing—would stumble into Nelson's base hospital with a bullet wound. The injured visitor would explain through broken English that the wound was the result of an accident. Nelson or one of his aides would render medical aid. Often, it turned out that the wounded person actually was an enemy Vietnamese soldier who had been hit in battle with American or allied forces, but figured a quick way to get medical attention was to visit an American medical station. Riddles came from many directions.

Since fewer than 2 percent of the officers in Vietnam were Black—the bane of Major Lavell Merritt's career—the average Black soldier with whom Elbert Nelson came in contact was in the 98 percent of Black enlisted men. He took care of their injuries and decided where they needed to go next if an injury required specialized treatment. When certain soldiers got comfortable enough around him to feel a sense of trust—not a given, because the average Black soldier had started growing wary of the officer class, no matter the color of their skin—they began telling him their complaints concerning Army life. The more Elbert Nelson listened, the more he began to sympathize with them, and even understand them. "What I can say is that there was a difference between the young Black soldier from the North, the East, the West, and the Midwest. These Black kids from the North—who had been compulsively conscripted from Harlem, the Bronx, Watts—they didn't like being in the military. They were often one year removed from riots. So they would create havoc. They would disobey orders. They would do things to get a dishonorable discharge."

Some white officers wanted to give Black soldiers a second chance if they had broken rules, wanted to help them survive military life without bad write-ups in their files. Rather than punish a soldier—because they saw potential—they'd march him to Elbert Nelson in hopes that he could provide the soldier with some direction and career advice. "A lot of the Black kids would fake illnesses, and they would bring them to me for a general evaluation. This happened on so many occasions," Nelson recalled. "I'd get the Black kid, examine them. I'd say, 'I can't find anything wrong with you. You should return to your unit.' Well, he does. But he comes back to me again! So I devised a speech. I'd say, 'If you had an orthopedic problem, I'd send you, via helicopter, for an evaluation. They are going to make a disposition and evaluate you limb to limb. They are then going to tell you there's nothing to prevent you from returning to full-duty status. And they are going to tell you that you have to go back to duty.'" The conversations went around in circles between Nelson and many of the young Black soldiers. "I'd say, 'I know you don't want to fight this "white man's war."' I was trying to use their language. I'd tell them that they didn't have anything wrong with their health. And they'd end up calling me an Oreo."

"Oreo" was a derisive term, akin to being called an "Uncle Tom"—someone who was Black on the outside but white on the inside, who had forsaken honesty around the topic of race for appeasement with whites. The charge stung Nelson and left him feeling the way a father might when he couldn't get through to a son about an important matter.

As the weeks and months passed in Vietnam, when Elbert Nelson thought about the young Black boys who were dying—most of them eighteen or nineteen years old—a sorrowful feeling would start to come over him. "Those young Black boys gave me a new perspective on what they had seen in terms of Watts, the 1968 Olympics, the civil rights murders. And some of them decided they'd take whatever punishment was coming to them when they refused to fight, by going to the stockade. It was those young soldiers that opened my eyes. It was those young soldiers who didn't have the ability to go beyond high school. I don't think I could have handled what they had to handle at eighteen or nineteen years old." He went on: "If I had to line up ten Black guys—five from the North and five from the South—the Black guys from the North would have a far different attitude about the war than the guys from the South. The kids who grew up in Detroit and Chicago didn't have to put up with what the Southern Black boys had to deal with."

—

When he was in Vietnam and writing letters back home to friends in West Virginia, Newman Jackson had to explain to them that there were Navy men, like him, who were not floating at sea but were on the ground in Saigon. The Navy would assign sailors to ground duty. Many worked in hospitals or, like Jackson, on security details. Jackson didn't think there was much of a future for him as a young Black man growing up in West Virginia, so he joined the Navy in 1966. He was just the kind of soldier Elbert Nelson worried about. "I noticed there were rebel flags in my base camp. This was the year of the 1968 Olympics. I wore a black glove to support Tommie Smith," Jackson says, speaking of the Black track star who had donned a black glove on the winners' podium to protest American discrimination. "I got called before a disciplinary council. Well, I stood in front of that council and asked why were they complaining about my black glove when you got rebel flags on base? They ended up taking my black glove."

There were days when the American soldiers in base camps or on patrol would come across leaflets that had been distributed by the North Vietnamese Army, sometimes pinned to logs floating downriver. The leaflets were directed toward Black soldiers and often drew a lot of discussion in the base camps. "We weren't the only ones who dropped leaflets," remarks Nelson, referring to leaflets Americans dropped over North Vietnamese outposts trying to encourage desertions.

Elbert Nelson kept one of the leaflets from North Vietnam:

> Colored GIs. The South Vietnamese people, who are struggling for their independence and freedom, are friends with the American colored people being victim of barbarous racial discrimination at home. Your battlefield is right in the USA! Your enemy is the warlords in the White House and the Pentagon.

Years later, talking about that leaflet—which he held on to—Nelson wondered: "Is it possible to understand one's feeling when you are in a combat zone knowing that your life could end in a millisecond and you read that leaflet?" He added: "To this day, I find it troubling to understand. 'Twoness' is real when you're the 'darker brother.' "

It was the writer-sociologist W.E.B. Du Bois who first talked of "twoness," angling it to mean having "two souls, two thoughts, two unreconciled strivings; two warring ideals in one dark body."

The longer he was in Vietnam, the more Elbert Nelson realized that a lot of the young Black soldiers may not have always been book-smart in the traditional sense, but they were certainly culturally alert: most of them were quite aware of the political leanings of Malcolm X, of the tactical positions of the Black Panthers, of the Black Power salute that Tommie Smith and John Carlos had displayed to the world at the 1968 Olympics in Mexico. So many of the young Black soldiers had been sprung from the racially charged urban environments of America. "These young Black soldiers opened my eyes," says Nelson. "In their minds, they literally had nothing to go back to."

The young *New York Times* reporter David Halberstam, sent to cover Vietnam in 1962, had earlier covered the burgeoning civil rights movement. "There are several parallels between Mississippi and Vietnam," he later said.

While Elbert Nelson was in Vietnam, *Newsweek* conducted a poll about Black attitudes toward the war. To a whopping seven-to-one degree, Blacks felt that the Vietnam War was harming the effectiveness of President Johnson's War on Poverty. *Newsweek* summed up the attitude of Blacks: "Vietnam was their own particular incubus—a war that depletes their young manhood and saps the resources available to healing their ills at home."

It was the paradox of the Black soldiers that they were escaping one war—in America—only to be given mercenary tools to fight another war—in Vietnam. When it came to race, Vietnam had become a crucible for America. The Black soldier had come of age in a segregated landscape—white TV shows and white authority figures and white draft boards and white law enforcement and white teachers. Now white military leaders were telling them to go and kill. Just when there had been a sense they might be on the precipice of freedom—those civil rights bills!—they found themselves in a jungle. The youngest of them—teenagers who were sometimes quick to unleash their emotions and anger against authority—had come face-to-face with something else: a class struggle between them and the very few Black officers in Vietnam. The dynamic tugged at Elbert Nelson's conscience, but there were not enough Black officers like him to try to save them. The tide of cultural pride was now rushing forth.

CHAPTER TWO

REFUGE IN SOUL ALLEY

The prospect of a fully integrated war was novel for American military leaders. The racial advancements that had occurred in the country before Vietnam had been ignited by the spilling of blood, long and sweaty marches, a civil war, the unspooling of legal strategies, and courtroom victories. It was hardly surprising that white and Black cultural customs would be different. America was a nation—and a world inside that nation—composed of separate but hardly equal parts.

In the 1960s, a potent phrase popped up in the American lexicon: Black Power. It arrived with the force of a hurricane, quickly and easily confusing the white populace of America while instilling pride throughout Black communities. During the Vietnam War, it was akin to a siren call and became its own kind of firepower. The phrase itself had actually been cribbed from the title of a book written by Richard Wright.

Wright, born in Roxie, Mississippi, in 1908, had led a Dickensian childhood, with a sickly mother and a father who abandoned the family. He found his calling after moving to Chicago, where he started writing for small literary journals. He got a further boost

Saigon merchants catered to the needs of Black soldiers, ordering items they needed, such as hair-care products, and preparing meals they requested in restaurants. The soldiers christened the area "Soul Alley."

when he joined the Works Progress Administration, started by the FDR administration to put writers to work gathering oral histories. Wright acquired a literary reputation in 1940 with the publication of his bestselling novel, *Native Son.* The novel revolves around a young Black man, Bigger Thomas, who tragically and accidentally kills a young white woman. It also revolves around that timeworn bogeyman: communism. Wright rose as one of the very few Black literary stars of the decade, but American racism drove him to relocate to Paris. While in Europe, he traveled and wrote about political developments on the African continent. He had popped up at the Bandung Conference in Indonesia, attended by the likes of Adam Clayton Powell, Jr., and others to debate a postcolonial world. He took a trip to a region known at the time as the Gold Coast (later Ghana) and wrote a book about different tribes and their political posturing. The book's full title was a mouthful: *Black Power: A Record of Reactions in a Land of Pathos.* Wright's book predated the 1960s civil rights movement, yet in that title he had introduced a phrase that was prime for future plucking. Stokely Carmichael, roaming leopardlike around the contours of the movement, would be the one to reach back into the past and snatch Wright's title as a calling. As a movement all its own.

Although he was born in Trinidad, Carmichael had arrived in New York City by the age of eleven. Smart and quick of mind, he was enrolled in the Bronx High School of Science. From there it was on to Howard University, from which he graduated in 1964. He joined the Student Nonviolent Coordinating Committee (SNCC) and bravely traveled about Mississippi and Alabama, protesting discrimination and getting arrested. He had a penchant for hopping atop flatbed trucks and screaming about injustice. Such scenes proved instantly cinematic. Publications found him good and exciting copy, a man with a quicksilver tongue and an aggressive posture. He drew different comparisons to traditional civil rights leaders when he came to succeed John Lewis as head of SNCC. If Martin Luther King, Jr., was the moral leader of the civil rights movement, Carmichael relished becoming its angry mascot. Here he is on the campus of the University of California in Berkeley:

> The white man says, "Work hard, nigger, and you will overcome." If that were true, the black man would be the richest man in the world! My dad believed in that hard work and overcome stuff! He worked like a dog, day and night! But only death came to that poor black man!—and in his early forties! My grandfather had to run, run, run. I ain't running no more! And hell no! We ain't going to Vietnam! Ain't no Vietcong ever called me nigger! If I'm to do any fighting it's going to be right here at home! I will not fight in Vietnam and run in Georgia!

Vietnam—and its intermingling of race, politics, and foreign affairs—suddenly provided Stokely Carmichael with a rich platform. Whereas many in the civil rights movement were not quite ready to question anyone's commitment to wartime patriotism, Carmichael took another tack. In his mind, Vietnam was but a minefield. It was a faraway place, sure enough, but it was already proving American hypocrisy when it came to true Democratic ideas. "If you want to train me," he had begun saying to Black audiences in America, "don't send me to Vietnam. Build a school in my neighborhood." And those Black vets arriving back from Vietnam after their twelve-month tour of duty—and who found themselves in the company of Carmichael—liked what they were hearing. They were quick to walk up to him and greet him with the "dap" handshake.

It was a handshake, but it was, in reality, so much more. Black soldiers in Vietnam had adopted the dap as a sign of esprit de corps. It told both soldiers—the one giving it and the one receiving it—that they were committed to watching out for each other in a racially charged environment. The handshake itself required a bit of arm-and-hand contortion. It was akin to a secret fraternity handshake: fingers interlocking, palms slapping and interlocking, elbows touching, all resembling a stretched-out moment of soulful pantomiming. It carried with it the decorum of being Black. White soldiers and white officers ignored it at first—the sight of two Black soldiers, sometimes more, shaking hands in some kind of ritual. But then came a point when whites in Vietnam decided to pay attention. They had worries and questions: Were these handshaking Black soldiers plotting something? Was the handshake—and grinning—a secret sign of something nefarious soon to take place at the Army base camp? The issue and concerns were reported to higher-ups. Dapping was going on in the mess halls, in and around the tents. Sometimes, the very act of dapping would annoy white soldiers so much that they exchanged heated words with the Black soldiers, and sometimes those words morphed into scuffles. To the Black soldiers, their handshaking was but a form of solidarity in the shadow of white officers. A good many of those white officers came from the still-segregated world of the American South. But the American military was not yet at the point of parsing differences when it came to cultural customs. "The demeanor of many young black soldiers is far more black than it is military," *The New York Times* reported. "They risk punishments with displays of varied and ever-changing symbols of dissent." Even the Afro—the thick, bushy hairstyle favored by Blacks in America and worn by many, among them Black fashion models, singers, athletes, actors, and actresses—had caused bouts of worry from military officials in Vietnam.

What the Army, Air Force, Navy, and Marines had to realize was that if you were Black and in Vietnam, you couldn't help but bring your Blackness with you, and that meant a certain custom and heritage—the soul music of Motown and the residue of the civil rights movement; some of Stokely and Martin, and some of the words Malcolm had left behind. It meant holding on to your dog-eared copy of James Baldwin's 1963 book *The Fire Next Time.* It meant that you were going to complain about there being no place on military bases to get hair grease for your bushy Afro; it meant you were going to complain when threatened yet again with thirty days in jail because that Afro had grown too big; and it meant that, when you could, you were going to take your righteous self over to Soul Alley: there, at least, you'd be able to commiserate with the other soul brothers who found themselves in—as they were so likely to call it—the muthafuckin Vietnam War.

It was early in the war when, by their very presence, Black soldiers had created enough of a cultural influence in Saigon to inspire the birth of Soul Alley. In earlier years, during the Indochina war, Vietnamese entrepreneurs had learned to cater to the French. Now they were catering to the legion of Black soldiers who hustled over to a street in Saigon not far from the airport and inspired it to bend to their cultural desires—food, music, hair products for their Afros in the stores. The street was only two hundred yards long, and populated by street urchins peddling goods from pushcarts, and mama-sans and pretty Asian girls who were the paramours of Black GIs. The businessmen and businesswomen of this street had begun serving barbecue, sweet potatoes, black-eyed peas, corn bread, and other food items popular in Black communities back in America. Black GIs who had gone AWOL hid out in Soul Alley, sometimes even feeling safe enough to be out in the open. Some participated in black-market activities. At night, soul music—the Temptations, the Four Tops, Sly & the Family Stone—blared from speakers and radios. Vietnamese barbers learned how to cut Black hair. It was a kind of sepia-toned Casablanca, a spot of feverish intrigue populated both by renegade Black soldiers and by Black soldiers simply enjoying their allotted leisure time. There were those who specialized in forgeries and selling rations. The daily goings-on in Soul Alley were all part of the war within the war for Black GIs. "I don't want to go back to the States, and certainly not back to Houston, Texas," explained one Black GI who had fled to Soul Alley. "They would call me a 'nigger' and my wife a 'gook' and they would never leave us alone." The military thought it wise to tolerate Soul Alley, although they were certainly not above staging the occasional raid, especially if white soldiers had ventured there and lost their jeeps or money. One such Christmastime raid upon the Black GIs of Soul Alley was described in *Time* magazine:

> Just after the 1 a.m. curfew one day last week, 300 heavily armed American and Vietnamese MPs, civilian police and militiamen, supported by 100 armored cars, trucks and Jeeps, swooped down on a narrow dirt alley in Saigon and sealed it off. As their house-to-house search began, G.I.'s groggy with sleep and drugs, scampered in every direction, a few over rooftops, trying to escape. Their women followed, some stark naked, some wearing only pajama bottoms, as spotlights from two helicopters above played on the bizarre scene. When the roundup ended four hours later, 56 girls and 110 G.I.'s, including 30 deserters, were hauled off into custody.

Stewart Kellerman, a correspondent for United Press International, was so intrigued by the power of the dap handshake that he decided to trek to Camp Holloway—located in the Central Highlands of Vietnam—in search of the meaning of this news-making gesture. He had heard that there were a good many Black soldiers at the camp. Kellerman and other reporters were grateful that, unlike in previous wars, reporters in Vietnam were not operating under censorship rules, save for the military's directive that their stories not reveal troop locations and map coordinates. Kellerman had been covering Vietnam long enough to make dependable contacts, and he had earned the trust of some Black soldiers—thus his invitation to Camp Holloway. Once he reached the camp, a group of Black soldiers welcomed him into their tent. He walked in, past a sign—NO RABBITS ALLOWED—code for "whites not welcome." One of the soldiers put on some music, *Black Talk!,* an instrumental by the organist and jazz musician Charles Earland. (Earland had gained popularity on the airwaves back in America, from Black communities and jazz lovers.) With the beat of the music, the mood inside the barracks between Kellerman and the soldiers lightened and became relaxed. One soldier lit up a joint and began passing it around. Someone popped open some cans of beer. The soldiers quickly realized that Kellerman wanted to know about more than a handshake; he wanted to know how they felt about being in the military and fighting a war in a racially charged environment so far away from racially haunted America. "Man, the Army's the most racist pig organization you ever seen," twenty-one-year-old Specialist 4 Robert McCarthy, from Newark, New Jersey, told Kellerman. "It's set up by dudes for dudes. Nothing for the brothers except trouble." McCarthy's thick Afro dominated his face. Twenty-four-year-old William Toliver of Los Angeles was nodding, and broke in: "Yeh, man. That's the way to tell it, you dig. You tell me I should be a good soldier. Man, what do you want? I'm getting the same gooks as the rabbits. But all I get is troubles from the pigs."

It was a war that went about creating its own slang. "Gooks" were the Vietnamese; "pigs" were the military police. And "rabbits" were white people, specifically soldiers.

Throughout the night, Black soldiers kept waltzing in and out of the tent. Every soldier, upon entering, went around the room dapping the other soldiers. Twenty-three-year-old Gary Terrell, a native of Birmingham, Alabama, began talking about the angst he felt when superiors demanded he get his Afro cut, or told him to stop dapping. "I tell them no," he told Kellerman and the others. "You ain't gonna take my soul away from me, you dig. So what happens? I got every rotten job the rabbits can think of." This prompted some aggressive nodding. It had all turned into a kind of rap session—the music vibrating, the beer being swilled, the white reporter, Kellerman, taking it all in. Tommy Gladney, who was just twenty-one and came from Chicago, had a story to tell of an encounter with communist troops in a Montagnard village that left him feeling rather strange about the enemy: "Man, we figured we were in for it," he related. "They jumped us and there was nothing we could do. But then, man, it was fantastic. Charlie [another word for the North Vietnamese] just sits down and has supper with us. We smoke some good stuff and then they let us go." Gladney—who admitted to Kellerman he had once been jailed for going AWOL—claimed that the Army's dispensing of discipline was also unfair. "A white guy goes out and kills 13 . . . babies and gets away with it . . . A brother doesn't shine his boots one day and he gets nine months." The beer supply was finally getting low. And there was a war to get back to. Kellerman began bidding his farewells to everyone who had come to meet with him. They all began dapping one another. They paid special attention to Kellerman himself, just to make sure he got the intricacies of the dap down correctly. And they told him it was absolutely fine to quote everything they had said. This wasn't their grandfather's World War II or their father's Korea. This was Vietnam. This was the war where it was time to speak one's mind.

Stewart Kellerman had gone to Camp Holloway to try to unravel the roots of why there was so much rising bitterness on the part of the Black soldier. It was a mystery the American military itself had yet to understand. A good many Black soldiers, once they completed their twelve-month tour of duty and were back on American soil, would share stories, in cinematic detail, of their Vietnam experiences. Their soliloquies—from front porches, beneath corner lamplights, in barbershops, in basements, where they sometimes congregated, in drug rehab centers—were often vivid enough to draw intent listeners. They became young griots—oral historians—of the country's first fully integrated war. Then another group of soldiers leaving America for Vietnam would share their own stories upon landing, of what was happening in riot-torn America. It was like a constantly looping cinematic movie reel, two kinds of hell, both of them mean and hot.

Marine Corporal Roger Harris had been in Vietnam for thirteen months. He was happy to be heading home to Boston. "I was feeling good because I survived and fought for my country," he recalled. "I got off the plane at Logan and I stepped out there in my uniform with my duffel bag and I'm just happy to be home. I walked out to the curb and the cabs just kept going by me. And there was a state trooper standing there. And I didn't realize what was happening, but he stepped in the street and he stopped a cab and he said, 'You have to take this man. You have to take this soldier.' And the driver looked over at me and he said, 'I don't want to go to Roxbury.' They don't see me as a soldier, you know. They see me as a nigger coming home."

These young Blacks returning from military service were so often seen as outcasts, because their people had no publicized roots yet, had no Black history that had been universally shared and documented across America. Television docudramas about slavery and segregation and civil rights were years away. What was happening in Vietnam was happening in America, and what was happening in America was happening in Vietnam—the Afro, the debates about heritage, the balled fist as the Black Power salute. During the Vietnam War, Ralph Ellison—author of the 1952 novel *Invisible Man,* about Black invisibility—sought to explain the significance of Black culture in white America, which had always been there: "In other words, had there been no blacks, certain creative tensions arising from the cross-purposes of whites and blacks would also not have existed," he wrote. "Not only would there have been no Faulkner, there would have been no Stephen Crane, who found certain basic themes of his writing in the Civil War. Thus also there would have been no Hemingway, who took Crane as a source and guide. Without the presence of Negro American style, our jokes, tall tales, even our sports would be lacking in the sudden turns, shocks and swift changes of pace (all jazz-shaped) that serve to remind us that the world is ever unexplored, and that while a complete mastery of life is mere illusion, the real secret of the game is to make life swing." Which pretty much explains why, inside that tent in the Central

Highlands of Vietnam, those Black soldiers felt right at home introducing their reporter guest to the jazzman Charles Earland. Even in war, make life swing!

It was the richest of ironies that young Black soldiers in Vietnam possessed a kind of newfound badge-wearing authority as they marched into villages—they were the law, they had come to bring order, they were pointing M-16s—and yet, back in America, they were often vilified by law enforcement. America had designed such a system of racial hierarchy that when teenage Blacks—their draft letter might be landing in the mailbox any day—stared into that system they couldn't help but see the country as it was: whites held the top jobs seemingly everywhere—in hospitals, at the movie studios, inside publishing houses, in newsrooms, on white-dominated college campuses, in corporations, and, among other professions, in law enforcement. The system, and mindset, had become so ingrained that it seemed to be the natural order of things. And when it came to justice, the system wasn't at all blind. To cite just one year, in 1967, Boston had twelve whites who had risen above captain in the police department and zero Blacks; Baltimore had twenty-one whites and one Black; Detroit had sixty-two whites and one Black; Memphis had forty-four whites and zero Blacks; San Francisco had ten whites and zero Blacks. In whichever geographical location one looked, the statistics rarely improved. In Philadelphia, twenty-three whites had risen above captain—and zero Blacks.

Trapped in a land of limited opportunities, the young Black "soul brothers" of 1964 through 1968, with the war showing no signs of easing, reenlisted at a higher rate than whites. Many of those who reenlisted had little to look forward to in the civilian world, and a steady military paycheck was nothing to be frowned upon. In Black communities, antiwar fever moved rather slowly, and the sense of patriotism remained strong. Eldson McGhee, a native of Georgia, felt the community's pride just before departing for Vietnam. "My dating opportunities flourished beyond description, and rest became an impossibility," he remembered. "I could never recall such fussing over me, such kissing, crying, and other carryings-on, even in my childhood."

As time passed, and the war inched closer to the length of World War II, military recruiters became more aggressive in their pitches to inner-city recruits. On recruiting visits into the homes of Black families, they played up the angle of seeing exotic locations during military service, and receiving college financial assistance afterward. Colonel William Cole was assigned to the Army's Sixth Recruiting District in San Francisco in the 1960s, an area rich for Black recruitment. Cole had his own personal feelings about aggressively recruiting young Blacks: "President Johnson wanted these guys off the streets," which he saw as the president's reactions to the urban crises.

Major American magazines (*Life, Look, Harper's,* and of course *Ebony,* with its Black readership) seemed particularly aware of race, and started printing photographs of Black and white soldiers lolling at base camps in Vietnam and fighting together on the battlefields. Photos of a white soldier carrying a Black soldier to safety, or a Black soldier carrying a white soldier, seemed to be about more than just war: they seemed to say that this racial experiment was working. Even if there were mighty deep fissures in race relations that were being kept from the American public.

Sergeant Clide Brown, Jr., a native of Brewton, Alabama, loved the Army. He'd been a soldier since 1961, after graduating from the all-Black Booker T. Washington High School. He was so gung-ho about the Army—anyone who met him could feel it—that when *Time* magazine reporters came to Saigon to do a cover story it was suggested they talk to Brown. "I don't know whether I would march if I became a civilian again," Brown told *Time.* "But nobody is going to shove me around." This was the kind of answer palatable to military officials: not radical at all, yet also manly. The magazine was so impressed with Brown that they put him on the cover of a 1967 issue, titled "The Negro in Vietnam." When the magazine reached Brown's base camp in Vietnam—his picture taking up the entire front cover—he got some ribbing from fellow soldiers. And some reactions that were not so good-natured. The morning after the magazine's delivery in Brown's camp, the cover boy woke up to see a burning cross, symbol of the Ku Klux Klan, that had been placed in front of his tent. There were many—white and Black, officers and enlistees—who were outraged. But there was also the reality that someone among them had placed the burning cross there. Brown's superiors dealt with the ugly situation by suggesting he forget about it.

At Christmastime in 1967, LBJ himself landed in Vietnam. Gliding among the gathered troops at Cam Ranh Bay, he seemed to tower over most of them, grasping their hands, asking about their hometowns. Hell, he said, he wished he could grab a rifle himself and charge into those hills in the distance! He might not have started all this, but he was responsible for it; it was his war. He came to talk about endurance, and about defeating the communists. "Please know that we are with you," he told the soldiers in a speech meant for the South Vietnamese as well. "We are for you. We will be there until the end."

Chapter Three

Ia Drang Is More Than Unforgiving

For weeks, everyone in small Leonardtown, Maryland, had been talking about the march. It was being advertised on billboards and posters. Those who could tune in to the Black radio stations over in Baltimore, eighty-five miles away, were inundated with announcements about the "1963 March on Washington for Jobs and Freedom." It would be taking place on August 28, in Washington, D.C. The aim of the march was to bring attention to inequality and the mistreatment of Blacks in segregated America. Many Blacks in Leonardtown had been feeling emboldened by the ongoing demonstrations over in Cambridge, Maryland. For the past two years, racial protests had been taking place there, often turning violent. Some of the town's Black citizens had taken to openly carrying firearms for protection. Cambridge's three Black police officers were not allowed to arrest whites, or even to patrol on the white side of town. Another example of the town's deeply rooted discrimination lay in the administration of health care: even if Cambridge Blacks were deathly ill, the local hospital would not admit them, instead telling them to get to Baltimore to receive attention. The Kennedy administration had arranged talks with the white power brokers in

During the infamous Battle of Ia Drang in 1965, George Forrest ran more than two hundred yards through enemy fire to help his men. He was one of many heroic figures during that days-long battle.

Cambridge in an effort to bring about agreements and some kind of peace, but, absent a federal civil rights law, they were unsuccessful.

For many Blacks in Leonardtown, their best job opportunities lay in going to work on one of the tobacco farms in the area. Jimmy Forrest and his wife, Harriett Ann, however, had been able to save to send each of their five children to college. As parents, they wanted a better and more just America. They were quite excited about making the trip to attend the March on Washington. The nation's capital sat just a little over sixty miles from Leonardtown. Among its scheduled headline speakers was Reverend Martin Luther King, Jr. King's reputation had been rising ever since the yearlong and widely publicized 1955 bus boycott in Montgomery, Alabama. Rosa Parks, who had been a seamstress on a military base, had been arrested for disobeying a city edict that stipulated that Blacks, when off base, had to ride in the back of city buses, or give up their seats to white riders who had come aboard. (The desegregation of military bases meant that Parks didn't have to suffer such an indignity when on base.) The King-led boycott spawned arrests, legal challenges, and, finally, a local victory for Black citizens. Ever since Montgomery, King had been the one civil rights figure across the country—pulpit by pulpit, march by march—garnering the most publicity from mainstream media.

Family photos and their children's athletic trophies adorned Jimmy and Harriett Ann's comfortable home. They were proud of all of their children, but their son George was on their minds an awful lot these days. He was in the Army, stationed at Fort Myer, in nearby Virginia. George was a member of the 1st Battalion, 3rd Infantry Regiment, also known as the Old Guard.

On the morning of August 28—with waves of people from all over the country rolling into Washington, D.C., for the march—George Forrest's Army unit was put on alert: they were told to be ready to go to the area of the Lincoln Memorial, where marchers were gathering, should there be any disturbances. Those inside the Kennedy administration feared some kind of clash; they also dreaded the optics of a mass demonstration against American discrimination. The Kennedy team suggested to the organizers that the march had the potential to derail any planned civil rights legislation. Besides, as Kennedy had reminded the leaders prior to the march, he needed the legislative favors of Southern Democrats—segregationists—if he was to pass any civil rights bills, and those politicians would certainly not be happy about a march. But King, Bayard Rustin, and other organizers refused to cancel it.

As his unit was being given orders about being on alert, a damnable thought crossed Captain George Forrest's mind: he knew his parents were attending the march, and now he just might have to go into the throngs and, if ordered to arrest them as protesters, figure a way to ignore those orders! Harriett Ann had never been known as anyone's wallflower. Thoughts also were swirling in her son's mind of having to protect his mother from rifle-toting fellow soldiers. He needn't have worried. "My mother later told me, if I had had to go and she crossed my path, she'd've said to me, 'Boy, you better get that bayonet out of here.' "

The march was a watershed moment in American history. The multiracial assemblage, estimated at 250,000 people, included some of those who had been beaten on the Edmund Pettus Bridge in Selma; many had come by bus or car, some from as far away as Watts in Los Angeles. The gospel singer Mahalia Jackson had the crowd swaying with her rendition of "I Been 'Buked and I Been Scorned." Rabbi Joachim Prinz of the American Jewish Congress spoke, testifying to the mix of religions in attendance. John Lewis, the young activist bloodied during the first Selma march, addressed the gathering: "My friends, let us not forget that we are involved in a serious social revolution." He blamed American politicians for building careers by making "immoral compromises." Such a massive march had first been proposed during World War II, to protest mistreatment of Black citizens. The Roosevelt administration, like the Kennedy administration, also didn't want a demonstration to take place at that time. They reached a compromise with organizers when they promised a Fair Employment Practices Commission (FEPC), which would ensure equal treatment in hiring in wartime industries. But by 1963—with racial murders still staining the land and civil rights legislation stalled—the guardians of the civil rights movement were ready. Many came with eagerness to hear Martin Luther King, Jr., who delivered a galvanizing speech that sang across the walls of history: "We will not be satisfied until justice runs down like waters and righteousness like a mighty stream." There were more words, about oppression and about the debt a powerful and rich America owed to its Black citizens, about that ticket not being punched. There came a moment when Mahalia Jackson interrupted him and said, "Tell 'em about the dream, Martin." And then it was as if the old lions—Frederick Douglass, Abraham Lincoln, all the great orators—were awakened. "I say to you today, my friends, and so even though we face the difficulties of today and tomorrow, I still have a dream. It is a dream rooted in the American dream . . ." Blacks around the country had heard him in their pulpits, surprising them with cool biblical logic week in and week out. These words, now, on this large stage, seemed to be for white America. It was as if he had summoned them to a sermon, before the eyes and ears of the nation. "I have a dream that one day, every valley shall be exalted . . ." He continued: "And when this happens . . . we will be able to speed up that day when all God's children, black men and white men, Jews and Gentiles, Protestants and Catholics, will be able to join hands and sing in the words of the old Negro spiritual, 'Free at last! Free at last! Thank God Almighty, we are free at last!' "

When they returned to Leonardtown, Jimmy and Harriett Ann Forrest couldn't stop talking about the march, about King, about his "Dream" soliloquy. They talked about it for days, with family, friends, and neighbors. Their son George had checked in to make sure they made it safely back to Leonardtown. He was also mighty impressed with the words of King's speech.

George Forrest felt his own dreams of a good life would begin with his entry into the United States Army after graduation from Morgan State University in Baltimore. At Morgan State, he had studied hard. Though the coursework was not always easy, all it took were images of the tobacco fields back in Leonardtown to convince him to devote more time to library study. He became a member of the football team, as a tight end, but mostly sat on the bench, rarely getting into games. Still, sports exemplified good camaraderie, and he liked that aspect of it. And something else drew his attention: classmates who were marching on campus wearing starched uniforms. They were members of ROTC (Reserve Officers' Training Corps), and they looked so snappy and well organized. He inquired, and found out that the ROTC program provided students with military training and also a financial stipend—spending money—with the requirement that those students officially join the military upon graduation. Forrest decided to sign up. "You were guaranteed a job after graduation! Had I not gone into the military, I would have struggled to get a job. I'd have probably gone into teaching or the funeral business," he says.

There was a motto that had long swept through Black colleges and their ROTC programs:

Equal Soldiers. Equal Citizens.

The majority of Black colleges and universities, just like Morgan State, were located in the South. In their early years, in the 1920s, the schools were wedded both to philanthropy and to a Southern ideology espoused by many of their patron saints. William H. Baldwin, Jr., was considered a friend of the Negro colleges. A Harvard man and a philanthropist, he had befriended many respected Blacks, among them clergymen and educators. Baldwin's financial contributions on behalf of Black education may have been generous, but they most assuredly hewed to an antebellum mindset. As he advised Negro students during one address:

> Face the music; avoid social questions; leave politics alone; continue to be patient; live moral lives; live simply; learn to work and to work intelligently . . . learn that it is a mistake to be educated out of your necessary environment; know that it is a crime for any teacher, white or black, to educate the Negro for positions which are not open to him . . .

Upon receiving his military commission when he graduated from Morgan State, George Forrest hoped indeed to elevate his station in life. He became a member of those referred to as the last of "the Kennedy Class"—men who became officers during Kennedy's White House years. Because Kennedy himself had been a World War II naval hero, the designation meant quite a lot. These last of the Kennedy men would come to be among the first to land in Vietnam as armed "advisers."

George Forrest, after collecting his college degree in 1960 and serving a military assignment in Germany, could not see that he would soon find himself on Chu Pong Mountain in Vietnam, in one of the bloodiest and most unforgettable battles in the history of the Vietnam War.

There was a peculiar thing about war—the actual bloody fighting itself—when it came to race and racial identity. In the midst of battle and smoke and grenade explosions, the adrenaline kicked in, and racial identity, the color of one's skin, just faded away. In battle, things became grainy one second, then exceedingly vivid the next, then back to grainy, then came more explosive vividness. More shrapnel, more slicing bayonets, more bullets in the back, the face, the shoulder, the head, the torso. When the bodies started falling, it was a brotherhood of the saved, the lucky, the doomed, the dying, the alert son of a bitch who told you to duck, to put that helmet back on, to move to the left, to the right. It was the soul brother dragging the white dude to safety; it was the white medic whispering to the Black cat to breathe, damn it, breathe! So often, it was in those nanoseconds of time between silence and explosive noise, between life and death, between wise decisions and unwise ones, that the white soldier and the Black soldier instinctively abandoned all historical memory. The hell with what had happened on that bridge in Selma. No one cared now about Watts and the blood spilled there. They were dancing together in the horrifying ritual of war. They would survive together, or die together. Let's save each other! Let's get our asses back home! Let's get out of Vietnam alive!

When George Forrest landed in South Vietnam, he didn't feel any need to talk about the fact that the battalion he was assigned to had once been General George Armstrong Custer's battalion. No one spent a lot of time talking about Custer's fate—too spooky. Forrest was headed into battle, sure enough, with Hal Moore and his men already ahead of him. The two men were destined to meet up.

In the second week of November 1965, Lieutenant Colonel Hal Moore of the 1st Battalion, 7th Cavalry Regiment, stood in an area south of Plei Me, in the Highlands of South Vietnam, to receive his orders from Colonel Thomas Brown. "Hal, I'm moving your battalion west tomorrow morning," he told Moore. He pointed to the map laid out before them. "Here is your area of operations—north of Chu Pong in the Ia Drang Valley. Your mission is the same one you have now: Find and kill the enemy." Brown knew that Moore's troops were inexperienced in serious combat. Though they had been in Vietnam for two months, they had yet to face a full regiment of enemy soldiers. He told Moore to make sure his rifle companies did not stray too far from one another once they helicoptered into the Ia Drang Valley. The Americans had the feeling that the North Vietnamese might be using the valley as a watering hole—a place to replenish themselves after fighting. It was also close to the Cambodian border, which allowed the North Vietnamese to cross over and back for supplies, a luxury American forces did not have.

The ongoing riddle of Vietnam lay in its complex history of coups and thwarted alliances, in its having fought colonialism, in its Buddhist religion, its homegrown peasant life, and its Chinese influence. To the Americans, Vietnam's history meant little. The Americans cared about stifling communism, afraid it might wash ashore in America like dark ocean waves, sweeping over everyone and corrupting millions upon millions.

Barry Zorthian was a Yale man whom LBJ had sent to Saigon; he was among the many Ivy Leaguers atop the growing war machine. Zorthian thought he had a fantastic job. He handled psychological warfare for the Americans. A tough former Marine, he spoke with General William Westmoreland a lot, sometimes several times a week. Some of his planning consisted of having flyers printed up and dropping them over villages where the Americans thought Viet Cong soldiers had lived but were now away in battle. "Daddy, Daddy, please come home," the flyers said in Vietnamese. What Zorthian failed to realize was that the Viet Cong were *home.* This was *their* country.

The American soldiers, at times, talked of the lush landscape, the verdant hills, the greenery that spread for miles in and around Vietnam. But now topography wasn't on Hal Moore's mind. As Lieutenant Colonel Brown had ordered him: Find and kill the enemy.

It was routine for soldiers to ask one another where they were from, and they'd try to imagine what someone's hometown might be like. These exchanges gave them a wider sense of their own country. The soldiers of 1st Battalion, 7th Cavalry Regiment, who had checked their canteens and ammunition belts and grenades and were getting ready to helicopter into the Ia Drang Valley, were from everywhere:

Aliceville, Alabama; Pass Christian, Mississippi; Oakland, California; Miami, Florida; Hartford, Connecticut; Steelton, Pennsylvania; Rigby, Idaho; North Bergen, New Jersey; Bangor, Maine; Hayfield, Minnesota. It was as if you uttered the name of your hometown to someone, then you had a fighting chance to get back home, through some kind of spiritual calling. Everyone had seen *The Wizard of Oz.* And, hell, everyone wanted to get back home. No one wanted to die.

On Sunday morning, November 14, Lieutenant Colonel Moore and his troops began arriving at a landing zone in the Central Highlands of the Ia Drang Valley, which Moore had code-named "X-Ray." They brought Chinook helicopters with as much weaponry as they could carry. They flew into X-Ray in groups of four helicopters. With mountains in the distance, and thick trees all around, they hustled through the elephant grass to cover. "By God," Moore howled upon landing, "they sent us over here to kill Communists and that's what we're going to do." Moore was worried about the time it would take to get all 450 of his men to the landing area from their base camp. (George Forrest and his men remained behind, on standby.) Each quartet of copters ferried about eighty men. The back-and-forth trips took more than four hours—four hours until they were at maximum strength.

Nearly sixteen hundred North Vietnamese soldiers were on Chu Pong Mountain, just above the American forces. They were watching from an observation post. The enemy, wearing khakis and sandals, were carrying a lot of hand-me-down Russian-made weaponry. And, just as they had done to the French, they were determined to drive out the Americans to keep and honor their independence. "I had a strong sense that we were under direct enemy observation," Moore recalled, describing the minutes after their landing. "That, and the fact that everything had gone well so far, made me nervous. Nothing was wrong, except that nothing was wrong." The Americans caught sight of a lone Vietnamese soldier in the brush, gave chase, and caught him. He appeared to be a deserter. Under questioning, he admitted that there were many Vietnamese soldiers in the area—and they were ready to engage.

It was noontime when the Americans were first fired upon.

Moore was determined to keep the enemy away from the landing zone—about the size of a football field—because that was where the incoming helicopters had to land, where George Forrest would have to arrive with his troops. Moore knew they'd have to go confront the enemy to keep them away from that zone. The sudden exchange of gunfire was relentless, from both sides. Soldiers were twisting and dropping dead, their howls of pain filling the smoky air. Sergeant Jimmie Jakes, a rifle-squad leader from Phenix City, Alabama, recalled: "As we were advancing toward the enemy, two of my men and one from another squad were hit by machine-gun fire. I was ordering men to my left and right; some didn't even belong to our platoon. I yelled to them to lay down a base of fire; then I crawled to aid the wounded. I was able to drag two of the wounded back to our defensive line. We had stopped advancing at this point. As I attempted to drag a third back I was wounded." Platoons and rifle squads were chasing Vietnamese troops deeper into the bush, as they were spotting more Vietnamese troops coming down from the hills. The noise was deafening. "There were the steady, deep-throated bursts of machine-gun fire; rifles crackling on full automatic; grenade, mortar, and rocket explosions," Moore recalled. The tall elephant grass was impeding visibility; Vietnamese troops kept coming; the wounded needed transport back to base camp; the fuselage of bullets was nonstop. Good news suddenly came with the arrival of another convoy of helicopters, bringing more soldiers, among them Sergeant Tom Keeton. He remembered: "Between one-thirty and one-forty-five p.m. we came in over X-Ray trailing a flight of four helicopters and you could see our soldiers and the North Vietnamese. The NVA were in the wood line shooting at the helicopter[s] . . . We never did come to a complete hover. All aboard had to dive out on the ground from about six feet up in the air. We ran in a crouch over to where Colonel Moore was, near an anthill. There were twenty to twenty-five wounded there, all huddled on the ground. We put the dead over in a separate area and started to work." Joe Galloway, a United Press International reporter, had been on one of the helicopters. "I could see these streams of light coming down the mountain, little pin-pricks of light," he remembered of the helicopter's approach. "This was the enemy approaching for the next day's attacks. They had little oil lamps tied to the back of their packs so that the guy behind them knew where to follow." Air cover zoomed in out of the blue skies, dropping 250- and 500-pound bombs. By the end of the first day, more than four thousand artillery rounds had been fired, and the American platoons had ordered more than three hundred fighter-bomber sorties.

The Vietnamese kept massing. Soon the American pilots were dropping their bombs.

American soldiers were sloshing across creek beds into the second day of fighting, flushing out the enemy while being shot at. "The enemy knew the area," as one soldier would succinctly put it. There was nary a moment to grieve for the fallen dead, just time to grab whatever maps or codebooks they might have been carrying. A cardinal rule: never leave maps or codebooks behind, because the enemy would certainly retrieve them. It was gut-wrenching to hear fallen men, dying, yelling for their mothers, who were thousands of miles away. Platoons got cut off from other units and were engaging in hand-to-hand combat. Some Vietnamese soldiers had roped themselves high up in trees and were firing down on Americans. When Vietnamese soldiers were shot in the trees, their rifles would spiral to the ground while they remained fastened in the branches, like a trapeze act frozen and suspended in air.

For three days, there were bombings, deadly night patrols, rolling grenades, bullets ripping into necks, men who had forgotten since childhood how to shed tears but were crying now for the dead and dying. For three days, the Americans held their ground against the relentless and combined Viet Cong and North Vietnamese Army forces. For three days, Vietnamese forces kept throwing their bodies into the line of fire, for they outnumbered the Americans nearly four to one.

George Forrest finally heard a crackle on his radio. "I got a call from my battalion commander, who said, 'Move four klicks, then three klicks to the west, and you will run into Hal Moore's battalion.'" His men moved as quickly as they could. George Forrest was the only Black company commander in his battalion, one of the few

Black commanders in this integrated war. He was not going to let anyone down. "And so we walked into LZ X-Ray not knowing what the hell was going on there. And when I got there, Hal Moore pulled me up and said, 'Who [are you] and where did you come from?'" With the battle raging all around them, Forrest thought of his young men and the life-and-death decisions he now had to make, minute by minute: "My job was to make sure they got home." George Forrest was actually right where he wanted to be. He wanted to climb the Army ladder of promotion, and an important step for an officer to rise in the ranks was to get combat experience. "I got command of a combat unit. That was the ticket to get a promotion. Normally, Black officers were not given combat infantry commands."

In battle, they barely slept, just stealing catnaps when possible. They dozed, free of dreams—dreams took time, and they had no time. Movement awakened them. Or another volley of bullets. Because this was the first big battle for most of them—including George Forrest—the number of soldiers falling dead around them was shocking. They ran their wounded to the approaching helicopters, then ducked beneath the blades and got back to the battle.

On November 17, the Army sent orders that the soldiers who had landed at X-Ray had to move out: Air Force B-52 bombers had taken off from Guam and were going to drop bombs on Chu Pong Mountain in a matter of hours. "For safety, we had to get at least three miles out," says Forrest.

The Americans were sent to an area known as Landing Zone Albany, six miles away. They started marching. "This was the least airmobile operation that occurred probably in the entire Vietnam War," Colonel Robert McDade would remember of the orders. "It was right back to 1950 Korea or 1944 Europe. All we got were verbal orders: Go here. Finger on map."

Captain Forrest realized that any move, with the enemy watching, was going to be risky. Furthermore, his men would be bringing up the rear, which was rarely a safe position. "McDade said we'd be the last company out," Forrest recalled. "I knew we were getting the tough job because we were reinforcements. McDade's instructions were very vague. At the time I thought it was because he didn't have a whole lot of information himself. We only had one map, and I had my weapons guy take an overlay and make himself a makeshift map. I told him to plot some fire support for us along this route so if something happens we can support ourselves. I put my company in a wedge formation, sent out some flankers, and moved out." The trees and tall grass provided some cover. The Americans captured two Vietnamese soldiers on the march. Though they cried to the translator that they were deserters, the Americans didn't believe them, were certain these were scouts who simply got caught. Their capture told Colonel McDade that more Vietnamese were close. He sent orders down the trail that he wanted to convene a meeting. Captain Forrest had to hustle along the line and join McDade and the others: "I'm going forward; you take over and deploy the troops in a herringbone formation, and spread them out good," he told one of his men. From front to back, the column of soldiers stretched about 550 yards.

A North Vietnamese reserve force had been hiding in the jungle. As the Americans reached Landing Zone Albany, the Vietnamese attacked, opening fire. It was ceaseless. Lieutenant Colonel Nguyen Huu An, a North Vietnamese commander, would come to recall the day of the Albany battle: "I gave the order to my battalions: When you meet the Americans divide yourself into many groups and attack the column from all directions and divide the column into many pieces. Move inside the column, grab them by the belt, and thus avoid casualties from the artillery and air." He had little doubt about the ability of his attacking forces: "This was our reserve battalion and they were just waiting for their turn. The 8th battalion had not been used in the fighting in this campaign. They were fresh." Hal Moore's men had yet to face the kind of mortar fire they suddenly were experiencing. Everyone was trying to set up positions. An American soldier raced to an anthill for cover: "I found stacks of GIs." Radio operators went down and died, making communications much more difficult and haphazard. It didn't take long for the North Vietnamese to have the Americans surrounded. As one soldier remembered: "It was clear that to leave this perimeter was death." Inside the perimeter, Moore and his men could see Vietnamese in the distance, just above the tall grass. It was the oddest scene: They were walking around—as if in a department store—stalking wounded Americans who were lying in the tall elephant grass, and killing them. In less than thirty minutes, the Americans had lost more than fifty men, and many others were wounded.

George Forrest knew he couldn't stay around McDade and the other officers who had gathered. "I knew we were surrounded," he says. "And so did the higher-ups." As soon as the enemy fire started, he immediately thought of his men, who were back down the trail, at the end of the column, and knew he had to get to them: they'd be looking to him for guidance. He huddled with his two radiomen, Larry Hess and Jimmie Smith, who had accompanied him to the gathering. They only needed to exchange a few words, because they all knew it was time to bolt back to their unit. It was important, Forrest emphasized, that they keep a distance from one another; bunched up, they could all fall in a hail of enemy fire aimed directly at them. About three hundred yards of tall grass and anthills lay between them and their unit, and invisible enemy soldiers could be anywhere—above them, in front of them, or behind them. Allowing twenty or so seconds between them, they took off; Forrest went first. Remembering his experience as a tight end on the Morgan State University football team as he ran, Forrest thought of how many opposing players he had knocked down or run over. He was back on the football field, grunting. Only, instead of a football, he was clutching a rifle and a bulky radio.

It didn't take long for the gunfire to start. Bullets were whizzing. He had to keep moving: "The firing was coming from all directions." The sounds of tree branches snapping behind him had to be his men, Hess and Smith, he figured, so he kept running. He couldn't see the snipers. Another round of bullets. Sometimes George Forrest saw figures off to the side, but he moved by them so quickly; the gunfire never stopped, and there was nothing to do but keep running. A rifleman who belonged to Forrest's unit would later comment: "Our company commander, Captain Forrest, came running along our line. He was stopping and telling everybody where to go. He acted as though he was immune to the enemy fire." He had fifty yards to go, then thirty yards. Finally, he reached his destination—his men, the men he had trained. He wondered if Smith and Hess had possibly zigzagged by him, had gotten ahead of him without his noticing and were already back. But he didn't see them. "My expectation was that I at some point would be able to reach out and touch them," he says about Smith and Hess. But his men told him that neither Smith nor Hess had arrived. He kept scanning the terrain and didn't see them.

When the two battles—at X-Ray and Albany—ended, by the fifth day, the toll was grim: 234 Americans—more than half the number of men who had fought—had died. Another 250 were wounded. And by the end of the long forty-three-day campaign, a total of 545 Americans would be arriving back in the USA in flag-draped coffins. It was an even grimmer toll, according to American figures, for the Vietnamese: more than 650 of their soldiers had died, and even more were wounded.

In 1876, at the Battle of the Little Big Horn in Montana, Lieutenant Colonel George Armstrong Custer, of the 1st Battalion, 7th Cavalry Regiment—now Lieutenant Colonel Hal Moore's battalion—lost 210 of his men and his own life in a battle with Sitting Bull and his warriors. The numbers were spookily close to the X-Ray and Albany losses. But spookiness was not something that soldiers allowed to unnerve them.

In a surviving photo of Captain George Forrest in the immediate aftermath of the Albany battle, he stands looking down over several dead soldiers. There is a forlorn look on his face as he regards the soldiers from both sides lying around. Some had been bayoneted, some felled by napalm. Forrest and his men launched a reconnaissance mission to look for Hess and Smith, the two radiomen. They found Hess, dead. They could not find Smith. A year later, Forrest and some of his soldiers returned to Albany, looking for any kind of sign of Smith's fate. They found his dog tags. "We didn't have to go out and find the bad guys," Forrest says of the two battles. "They found us." The losses still haunt Forrest. He would come to realize the hand of fate: "But this is why commanders often wonder, 'Why didn't I catch a bullet? What made me so special that they missed me?' And I was a couple of inches taller than either of [those] two kids."

Lieutenant Colonel Hal Moore realized that the Vietnamese were going to be formidable as the war went forward. "The peasant soldiers [of North Vietnam] had withstood the terrible high-tech firestorm delivered against them by a superpower and had at least fought the Americans to a draw. By their yardstick, a draw against such a powerful opponent was the equivalent of victory."

In the days and months following the Battle of Ia Drang, George Forrest thought about all the men the battalions had lost. "I personally lost seventeen men," he says. "I call them national treasures. I lost seventeen national treasures during the fighting." He thought quite a bit about Hess and Smith, his two radiomen, asking himself question after question: Should the three of them have stuck together? Did he provide the best instruction about navigating the terrain? There were a lot of heroes during the twin battles. George Forrest was one of them; his men told him as much. But he could never reconcile that with the loss of men under his command. Filled with guilt, he even found it hard to listen to those who called him a hero. Though his nearly three-hundred-yard run to get back to his men would live in their collective hearts and minds forever, and he earned a Silver Star for his heroics, the guilt of losing men haunted him. "I went into a shell," he says.

It was in 1965 that the phrase "the Vietnam War" officially took hold of the American imagination. It started to burrow its way into all those itty-bitty hometowns around the country, and up and through the big cities. This was the year when the big TV news organizations—CBS, ABC, NBC—beefed up their crews. Newspapers found reporters inside their newsrooms who wanted to go cover the ever-growing story. Everyday Americans started talking about it—the Vietnam War—on their lunch breaks, around the dinner table, inside factories, while doing their weekend grocery shopping. Soldiers who had joined the military during the Korean War, and who were determined to make a career in the military, now found themselves on their way to Southeast Asia, to Vietnam. This was the year of the Battle of Ia Drang, by the end of which General Westmoreland told Defense Secretary Robert McNamara that he was going to need more, a lot more, troops. The year when the chess pieces started to flip over. And the Vietnamese started to take control of the rules of the game.

Military officials couldn't help but learn lessons from Ia Drang. They learned that the Vietnamese would keep coming down from the hills, risking more soldiers than they imagined possible, and when their soldiers were depleted, there'd be even more soldiers coming over the horizon. Or up from the tunnels. Those Kennedy-era men who had first stepped onto Vietnam soil had to curb their optimism that things would end soon. "We had been fighting guerrillas," Forrest says. "But after Ia Drang we realized Hanoi was also willing to commit regular Army forces."

George Forrest returned to America after his first tour of duty in Vietnam ended. On the plane, he was told to take off his uniform before landing: the antiwar movement was gaining momentum and protestors were known to gather outside the terminal. He went back and did a second tour in Vietnam, and the folks in Leonardtown were mighty proud. He emerged from that second tour unscathed as well: fate.

CHAPTER FOUR

IN THE DARK-GREEN JUNGLE, A STAR IS BORN

At the time of the Vietnam War, West Point stood as the pinnacle of American military training, its legacy studded with famous names and personages. President Thomas Jefferson signed legislation establishing West Point as a military academy in 1802. The gray stone buildings are arrayed on hills above the Hudson River in Upstate New York, about fifty miles north of New York City. Its purpose was to train young men as officers, to churn out leaders to defend the United States of America. A legion of its graduates went into military lore, engaging in battles across wars at home and abroad—the Civil War, the Indian Wars, World Wars I and II, Korea. Among its famously known graduates were George Armstrong Custer, Ulysses S. Grant, William T. Sherman, John J. Pershing, Dwight Eisenhower, George Patton, Douglas MacArthur, and William Westmoreland. Westmoreland, West Point Class of 1936, was now leading the forces in Vietnam. "I have an intuitive feeling," Westmoreland said of the escalating battle, "that the Negro servicemen have a better understanding than the whites of what the war is about." This comment, however, demanded careful analysis, for it seemed a bit of sly propaganda: giving the Black troops intellectual

The Kansas native Joe Anderson showed great leadership skills at West Point. In 1966, Captain Anderson led his troops in a daring rescue mission in the Vietnam jungles. He later became a key subject in a documentary by a celebrated French filmmaker.

weight while, at the same time, ignoring racial issues tormenting the rank and file.

Those responsible for admission to West Point always had their pick of gifted young men (the academy did not become coed until 1976). Candidates had to be recommended by their congressional representative or one of their U.S. senators. Admission had long carried the same kind of cachet as being accepted to any of the Ivy League universities. But, beginning in the early 1960s, a significant number of West Point grads came to realize that their immediate destination after graduation—at which time they owed Uncle Sam military service in payment for their free education—was going to be Southeast Asia and the elephant grass of Vietnam.

Joe Anderson, born in 1943, grew up on the plains of Kansas, in the state capital of Topeka. His father worked for the Santa Fe Railway, his mother at a local department store. He had an idea he wanted to become an engineer. While he was in high school, some of his relatives were in the military. He liked their crisp, neat uniforms. "My brother would bring back these beautiful jackets from Korea," he says. The idea of West Point—great place to learn engineering!—caught his attention. But in Kansas—and everywhere else for Black children—education was limited by the rituals of school segregation. Segregated schools meant lesser funding for Black students, lesser pay for their teachers. And that battle for integration was now coming to Joe Anderson's hometown. So, before hearing about West Point, he heard about Thurgood Marshall.

Most every Black kid growing up in Topeka in the 1950s had heard either about the NAACP or about Thurgood Marshall. Marshall, founder of the NAACP Legal Defense Fund, had carved out for himself a staggering reputation as the premier civil rights attorney in the nation, roaming America and filing lawsuits on behalf of Blacks and their causes. In 1944, he had won a U.S. Supreme Court victory dismantling the all-white primary voting system in Texas; in 1948, he and fellow attorneys were successful in *Shelley v. Kraemer,* a case in which the U.S. Supreme Court ruled that racial covenants in housing deeds (a wicked tool used to thwart Blacks) were unlawful. The American military was also quite familiar with Thurgood Marshall. In 1944, a group of Black sailors, some of whom had been injured in an explosion that occurred while they were loading bombs on a ship at the Port Chicago Naval Station in California, staged a work stoppage aboard another ship, fearing another explosion. The Black sailors were soon charged with mutiny. Marshall flew to California. "Negroes in the Navy don't mind loading ammunition. They just want to know why they were the only ones doing the loading!" Marshall bellowed to an audience. "They want to know why they are segregated, why they don't get promoted." After the war—with mounting pressure upon Navy Secretary James Forrestal—many of the men who had been convicted and sentenced had their sentences reduced and were able to return to active duty.

It was during Joe's school years of 1952 and 1953 that the genius of Thurgood Marshall came to touch the world of the young man. While growing up in Topeka, Anderson and his classmates endured the challenges of a segregated education. It was clear to all that white schools were better financed. The overcrowding of the four Topeka elementary schools bothered McKinley Burnett, president of the local NAACP. City officials kept telling Black parents that they were only following the 1896 *Plessy v. Ferguson* Supreme Court ruling, which, for generations, had all but ensured a segregated American public life. Life in Topeka meant a segregated existence for Blacks: Their Black friends who traveled into town were obliged to stay at the Dunbar Hotel. The Apex movie theater was segregated. And they had a better chance of sprouting wings than of securing a loan from one of the banks in town. Thurgood Marshall and his legal team had been devising a plan to overthrow the segregated education system of America. It meant choosing jurisdictions, filing lawsuits, and, they hoped, having those lawsuits reach the U.S. Supreme Court to upend the brutish words and mindset of the *Plessy* ruling. Marshall dispatched Robert Carter—another NAACP lawyer, and a World War II veteran—to Kansas. Carter did not have fond memories of the American military. "I thought I was pretty well balanced regarding the race problem," he would recall, "but once I got in the Army, the thing was ground into my face everywhere I turned: blacks acting as lackeys to whites, and whites acting oppressively toward blacks."

One of Joe Anderson's classmates was Linda Brown, about to take her place in the annals of Black history, American history, and constitutional law. Linda Brown's father, Oliver, allowed his daughter's name to be used as one of the lead plaintiffs of the desegregation lawsuit filed on behalf of the Black plaintiffs of Kansas. That lawsuit drew in cases in other locations: South Carolina, Virginia, Delaware, and Washington, D.C. These five cases pitted NAACP attorneys against the brightest minds in America who were defenders of segregation. When the Supreme Court ruled in 1954 in favor of Linda Brown and Joe Anderson and the other Black schoolchildren of Topeka and elsewhere, it was a titanic decision, and began the process of altering American life. "To separate [Black children] from others of similar age and qualifications solely because of their race generates a feeling of inferiority as to their status in the community that may affect their hearts and minds in a way unlikely ever to be undone," the court wrote.

—

Six years after the *Brown* court ruling, Joe Anderson had grown up with his heart and mind set on entry to West Point. His parents would certainly appreciate the free education provided to cadets. In the summer of 1961, young Joe went through the process of filling out the West Point application forms. One of the state's U.S. senators, Frank Carlson, supported his application. He was full of anticipation, awaiting the results of his application, but then disappointed when he was informed he was not accepted, although he was told he had been named as an "alternate"—someone to be offered admission should someone who had been admitted not attend for some reason or simply change their mind. Joe Anderson began to make plans to attend the University of Kansas. But one day not long after, the phone rang at the Anderson household. It was West Point. They told Joe a spot had opened up in the incoming Class of 1965 and asked him if he still desired a West Point education. He excitedly told them he did, and started packing.

Anderson entered West Point in 1961 with nine hundred other cadets; there were five other Black cadets in his class. It quickly became clear to the Black cadets that a mentor would serve them well. One of Anderson's fellow cadets happened to be James Fowler, Jr., whose father, James Fowler, Sr., had been a member of the Class of 1941 at West Point. While at the academy, he had been subjected to "the silent treatment"—fellow cadets only spoke to him when necessary because of academy duties. He'd found vile liquids poured into his shoes. The elder Fowler was eager to offer knowledge and guidance about the road ahead for the new young Black cadets. "We got a lot of people who can sit at lunch counters and get their heads beat in," the elder Fowler, only the fifth Black graduate of West Point, told Anderson and the others. "Your job is to get through West Point."

This advice meant a lot to the group. Anderson put his head down and gritted through the drills and challenges. There were times when he thought he might not make it. There were days when he wished he were back in Kansas, enjoying himself at one of the state universities. But after his freshman year, he gained confidence and started feeling optimistic about his future at the academy. There were stories still circulating about "the Alabama Gang"—a group of white Southern cadets who had a reputation for harassing Black cadets. But Anderson never had a confrontation with them. He impressed the academy leadership enough with his singular determination that he became a battalion commander, then a regimental commander. Those were valued promotions for any cadet.

James Fowler, Sr.—the Class of '41 graduate—was living in Baltimore. Jim Jr., delighted in bringing Joe Anderson home, to enjoy a home-cooked meal and conversation with the Fowler family. One topic, something else that the elder Fowler wanted the young Black cadets to know, was the name Henry Flipper.

In 1877, Henry Flipper became the first Black graduate of West Point. He distinguished himself as an officer at various military postings until suspicious charges of wrongdoing destroyed his career. In 1999, President Clinton issued him a posthumous pardon.

It seemed that every Black cadet who entered West Point had to pass the ghost of Henry Ossian Flipper.

In 1873, Henry Flipper, of Atlanta—who had been educated in American Missionary Association schools—was accepted into West Point. He studied engineering. A few other Blacks had preceded him, but none had graduated, and all had been met with a series of harsh racial abuses and insults, for which little was done to the perpetrators. It was Georgia Congressman J. C. Freeman who recommended Flipper to the academy. For his faith in Flipper, Freeman received vicious hate mail and public excoriation. "Freeman, the only white man in Georgia that ever disgraced the military of the United States," one Georgia newspaper wrote of the congressman. Despite the daily insults, Henry Flipper seemed to realize intuitively that his main job was to get through West Point. Fellow cadets, not surprisingly, also gave him "the silent treatment." As Flipper would recall: "There was no society for me to enjoy—no friends, male or female, for me to visit, or with whom I could have any social intercourse, so absolute was my isolation." Visitors to campus who knew of Flipper's presence looked for sightings of him. "There's the colored cadet! There's the colored cadet!" It was as if he were some kind of freak.

After Henry Flipper graduated from West Point, on June 14, 1877, he received his commission and was assigned to the 10th U.S. Cavalry, an all-Black unit. There followed a series of postings across Texas and the Indian Territory, which later became Oklahoma. He fought in the 1880 Indian War, battling the Apache leader Victorio. Many of the white officers loathed Flipper's rank, and even his presence. In 1881, he was stationed at Fort Davis in Texas. By then, he had also become a very able engineer. When some commissary funds came up missing at Fort Davis, Flipper was accused of stealing $3,791.77. In the ensuing court-martial all of Flipper's fears about being judged unfairly in the military were tested. He was cleared of the theft charge, but speciously found guilty of "conduct unbecoming an officer and a gentleman." On June 30, 1882, Flipper was dishonorably discharged from the Army.

He refused to become undone, however, and over the succeeding decades found work as an engineer and a cartographer. He wrote articles about Mexican law, having become adept at picking up foreign languages. After working for an oil company in Venezuela in the early 1920s, he wrote a book about the laws of that country. Flipper died in 1940 in Atlanta. He was eighty-four years old. Though he did not appear to be bitter about his military treatment, he died disappointed that his rank had been taken from him. In the succeeding years the small number of Black graduates from West Point did what they could to keep his name alive. In the late 1970s, the name Henry Flipper finally came back into the news. In 1977, the U.S. Army granted Flipper a posthumous honorable discharge. In 1978, a television movie was aired, *The Trial of the Moke,* about the embezzlement case he had to endure, starring a quartet of rising Black actors at the time: Samuel L. Jackson, Howard E. Rollins, Franklyn Seales, who portrayed Flipper, and Alfre Woodard.

It was not lost on Joe Anderson or his fellow Black graduates in 1965 that there was not a single Black general in the U.S. Army. Of the six Blacks who had entered West Point in 1961, only four remained on graduation day—Art Hester, Hal Jenkins, Jim Conley, and Anderson.

It was time to go out into the world.

Joe Anderson was first assigned to Fort Bragg in North Carolina. The community was still getting accustomed to the recently passed 1964 Civil Rights Act—to a world of evolving integration. Life on American military bases had been integrated, but beyond those bases, particularly in the South, Black soldiers were still complaining about having white rental agents refuse to rent apartments and houses to them. Army officials had to visit local rental agencies to remind them they were breaking the law. Anderson was eager to acclimate himself to life at Fort Bragg. The greeting he received upon first arriving there, from a white noncom, was: "Welcome Lieutenant [Anderson], I've been in charge of the Platoon, and I'll keep things going. You just sit back and take it easy." Anderson did not know what degree of racial condescension might have been involved in the greeting, but he was not amused. "No," he replied, the leader in him quickly surfacing. "I'm here to lead the Platoon, and you're my Platoon Sergeant. Let's get that straight right now." It didn't take long for Anderson's talents to be noticed. At Fort Bragg, he was often singled out for praise, just as he had been at West Point. Superiors took note of his cool demeanor and his skilled leadership abilities. He applied for Airborne School and completed the course. Then he went to Ranger School, a process that required top exam grades as well as uncommon physical stamina. Not only did he soar in Ranger School; he was named a leader of his class. And by June 1966—a year after graduating from West Point—Joe Anderson was on his way to Vietnam.

A monthlong pause in U.S. bombing in Vietnam had begun in late 1965. Senator J. W. Fulbright, chairman of the Senate Foreign Relations Committee, was growing more and more concerned about the war. "As we continue our efforts to bring the Vietnamese war to a satisfactory end, I think we should keep in mind that nationalism rather than communism is the dominant political force in Southeast Asia," Fulbright said. Such concern from a powerful senator should have worried the White House, but it did not. The White House mindset was unwilling to let go of the spread of communism as the primary reason for fighting this war. The bombing resumed in late January 1966. By April 1966, the Johnson administration had ordered B-52s to take off from Guam and, for the first time, drop bombs on North Vietnam. "I am not happy about Vietnam," President Johnson had confided to aides inside the White House, "but we cannot run out."

Upon his arrival in Vietnam, Joe Anderson took over the 1st Platoon of B Company of the 12th Cavalry Regiment. He didn't get much time for acclimation, because soon thereafter he was out patrolling through the elephant grass with his men. A field report informed him that a group of soldiers who had earlier been on a search-and-destroy mission were under severe attack in a landing-zone area referred to as LZ Pink, in the Central Highlands. Their radios had been damaged, and communication was spotty. Anderson and his platoon of thirty-three men had to get to the area where the soldiers were thought to be and help them. They were soon up against darkening skies, so Anderson directed his men to form a perimeter and settle in for the night. "Headquarters wanted me to keep moving and keep searching through the night," he recalled. "I knew it wasn't a smart thing to do, because you could get ambushed. You can't see what you're doing in the dark." Anderson stayed put. Just before midnight, enemy fire sliced the air and surprised them; they were surrounded by a Viet Cong battalion. Anderson's platoon returned fire. He called in flares to light the terrain for visibility, then began calling in artillery. Enemy soldiers were being hit and falling. Anderson knew his men would be judging his actions: "This is my first operation. I'm new in-country. People don't know me. I don't know them. They have to be thinking: Can this platoon leader handle it?" But it was war; there was simply no time for fear. "I can't remember wondering if I was ever gonna get out of this," Anderson remembered. "I just did not have time to think about it. I was just too busy directing fire to be scared." By his own estimate, Anderson and his men seemed to be outnumbered ten to one. At one point, knowing his men were nearing the end of their ammunition, Anderson instructed them to fix their bayonets. "There may have been 300 to 400 of them," he said, estimating the enemy forces. When Anderson's men realized they had either killed the enemy soldiers—with the help of the artillery fire—or forced those still alive to flee, they could finally reassemble. They had won this mean battle. They checked their weapons and the immediate area around them. With a lost platoon still to locate, they started moving. They came upon the scene just fifty yards away. "A bloody massacre" is how he summed it up. When they checked the area for the American soldiers wounded and dead, they counted twenty-five dead, four badly wounded. There was some noise in the weeds; everyone poised to shoot. Four fellow soldiers emerged from the jungle, breathing heavily but still alive. The survivors were animated in expressing thanks to Anderson and his men; it seemed like a near miracle to them. Throughout all of the hours of marching and firing, and finding the platoon, only one of Anderson's men suffered an injury, a hip wound. His men immediately became enamored of their new leader. It was sheer courage, as well as the manner in which he had talked to Headquarters: no matter what they had ordered, he let them know what was best for him and his platoon. They were in the jungle; they were the ones being shot at. The men of his platoon had heard him taking a stance, and making judgment calls, and they had seen that his judgment calls had been the right ones to make. In his first engagement with the enemy, Joe Anderson had shown his men what a leader does under extreme pressure. He had capitalized on what he had been taught at West Point, and this was now his platoon—the Anderson Platoon.

Word quickly spread about what Anderson and his men had done in the Central Highlands. (He would be awarded the coveted Silver Star for leading the rescue of the missing platoon.) He came to realize that he had a gift for leading men, a gift for battle: "I was gung-ho. And I thought the war would last three years at the most." Meanwhile, something else began to dawn upon Anderson: he was receiving a special kind of respect, the very kind he might not have received back in America. "I was an officer and a gentleman by act of Congress. Where else could a black go and get that label just like that?" Anderson was also impressed with the racial makeup of his platoon, which he thought was unique: Two of his squad leaders were Black. A third of his thirty-three-member platoon—made up of whites, Blacks, Mexicans, and a few Native Americans—were Black. Even though he himself was the product of an elite education, Anderson realized the plight of so many young Black men back in America: "For many black men, the service, even during a war, was the best of a number of alternatives to staying home and working in the fields or bumming around the streets of Chicago or New York."

Joe Anderson had never heard of the Frenchman Pierre Schoendoerffer. But Pierre Schoendoerffer, whose history in Vietnam dated back to the French Indochina War, had heard about Joe Anderson and his platoon's exploits. And he badly wanted to meet him.

Vietnam, and its war history, was always tethered to politics and the foreign-policy muscle of America. In late 1951, Massachusetts Congressman John F. Kennedy was plotting a U.S. Senate run. Wanting to acquire more foreign-policy expertise, he undertook a trip around the world, and made a stop in Saigon. At the time, the French were waging war against the Vietnamese. Anticommunism was the common denominator between the French and their Western allies. Kennedy expressed worry to some of his traveling companions that the war might eventually result in American involvement. A year later, when Chinese forces marched into North Korea to aid in battling against UN forces, American leaders felt they had to noticeably increase their support for the French in Indochina. Kennedy's prophecy had come true.

The ongoing French Indochina War, begun in 1946, did not seem to derail the French. But by the time the calendar turned to 1953, many French citizens had grown weary of the war. There were reports of French brutality, of innumerable human rights abuses, of the use of napalm—a nasty gel that burned through flesh and forest. The French who had tired of the war began referring to it as *la sale guerre*—the dirty war. Colonialism was an ugly political pastime. In the early spring of 1954, French commanders devised a plan to lure the pro-communist Viet Minh into a battle at Dien Bien Phu. Unbeknownst to French forces, the Viet Minh had directed men and women through the dense countryside and up along mountains, all while ferrying weapons to the location. The battle that erupted lasted almost two months. The French counted on air support, but the Viet Minh had weaponry to counter those attacks. The battle eventually resulted in a devastating defeat for the French. It also saw the country split into two, North and South Vietnam. Approximately eleven thousand French troops were captured by the Viet Minh and imprisoned. Of those imprisoned, only thirty-three hundred made it out alive.

One of those injured at the Battle of Dien Bien Phu was Pierre Schoendoerffer. His life could have outdone that of any figure sprung from the pages of Ernest Hemingway. Born in 1928 in Chamalières, France, Schoendoerffer came to decide he wanted to be an adventurer. His favorite writers were Henry Melville, Joseph Conrad, and Robert Louis Stevenson. "I've always dreamed of being a sailor," he once said. "All my great books have been in English, starting with 'Treasure Island,' the best first pages of any novel I've ever read." Determined to travel the high seas, he did so in his early adult years, aboard cargo and merchant ships. These were risky endeavors, but his father had died in 1940, and he was pretty much left to his own prowess and decision making. His travels kept him dreaming. He became fascinated with photography and filmmaking. A story in *Le Figaro* caught his attention, about Georges Kowal, a photographer assigned to the French Army in the Indochina war, who had been killed during the conflict. This death ignited Schoendoerffer's passion, and he decided to enter the French military service. He was given photography and cameraman duties. The work was both exciting and, of course, dangerous. He suffered a wound at the outset of the Battle of Dien Bien Phu. Following his recovery, on March 5, 1954, he parachuted back into the war zone with Vietnamese paratroopers. In May, the camp he was attached to was overtaken by NVA forces. Schoendoerffer sat in a crowded prison camp for four months, until finally freed. Now he knew he was going to be a filmmaker. Men at war fascinated him, especially men who had shown uncommon bravery while surviving against overwhelming odds. He made a film, *The 317th Platoon,* which was released in 1965, extolling the exploits of bravery at Dien Bien Phu, which won the Best Screenplay Award at the Cannes Film Festival. He was the rare filmmaker who had actually been in war.

In 1966, Schoendoerffer found himself back in Vietnam. He had been hired by French National Public Television and, accompanied by a two-man crew, was interviewing and filming footage of the war. When word reached Schoendoerffer about the Anderson Platoon—their successful rescue mission in the Central Highlands, that they were led by a Black man, a West Point graduate no less, and were skillful in the art of maneuvering around the Highlands by helicopter—he told himself he had to meet this Lieutenant Joe Anderson.

The French populace had long had an enviable rapport with Black Americans. They had welcomed Black soldiers into their ranks during World War I—when America shunned them—and honored scores of those soldiers for their bravery with the Croix de Guerre medal; in 1925, they had welcomed the Black chanteuse Josephine Baker to Paris, where she became a nightclub sensation and later a heroine during the French Resistance; and they had welcomed Black writers such as James Baldwin and Richard Wright into their orbit during the 1950s. The racism that had become all but cemented into law, and into the attitudes of many in white America, was far less powerful in France. White American filmmakers had shown no inclination to highlight the exploits of Black soldiers in either World War I or World War II.

When Schoendoerffer met Joe Anderson, it seemed a delightful coincidence that Anderson spoke French. He wasn't fluent, but, thanks to his West Point education, he was conversational. Schoendoerffer, who spoke English, shared with Anderson his decade-long experiences in Vietnam. Anderson quickly realized that the fearless Frenchman had a proposal for him: he wanted to embed himself and his two-member film crew into the Anderson Platoon and accompany them on patrol. It sounded a bit crazy to Anderson, and the pitch made him wary—"not knowing who they were and what they were going to do to get us in trouble." But he soon found himself intrigued. He wanted to know how long Schoendoerffer and his crew wished to travel with the platoon. At least six weeks, he was told. Anderson, who was both cerebral and macho ("gung-ho," as he had put it) and hardly shy about either attribute, continued rolling this proposal around in his mind. He knew that such an involved request had to go up the chain of command. The Army had always been cautious regarding the media, and at the time many believed that the war would be over soon. Also, Joe Anderson had become an instant hero. Even if many from the outside world were not yet aware of it, Army higher-ups were quite cognizant that a Black West Point graduate had distinguished himself on the battlefield, and such a development was bound to have a positive effect upon recruitment, though the military was experiencing a myriad of racial problems. Besides, if the Schoendoerffer gamble went haywire, the disaster would be traced to French TV executives and their decision to send him into battle—not to the American military.

The Army—somewhat to its own surprise, and once Anderson himself agreed to it—signed off on the Schoendoerffer proposal.

Schoendoerffer was aware that in 1966 America was only two years beyond passage of the 1964 Civil Rights Act, upending centuries of a certain way of life. Even before they all—the soldiers, Schoendoerffer, and his crew—set out, he was curious about race inside the platoon. Anderson was quick to admit that, because they had been in a serious battle, because they had had a chance to bond, because they all knew the value of saving one another's asses, they had yet to experience any racial turmoil, as existed in so many other units. They were from all over—Illinois and Alabama and the Dakotas—and represented the mix of America. "There was only one significant area of conflict," Anderson admitted, regarding race among his men. "It was over music." The music was piped in by the American Forces Vietnam Network, which blared twenty-four hours a day and seven days a week. And it was in the base camps where arguments would erupt over that music, about which music was better, Black or white. Sometimes the arguments were playful, other times not so much. The American Forces Network played a lot of rock and roll, a lot of country music. The Black soldiers didn't like it, and complained that their culture was being ignored. Music from 1966:

White Music
"California Dreamin' "—The Mamas & the Papas
"Last Train to Clarksville"—The Monkees
"These Boots Are Made for Walkin' "—Nancy Sinatra
"Working in the Coal Mine"—Lee Dorsey
"Secret Agent Man"—Johnny Rivers
"Yellow Submarine"—The Beatles

Black Music
"Ain't Too Proud to Beg"—The Temptations
"Uptight (Everything's Alright)"—Stevie Wonder
"Don't Mess with Bill"—The Marvelettes
"634-5789 (Soulsville, U.S.A.)"—Wilson Pickett
"This Old Heart of Mine"—The Isley Brothers
"My World Is Empty Without You"—The Supremes

It was the music white and Black soldiers had heard back in America in their respective communities, on their local radio stations, while dancing with their girlfriends in their basements on Friday nights. It was the music that spoke to them. And it was the music they wanted to hear during wartime. The situation became so charged that Army officials let it be known to the American Forces Network (its radio operators were mostly white) that the music they played indeed lacked diversity, that it skewed more toward white music. The network began instituting changes.

Each time he led his platoon out on patrol, Joe Anderson had one mission in mind: "I was there to keep them alive—and get them home. That was all that mattered." He understood that the Viet Cong were a formidable foe. "They were trained and familiar with the jungle," he said. "They relied on stealth, on ambush, on their personal skills and wile, as opposed to firepower."

In September, Anderson's platoon, accompanied by Pierre Schoendoerffer and his two-member crew, set out on another search-and-destroy mission up into the Highlands of Vietnam. For the next six weeks, Schoendoerffer captured as much of the war as he could: the soldiers sloshing through swamp and mud, and wolfing down food while keeping their eyes alert; helicopters swooping overhead; Viet Cong guerrillas startled by the American firepower when it came; soldiers shooting the breeze as if they were in some kind of clubhouse, then bolting into action at the rustling of bushes; Vietnamese kids appearing from the bush, hungry, begging for food. The camera crew caught Anderson shaving and washing in a waist-high swamp along with his men. Sometimes while shooting his reams and reams of film, Schoendoerffer had no idea what it would mean, how he would edit it. But he kept filming: soldiers playfully gambling with dice as if this were some kind of Las Vegas dream; a helicopter taking off, only to suddenly crash; the sometimes eerie stillness of war. Stillness always made one more nervous than gunfire itself, because stillness invited surprise. The film crew accompanied a tall white soldier on an R&R respite back to Saigon and into a nightclub, where he dwarfed two pretty Vietnamese women, full of laughter and whispering and kissing. And, of course, the crew filmed the wounded, the dying and dead, the limp bodies of breathless soldiers killed in battle being lifted onto pieces of cloth, the eyes of their fellow soldiers frozen at the loss. Anderson describes one assault during that six-week outing:

> We blocked a northern route of egress, and then we started to sweep south through the village . . . We walked through the village, through their entire battalion, to link up with our company on the other side. And they never fired a shot. To this day I don't know why. Meanwhile, the divisions piled on. We put about a brigade in, three battalions, and surrounded the village about a mile across. We did it so quick, they were fixed. They couldn't escape. And with artillery, aircraft, and naval gunfire off the coast, we really waged a high-powered conflict. But not without casualties.

Schoendoerffer and his crew kept trudging right along with the soldiers, filming, and fighting the snakes, mosquitoes, malaria, tall elephant grass, intermittent gunfire, and grenade blasts, just as the platoon had to do. This was what he wanted; it was the stuff of his literary hero Joseph Conrad.

Anderson believed in the anticommunist mission, but his background seemed to imbue him with a respect for the innocents of war: "Whenever we would go into villages . . . we would set up our medics to treat the children and the people. We would tend to scars, wounds, whatever. Give them aspirin and soap. We'd give the kids gum, cookies, C-rations. If we wanted to eat off the land, we would buy a chicken or buy a pig."

Both U.S. Army officials and French military officials were happy when the Anderson-Schoendoerffer excursion came to an end with no casualties among the film crew. Schoendoerffer and his crew had proved their mettle to Anderson and his men, and had even formed a bond that would last a lifetime. When Schoendoerffer made it back to Paris after his six-week sojourn, he set about making sense of the many hours of footage he had shot. Like any filmmaker, he went off to a darkened room to assess his material. The editing process involved cutting, and more cutting. He had to adjust the sound; he decided he himself would do the voiceover. While he was getting the material into shape, the filmmaker began to feel optimistic that he had something unique; there was even a giddiness. It all took him back to 1954 and Dien Bien Phu, when he had been filming as the French were defeated by the Vietnamese, and he just knew that the footage was special. But that footage got taken from him when he was captured and sent to the prison camp. Some of his friends wondered if his trek with the Anderson Platoon would be a kind of cinematic revenge.

On February 3, 1967, *La Section Anderson* premiered in France on French National Public Television. Schoendoerffer explains himself in the opening: "I went back to rediscover the Vietnam I had left thirteen years ago with the French Army. Except for a few poignant scenes, I discovered, above all, America."

Here are Schoendoerffer's words as a helicopter hovers above the jungle of Vietnam at the beginning of *La Section Anderson:* "It began on a Sunday in September 1966. On this day, the Vietnamese in their pagodas try to appease all the souls of the unburied dead—wandering souls—those of beggars, prostitutes, and soldiers."

What the French audience saw was one of the first documentaries of the Vietnam War—a frontline exposé of the rhythms of war, a platoon being led by an American Black man. The black-and-white film showed homesick soldiers, soldiers taking communion, soldiers gambling and smoking cigarettes, soldiers crying tearlessly over dead comrades. There's a scene of soldiers sloshing through water and mud with Nancy Sinatra's "These Boots Are Made for Walkin'" bouncing off the screen. There are helicopters and cannon fire and bombardments coming from what appear to be far distances. To the French this was *cinéma vérité,* the truth on celluloid. When the reviews came in, they were such as would have made any filmmaker proud. "The mere sight of a white soldier holding the hand of his Negro buddy who has been wounded tells of the brotherhood of battle without words," wrote a *Time* magazine correspondent in France. Schoendoerffer was soon besieged with phone calls from friends and *cinéastes* praising the film. "It took the country by storm," Anderson himself admitted of the French reaction. The director was stopped on the streets and in the Parisian cafés he frequented. "U.S. T.V. officials who have seen it consider 'The Anderson Platoon' the best documentary of the war to date," the *Time* correspondent wrote. "It may soon be shown on a U.S. network." In 1967, *The Anderson Platoon* was awarded the Prix Italia in Italy for Original Dramatic Program.

The *Time* correspondent who had mused that the film was drawing curiosity among decision makers in the American film community was correct: Now with an American title, *The Anderson Platoon,* and an American actor, Stuart Whitman, narrating, it was scheduled to premiere in America on CBS on July 4, 1967. The Army, encouraged that it was an apolitical film—which, to them, meant pro-war with a powerful ode to patriotism—sensed a publicity moment: they allowed Anderson to return to Kansas to watch the film with his family and friends. There was quite a bit of publicity, both in his hometown of Topeka and around the country. Anderson marveled at the attention the film was garnering. By year's end—with its positive word-of-mouth steadily growing—*The Anderson Platoon* was playing in art-house movie theaters around the country. And what appeared so searing about the film for audiences was the interracial play among soldiers, inside this integrated war. This was a kind of cinema American audiences, white and Black, had never seen before. *The New York Times* called the documentary "a many-sided experience that was related with compelling human understanding." The reviewer also referred to the film as "not only a lean and stark account of individuals in battle but a composite glimpse of the American character responding to the ultimate stress." Black publications picked up on the film's release, which introduced the Vietnam War to them in a new way: with a Black leading man.

Cinema had long had a difficult time with Black figures, let alone heroic Black figures serving in the military. The genre was so fraught that there was a bizarre backstory to the 1949 film *Home of the Brave.* The movie starred James Edwards, a rising Black actor in Hollywood. During filming, one of the producers, the socially conscious Stanley Kramer, decided to mislead the film studio by telling them he was filming a different movie from the one he was actually making. What he was filming was a movie about racism in World War II, a subject that had never been addressed in film with any depth. Kramer and his team knew that some Southern theaters wouldn't show the movie. In Houston, it was announced Blacks would only be allowed to see it at midnight showings. The film "abashes the white man for both his habit of Negro prejudice and worse, his unconscious tactlessness," *The Dallas Morning News* wrote. From *The Commercial Appeal* in Memphis: "Let no smug section of the nation think [the Negro problem] is exclusively the South's baby. It belongs to us all." Between *Home of the Brave* and *The Anderson Platoon* lay a huge gap in modern war movies with a Black hero.

French cinema officials were so surprised by the critical praise of Schoendoerffer's film that they decided to enter it in the documentary section of the American Academy Awards. On February 19, 1968, when the announcements for the 40th Academy Awards were shared with the worldwide public, the nominees for Best Documentary Feature were *Festival,* produced by Murray Lerner; *Harvest,* produced by Carroll Ballard; *A King's Story,* produced by Jack Levin; *A Time for Burning,* produced by William C. Jersey; and *The Anderson Platoon,* produced by Pierre Schoendoerffer.

On the early evening of April 10, Schoendoerffer was among the well-dressed crowd gathered inside the Dorothy Chandler Pavilion for the Academy Awards ceremony. Bob Hope served as the evening's host. The actress Barbara Rush was given the task of opening the envelope for winner of Best Documentary Feature: *The Ander-*

son Platoon and Pierre Schoendoerffer. This win seemed stunning. Schoendoerffer gave a short speech, thanking the members of the Anderson Platoon—"above all because of the human quality of their leader, Joe B. Anderson." But that wasn't the only prize the film won: it went on to win an Emmy Award and a BBC Merit Award.

Lieutenant Joe Anderson had become the first acknowledged cinematic Black hero of the Vietnam War, celebrated by both the Army and French cinema itself.

But another war movie came along, in 1968, *The Green Berets,* starring John Wayne, and its make-believe jingoism dwarfed the real-life story of *The Anderson Platoon.* Wayne—one of Hollywood's most pro–Vietnam War figures—appealed directly to President Johnson to get permission from the Pentagon to help with his film. LBJ loved *The Green Berets,* and kept silent on *The Anderson Platoon.* Critics howled at Wayne's film, and not in a good way. Renata Adler, writing for *The New York Times:* " 'The Green Berets' is a film so unspeakable, so stupid, so rotten and false in every detail that it passes through being fun, through being funny, through being camp, through everything and becomes an invitation to grieve, not for our soldiers or for Vietnam . . . but for what has happened to the fantasy-making apparatus in this country." The *San Francisco Examiner* called it "the phoniest, most laughable war picture in many years." Two years before Wayne's film, a song called "Ballad of the Green Berets," sung by Barry Sadler, had climbed to the very top of the record charts. It had played on every rock-and-roll and country station.

The Army had a real hero in Joe Anderson, and they were going to show him their appreciation. He got a promotion; he became a Stateside aide-de-camp to a general. "Being featured in *The Anderson Platoon,*" he knew, "had obviously helped my career." Now that he was Stateside, he began to wonder if his estimation of a three-year war in Vietnam was still valid; he had enough insight to know it was not. At heart, he was a warrior, so he signed up for a second tour of duty.

Joe Anderson was hardly the only one wondering about the direction and duration of the war. The hosts of the popular TV news program *Face the Nation* were also quite curious. They invited President Johnson's ambassador to Vietnam, Ellsworth Bunker, onto the show.

> ELLSWORTH BUNKER: I think we're now beginning to see light at the end of the tunnel.
>
> BERT QUINT: Mr. Ambassador, you talk about light at the end of the tunnel. How long is this tunnel?

Anderson, by virtue of his latest promotion, landed back in Vietnam as Captain Joe Anderson. He was also now a company commander, and there were not many Blacks with that title. Now back in the war zone, he noticed changes. Soldiers—especially those dapping Black soldiers, who were dapping more aggressively now—had a lot more questions about the war and their mission. "What was very clear to me was an awareness," Anderson felt, "among our men that the support for the war was declining in the United States. The gung-ho attitude that made our soldiers so effective in 1966, '67, was replaced by the will to survive. They became more security conscious. They would take more defensive measures so they wouldn't get hurt. They were more scared. They wanted to get back home."

CHAPTER FIVE

THE PIANO PLAYER CAUGHT IN A RACIAL QUAGMIRE

They had been showing up along the streets and alleyways of Saigon. They were hard to miss, because they looked different from the usual Vietnamese children. American soldiers fathered babies in Vietnam, just as soldiers had done in other wars. There were brothels in Saigon; there were desperate women who needed food and money. Honest sex doesn't exactly exist in wartime. The kids who had been fathered by Black GIs in Vietnam had a darker complexion; they couldn't help but stand out. They had an even harder road to traverse than poverty and war: they would often be ostracized for their complicated racial appearance. They came to be called *bui doi*—"the dust of life." The Black GIs, many from broken homes themselves, suddenly had to confront playing a part in another broken family, caused by war. Some of them, after their tour of duty, brought their Vietnamese lovers to America so they could get married. The red tape was always hellish, because the children's paternity had to be proved. Many of the children would be left behind. "These children are doomed by the racism of their countrymen to be blown about in the streets and alleys, to fend for themselves," the acclaimed Vietnamese writer Viet Thanh Nguyen wrote.

Philippa Schuyler, a renowned concert pianist, grew dismayed by the harsh racial climate of America. She largely abandoned her career in the mid-1960s to go rescue orphans in Vietnam who had been fathered by American soldiers. A selfless and fatal decision.

—

If one was looking for a family in mid-1960s America that illuminated all the painful realities about Blackness in the nation—and about whiteness, and about racism, and about genius and fame, and about writing, and also about the pull of the wicked, headline-making body count of the Vietnam War—that family could be found behind the door of a small, elegant apartment at 321 Edgecombe Avenue, in New York City. The address was in Black Harlem. The occupants of the apartment—all fearless totems of the times—were the Schuylers, a preternaturally close family consisting of three members, George and Josephine, husband and wife, and their daughter, Philippa. All were proud anticommunists and strongly supported America's incursion into Vietnam. They were also considered strange. Two members of the family, George and Philippa, gave off vibes of being downright embarrassed about being

Black. Josephine didn't have such a malady. She was white, even the granddaughter of onetime slave owner.

Not every Black in America was born into a onetime slave family, and George Schuyler—born in 1895 in Providence, Rhode Island, raised in Syracuse, New York—was proud to tell classmates his family had no slave lineage. He even refused to believe he had any Southern relatives at all. His parents—George and Eliza—were cooks, who made enough income to give him a comfortable upbringing. Missing from young George Schuyler's life in Syracuse, however, was the sight of Black figures who held any kind of authority or community respect. That changed when he saw Black soldiers in uniform on military exercises. He was entranced. So much so that he abandoned school and, at age seventeen, enlisted in the Army. Young George Schuyler became a member of the famed all-Negro 25th U.S. Infantry Regiment. During the next several years, he was posted to various locations in the Pacific Northwest. Another posting landed him in Honolulu, where there was much "rum and roistering." During World War I, he found himself writing for an Army magazine, *Service,* and he began imagining—because he liked writing and reporting so much—that the experience might lead to a full-time job someday. But he was thrown off course one day when, in 1918, in Philadelphia, he walked into a restaurant to get something to eat and was refused service because of his race. He was standing in the city of freedom, the city with the Liberty Bell, and couldn't get a burger. This angered him. "I'm a son-of-a-bitch if I'll serve this goddam country any longer!" he howled. He left the establishment. Then he abruptly left the Army. He went AWOL. Army investigators began looking for him. After three months of solitary roaming, he decided to turn himself in while in San Diego. He served nine months of a five-year sentence for desertion.

After prison, and without telling anyone about his prison time, George Schuyler finally launched a career, writing for periodicals that focused on a Black readership. His reputation grew as someone with a sharp eye and an enigmatic writing style. He secured a job in 1923 with *The Messenger,* a progressive newspaper founded by A. Philip

Randolph, who was soon to carve a reputation as a civil rights and labor figure. Schuyler was given a column, in which he aimed to "slur, lampoon, damn, and occasionally praise anybody or anything in the known universe." Blacks would not be spared. Adopting a satirical bent, Schuyler for years toyed with the sensitivities of both Blacks and whites. Blacks soon found his tone and philosophy off-putting. He even criticized the talents behind the epochal Harlem Renaissance: "the Negro-Art Hokum" is how he summarized the movement.

In the mid-1920s, George Schuyler took his act (or show!) to *The Pittsburgh Courier,* and became one of the most widely read Black columnists in the country. White Southerners came to read him because of his put-downs of Blacks; Blacks read him because he claimed reading space in the pages of *The Pittsburgh Courier* and had the ability to make readers chuckle. Now and then, H. L. Mencken, founder of *The American Mercury* and an acid-tongued critic himself, would also publish Schuyler.

In 1932, Walter White, who had been a seasoned lynching-and-riot investigator for the NAACP and now was operating as an NAACP official, sent Schuyler and another journalist, Roy Wilkins, to Mississippi to investigate reports of abuses against Blacks in the Federal Flood Control Project. Both went undercover, dressed in scruffy clothing, and visited nearly two dozen labor camps, from which they sneaked reports back to White about the galling abuses they were uncovering. The Black workers were being paid less than the white workers. Their segregated living quarters—of which Wilkins and Schuyler knew firsthand from having slept in them—were inferior to accommodations given to whites. It was dangerous work. Schuyler and Wilkins worked just like the Negro laborers, and when they could, in the evenings, they'd ask the Negro workers questions about their jobs and mistreatment. White recalled: "They found that Negroes, being paid an average of ten cents an hour, were required to purchase all their supplies from commissaries which charged exorbitant prices, and that any Negro who dared protest was beaten unmercifully. Some had been beaten to death and their bodies buried in the levees." It was the stuff of movies, of melodrama—two Negroes operating undercover and exposing racial abuses in a government program. One evening, Schuyler was rousted out of bed and his notebooks were confiscated by camp police. The police, hardly happy about this undercover impostor, threatened arrest. Schuyler managed to talk himself out of danger by saying that some of his work was for the War Department, and that government officials wanted to know the conditions of the camps so they could pour more money, if needed, into the Mississippi economy. Schuyler was taken to a nearby street and told, "Don't wait for the train." He had to flee town as best he could.

The year of George Schuyler's notable undercover Mississippi investigation, 1932, also saw another important moment in his life. He and his wife, Josephine, had their first and only child, a daughter, Philippa Duke Schuyler.

Josephine Cogdell had walked into the offices of *The Messenger* in Harlem and laid eyes on George Schuyler just as he'd laid eyes on her, which led to drinks. Schuyler was not a conventionally handsome man, but those who met him were often intrigued by his wit, even if it could be caustic. As for Josephine, she had alluring eyes and a buxom figure. She hailed from a wealthy white cotton-and-cattle family in Texas. They owned mills and plenty of West Texas land. The Cogdells crossed into Black life via sexual energies and scandal: There had been affairs with Black maids involving the men in her family. There had been lies and divorces and courtroom entanglements, often traced to furtive assignations with Black women. Their money shielded them from what otherwise would have been public scorn. Scientific studies led them to practice strict dietary protocols, heavy on grains and various herbs. Josephine's foray into Black

Harlem was par for the course. Already divorced once, and running away from a new paramour when she reached Harlem, she was intent on exploring what treats the city might hold for a brave Texas girl. It was 1927, and she had already been submitting articles and having them published in *The Messenger.* She settled into a Greenwich Village apartment. When it came time to visit the *Messenger* offices, the editors—she later claimed—didn't know she was white. Cogdell reported this in her diary, in which she wrote obsessively. One entry followed an outing with George: "Something marvelous has happened . . . and by all moral and social logic, I should now be feeling disgust, regret and contrition. I feel none of these," she wrote after her first night with Schuyler. "I cannot for the life of me conjure up a single shred of shame. This morning George possessed me. My blood is still ringing from it."

In due time, John Garth, the former lover whom Josephine had fled from, arrived unannounced at her apartment. He suspected she might be seeing someone. His suspicions were correct. "You, living with a nigger!" he howled upon the discovery. "What will your father say? . . . Your brothers ought to come up here and kill you both! And they will when they find out!" He wasn't finished: "You've always had a Negro complex," he told her. But when he left, she was free to continue her affair with Schuyler, who asked her to marry him. The private ceremony took place on January 6, 1928. Before they wedded, she wrote in her diary: "The Cogdells were all miserable with their legal mates, their good women and men. We have no place in the anemic, conventional world. We are savages. We like our meat and our whiskey raw. I've always liked the night better than the day because the night is still primal and can never be tamed. Our kinship is with people who frankly, lustily fight, and love, and break the soil, and sing. It is in our blood, the love of black people."

They married at the courthouse in Manhattan, a quick and quiet affair. A public wedding might have brought out the crazies, and they knew it—among them certain members of her own family, the ones not wild about Negroes.

—

In planning their family, the Schuylers believed in "hybrid vigor," a term associated with plant and animal genetics. It meant that their newborn, Philippa, would be raised on mother's milk and then raw foods. Sugar and salt and other items deemed harmful to the baby's health were forbidden.

Interracial married couples were not only very rare in America, but illegal in many states. The Schuylers were enough of an intriguing couple—George a writer with a following, Josephine an artist and a writer—that the birth of their baby was mentioned in many Negro newspapers.

As she grew, Philippa Schuyler began showing signs of being extraordinarily intelligent for her age. When she began playing difficult compositions on the piano, in 1934, at the age of three, some people started calling her a child prodigy, even a genius. The parents loathed the terminology, insisting that their child, their creation, was in an advanced state of mind because of their belief in "hybrid genetics." Newspapers wrote about her.

Before she hit her fourth birthday Philippa's IQ was measured as being between 179 and 185. An average child's IQ often fell between 80 and 120.

Two months shy of her fifth birthday, young Philippa was entered in the National Piano Playing Tournament in New York City. She played a variety of classical compositions and emerged as one of seven winners. No one her age had ever achieved such recognition. *Time* magazine—in prose tinged with the racial insensitivities of the day—wrote:

> Prodigious at more than music is this Harlem-born daughter of a white mother and coal-black father. Mrs. Schuyler paints, writes for Negro newspapers. George Schuyler was a day laborer and a dishwasher before he became a novelist . . . a contributor to American Mercury and Saturday Evening Post. All three Schuylers subsist on raw vegetables, raw meat, a diet which Mrs. Schuyler claims is largely responsible for her daughter's

> precocity . . . She is keen at mathematics, reads fourth-grade books, writes poetry, draws and paints, turns out neat letters on her father's typewriter.

The Schuylers were so enamored of their child that they would not allow her to attend just any public school. Her education came from a variety of sources and locations: the prestigious Convent Music School, which she integrated; lessons at Durlach and Emerson, a tony school affiliated with New York University; and finally, her parents began employing personal tutors. Husband and wife kept in touch about their daughter's progress via letters during George's long reporting trips. There were many musical events for little Philippa; more ribbons and prizes and news accounts. She was paid, sometimes as much as $175 for a performance, an amount that, in those Depression-era times, would have made any family swoon. "I often speculate on what she will become and what glory she will reflect upon us," George Schuyler wrote in one missive to his wife, in terms that read as if they had invented a product. "It is a wonderful thing to look forward to. I just know she is going to be a marvelously beautiful and intelligent woman. We must do everything to preserve her, like a hothouse flower. For she is a rare and exotic breed. There are few beings like her in the world."

It is hardly any wonder that Philippa soon began asking her mother why she was being physically beaten for the littlest infraction at the piano. The beatings, she said to her mother, were painful. Josephine told her it was for discipline, and to make her even better!

As the years rolled onward, Josephine and her a-star-is-born daughter embarked on constant journeys, notably throughout the Midwest. "Most of her concerts," the Schuyler family biographer recounted, "were sponsored by black organizations; those sponsors that were white were religiously affiliated, usually Catholic. Her reviews in the local and national press, both black and white, were outstanding."

Meanwhile, little Philippa's Texas relatives, when they gleaned information from press reports about her, referred to her as their "nigger" niece.

Continuing to travel with her manager-mother into her teenage years, Philippa Schuyler drew applause for both composing and performing music. But—as in most showbiz families—there was friction. Phillipa started questioning what her mother was doing with her money. Even when he was around, and not traveling the country as a reporter, George Schuyler avoided the mother-daughter confrontations. In 1947, Josephine was quoted in a Baltimore newspaper: "We have, as a matter of fact, used all our money above bare living costs, to give her advantages in music. We have no car, we take no extra vacations—we couldn't and give Philippa the things she must have . . . Of course she could have had a millionaire to sponsor her education, but there were too many strings attached to such an arrangement." Such tales were news to Philippa herself, who began to question the direction of her career under her mother's guidance.

Having been in a cocoon for so much of her life—no close schoolmates, no outside activities, shielded from the lash of direct racism—Philippa Schuyler started to ask questions about her racial heritage, too. People wanted to know more about her Black father. There were uncomfortable conversations with so-called admirers. When she was a child, her talent could be seen as cute and charming. When she got to be a grown-up, inquiring minds were beyond cooing; they wanted details about her life. Also, the world of classical music wasn't drawing sizable Black patrons like jazz was. Having avoided the warmth of Black friendship with common folk, in and around Harlem, she had no allies to depend on. As she would later write in her autobiography, *Adventures in Black and White:* "[I] encountered vicious barriers of prejudice in the field of employment because I was the off-spring of what America calls a 'mixed-marriage.' It was a ruthless shock to me that, at first, made the walls of my self-confidence crumble. It horrified, humiliated me. But instead of breaking under the strain, I adjusted to it. I left."

In 1950, nineteen-year-old Philippa Schuyler surfaced in the Caribbean islands, playing concerts for high-ranking politicians there. Through the coming years, she popped up in Cuba, Haiti, and

Puerto Rico, then throughout Central and South America. The farther away from America she traveled, the happier she seemed. It was as if she had found a whole new world. She told new friends that she didn't experience the kind of racism in these new locations that she witnessed in America. Trips back to the States only ignited her urge to flee yet again. And something else had evolved in Philippa Schuyler's mindset. She was letting it be known that she was like her father in one major respect: she was an archconservative.

George Schuyler had taken the bizarre step of defending Senator Joseph McCarthy, whose lashing attacks against those suspected of being communist damaged not only whites but Blacks as well. Schuyler even went so far as to claim that Blacks didn't suffer from marauding Klansmen during the poll-tax era of the 1950s. What was once seen as his iconoclastic style of journalism was now scorned for being painfully out of touch with the burgeoning civil rights movement. He attacked both Malcolm X and Martin Luther King, Jr., even aligning himself with the John Birch Society, the radical right-wing and anticommunist organization founded in 1958.

Philippa Schuyler, as the sixties came into view, clung to her father's reactionary political beliefs. Sliding from music halls into auditoriums, she began giving anticommunist speeches while traveling throughout the South. Inasmuch as many whites considered the civil rights movement to be aligned with communism, the white audiences who came to hear her were in energetic agreement with her. Blacks who had supported her previous forays into the South, which had often been publicized by the NAACP, now avoided this new persona of Philippa Schuyler, the one who ignored the pain roiling Black America—the Emmett Till murder, the Little Rock school crisis, the jailed children who had marched alongside King. There were opportunities to speak out against the horrors sweeping the land, but she avoided doing so. She could have befriended the likes of Eartha Kitt or Lena Horne, two Blacks in the world of music who undoubtedly would have embraced her as another Black woman in the challenging world of the arts. Such communion did not interest her. Evelyn Cunningham, a Black reporter at *The Pittsburgh Courier* and a colleague of her father's, would have embraced her. Cunningham knew all the stars of Black

America—Jackie Robinson, Sammy Davis, Jr., Duke Ellington, Dinah Washington—because she wrote about them and dined with them. Her Harlem apartment was a hip salon of Black artistes; the conversations were spirited and the wine flowed. But Philippa Schuyler didn't want anything to do with Evelyn Cunningham or her crowd of Black sophisticates. Or Black people.

Philippa turned thirty in 1961, and began thinking of other career choices. She began to write. Her 1962 book, *Who Killed the Congo,* struck many Black Africans as an attack upon them rather than the white colonizers. Shortly after it was published, she received a scathing letter from Kwame Nkrumah, a champion of African independence. He was the first prime minister of the Gold Coast and later the first prime minister and then president of the newly renamed Ghana—not someone an author would want to have disagreeing with the premise of a book about Africa. In his letter to Philippa Schuyler, Nkrumah wrote:

> What on earth could have led you to believe that one of the greatest champions of our liberty and dignity that our continent has produced [Lumumba] was a Trotskyite, that Gizenga is a Communist, or that Ghana, which is well-known for her policy of neutralism and non-alignment, is "leftist"? Have you ever found time to study the records of Ghana's international relations since our independence? What could have influenced you to take this most anti-African attitude in Africa's international relations?

If anyone needed more proof of Philippa Schuyler's disenchantment with being referred to as Negro or Colored, it came following publication of a reference book, *Who's Who in Colored America,* which featured an entry about her: she was furious. When it came time to publish her next book, Philippa wrote to her mother: "NOWHERE in my forthcoming book do I want the word Negro or colored mentioned in connection with me, NOWHERE." In another letter, she told her mother that she had spent "30 miserable years in the USA" being a Negro, and that she was now determined to alter her identity.

She kept looking for love—and a husband—in various countries. She met a Frenchman, Maurice Raymond, who wanted to marry her. She wrote her mother a letter about Monsieur Raymond: "Imagine if we had a child, it would be perfect: Have his eyesight; his green eyes, his health and stamina; his Aryan appearance; my talents; AND NO NEGRITUDE." The prospect of marriage, however, soon evaporated. There were lies and too much mystery in Raymond's background, the full measure of which Philippa could never unravel. He sent unhinged letters, threatening blackmail concerning explicit photographs. She felt lucky to have escaped him.

In 1963, the year Martin Luther King, Jr., led the March on Washington, Philippa Schuyler, wanting to distance herself even more from "Negritude," from Blackness, decided to alter her name: She became Felipa Monterro. She felt even more that she couldn't make a living in America because of her racial heritage. The new name, in her mind, would position her as a foreigner, so that she could garner more concert invitations. She figured she might be thought of as Spanish, or Eurasian, or Oriental.

She took, yet again, to the high seas and foreign lands. Friends abroad, when informed of her name change, thought it somewhat strange—not the name, but the fact that she had done it.

Felipa was now not only traveling as an itinerant concert pianist, she was also carrying press credentials, having decided to follow in her father's footsteps. George Schuyler had begun writing for New Hampshire's reactionary and right-wing *Manchester Union Leader.* Serious journalists considered the paper an organ for the likes of the John Birch Society, a racist organization that George and Philippa both joined. To George Schuyler, those who had challenged interstate segregation by riding on "freedom buses" were simply "brainchildren of crackpots and conspirators . . . no more than hitchhikers pressing their luck."

As it happened, the name-change experiment was short-lived. By 1966, Philippa Schuyler had begun using her birth name again. She had also started relying more and more on her Catholic faith.

And she began dreaming of a place she had never gone before: Vietnam.

During her worldwide travels, Philippa had met many American diplomats, giving performances for them and their staffers. In 1966, when Henry Cabot Lodge, the American ambassador to Vietnam, invited Philippa to the war-racked country, she was excited to go. War did not frighten her. In Africa, after all, she had witnessed coups up close. Ambassador Lodge wanted her to perform for wounded soldiers. Wounded soldiers, of course, might be amenable to a little Mozart along with their rock-and-roll and soul music. Philippa—who had not seen in her tarot card readings that any harm would come to her in Vietnam, and who also still had her press credentials—packed her bags.

She landed in Saigon on September 2, 1966. Four months earlier, U.S. forces had begun intensifying their bombing in North Vietnam. For safety reasons, she slept at the U.S. Embassy, with embassy personnel very protective of her.

In between and following her initial performances, she saw, up close, the jaw-dropping muscle of the American military—planes, jeeps, tents, helicopters, hospitals, doctors, nurses—war. As she interacted with them, always asking questions, white soldiers may have been confused about her racial background, given the very light complexion of her skin, but Black soldiers had no doubt this was a Black woman. Ambassador Lodge and his aides worried about her safety and implored her to leave Saigon after her performances because the dangers of being in a war-torn environment were always present. But she had no intention of doing so. She had traveled the world enough to talk and seduce her way past gatekeepers; her press credentials provided her with even more of an ability to move about. Additionally, she spoke French, just as many Vietnamese did. Black soldiers introduced themselves to her. They gave her tips on where to go and not to go. She certainly was not above using her race when she needed to. She wrote her mother back in New York City: "I have visited the Vietnam People's Hospital, asylums, orphanages, refugee camps. I interviewed ex–Viet Cong terrorists . . . have talked with student groups, priests, social workers . . . American officials. I have gone into poor Vietnamese homes . . . and have talked to the 'man in the street' and . . . I have interviewed Negro and white civilians, and military personnel."

In Vietnam, race was everywhere: white commanders leading a war; Black soldiers fighting that war in disproportionate numbers; and native Vietnamese peasants crisscrossing in front of everyone as either friend or foe. From another letter to her mother: "A disfigured girl, the victim of one of our napalm bombings, looks straight through you, with a blank . . . stare. Should one look back at her? Sympathy would make her even more bitter, curiosity would be an insult." American military intelligence sometimes followed her, and sometimes they lost sight of her, dressed as she was in Vietnamese clothing and moving swiftly in her sandals. She kept popping up in places, questioning people, jotting down their answers. As a military intelligence officer confided: "She did not seem to have a base of operation that I was aware of. I'd run into her in Da Nang, even Quang Tri—don't know how the hell she ever got the permission to go there . . . She was always looking for a ride on an airplane or some kind of transportation. And in a lot of places she was looking for a place to sleep."

Something else besides gathering a potential news story began to affect Philippa Schuyler in Vietnam: the children, the orphans. The echoes of their cries in the orphanages began ringing in her ears. She knew that children, unlike many adults, were nonjudgmental. They just needed affection; they didn't care about her racial identity.

Her initial Vietnam odyssey ended after six weeks, but she told herself she had to return.

In March 1967, Philippa Schuyler was back in Vietnam. She had contacts in military intelligence that she utilized to help her move about. She was warned to not stay in one place too long. She appeared fearless, now back in the country on self-appointed rescue missions. She began hitching rides with missionaries, visiting children in villages and in orphanages. She roamed around the countryside—if not with missionaries, then alone. It was a risky business. Black soldiers helped her when they could. Between the falling bombs and constant battles and eyeing dead soldiers in body bags, she might have been in a Graham Greene novel.

The more she traipsed around Vietnam, the more she began to pay attention to something else: the mistreatment of the Black soldier. She began including anecdotes of this mistreatment in the articles she sent to the Manchester newspaper. It was as if war—blood, death, the presence of Black soldiers who always seemed to be looking out for her—had awakened something in her that she had never before possessed: a kinship with Black culture. The heritage she had denied for so long took an emotional hold. From another letter to her mother:

> Concerning bravery: I would like you to appreciate the fact that accepting a segregated form of life and work is not bravery at all. Men like William Mann and Leonard Holsey who . . . brave the slights of the race- and color-prejudiced American white who resents them having a position even moderately compensating their talents—THESE ARE THE TRUE HEROES. The American white man resents a colored person being in any role but servant or entertainer . . . The Negro military officers over here are some of the finest men I've met . . . far superior to white officers of the same rank.

She had never been so outspoken about Black life. War seemed to be crystallizing so much for her. In the letters she wrote home during the late spring of 1967, Philippa had even started heaping praise upon the likes of Stokely Carmichael! The Black soldiers had opened her eyes not only to the reality of being a Black American in 1967, but also to being a Black soldier in a foreign war in 1967.

Visiting village after village, Philippa was confronted by something else that touched upon her own life—the presence of racially mixed children. They were the children from the brothels, sons and daughters of Black or white American soldiers who had fathered children with Vietnamese women. She couldn't stop thinking of the near-impossible odds of the helpless mothers and their children making it to America. But those were rare occasions. Philippa would see the children at the Catholic-run orphanages, or just scampering around villages. Other Vietnamese children sometimes mocked them because they looked different. This opened a psychological wound in her.

There were benefits to being a gadabout in war-torn Vietnam, and Philippa knew it. She had accumulated contacts while traveling around Southeast Asia. She knew U.S. Embassy personnel, and she knew military intelligence officials—though sometimes, of course, they could be one and the same. Webbed between her own racial awakening and the pull of her heartstrings seeing wandering and hungry children, she went to work organizing airlifts to get as many children as possible, mostly orphans, out of Vietnam. She began visiting officials at Catholic orphanages, quick to inform them of her own Catholic faith. There were times when she annoyed military personnel, but she didn't care. Day by day, she was becoming more and more determined to save the babies!

On Tuesday, May 9, 1967, Philippa Schuyler found herself in Hue, a Vietnamese city that had been the imperial capital during the French-Indochinese regime. It had boasted gardens, walls, and palaces. But the sacred city had also suffered great damage in the late-1940s fighting. Philippa had come to Hue because she had arranged an airlift to get nine more children out of Vietnam. As they were loading up, a member of the ground crew was heard to utter to another crew member, about Philippa: "If you can convince her not to come back, we will get you anything you want." Perhaps it was said in jest. Everyone knew it was always good to get out of Hue, a very dangerous spot.

There were sixteen aboard, eight orphans among them, on the fifty-mile helicopter flight over to Da Nang. The pilot and copilot received word that the weather would be just fine. Philippa felt wonderful when she had executed an evacuation to its "go" stage. In the helicopter, space was tight, and one of the children had to sit on her lap. Philippa comforted the child as the helicopter lifted off and was soon flying at an altitude of three thousand feet. The scenery was beautiful and lush. Most of the orphans had never been in a helicopter before, and there was excitement on their faces. But the pilot, not far out from Da Nang, entered a mountain pass and dropped down to about fifteen hundred feet. This was a maneuver often done to avoid enemy fire. When he tried to lift back up, however, the chopper wouldn't rise. There was audible confusion in the cockpit. No matter what the pilots tried, it wouldn't lift. The pilots tinkered with the dials, then passengers heard a dreaded word from one of the pilots into the radio: MAYDAY, MAYDAY. The chopper, swirling downward, was close enough to the water so the descent and boom-splash was quick. Bodies smacked about. They were in the water; there was yelling, screaming. Parts of the chopper had cracked loose upon hitting the water, and there was nothing to keep it afloat; it slowly began sinking. Some of the passengers wrested themselves free of seatbelts and swam up to the surface. Jet fuel was seeping into people's lungs. A shoreline was nearby, and those who had broken free and were not too badly injured were swimming toward it. Then came a voice: "I can't swim!" It was Philippa. "Try. Kick your feet and move your hands," came an urgent plea from somewhere. Philippa Schuyler would have seen the shore—where some of the kids she had gotten out of Hue were now standing—before she descended below the surface. Someone onshore scrawled an SOS message into the sand. The chopper had fallen close enough to Da Nang so that a Marine rescue helicopter was soon on the scene. Thirteen survived the crash. Three did not: an Army private, a young orphan by the name of Doan Van Lien, and Philippa Schuyler.

On November 4, 1965, Dickey Chapelle, a photojournalist, was killed while on patrol with a company of Marines near Chu Lai, in South Vietnam. She was the first female journalist to die in the Vietnam War. Philippa Schuyler was the second.

News of her death swept around the world, from Vietnam to the European capitals where she had given so many recitals, and on to America. Her parents were in a state of shock.

Her funeral was held on May 17 in New York City. The next morning, there was a procession to St. Patrick's Cathedral. The sight of children and nuns leading the procession forced many to weep openly.

In the months following her daughter's death, Josephine Schuyler was determined to write about her daughter, and she published a small tribute book full of poetry. She and George grew estranged from each other. As the second-year anniversary of her daughter's death approached, Josephine Schuyler remained as distraught as ever. On May 2, 1969, she walked into her bedroom and, after a short period of time, proceeded to jam the door. When her husband later looked in on her, she was dead. She had hanged herself.

In the end, it did not seem to matter much to Blacks that Philippa Schuyler had shown little affinity for Blacks during so much of her own life. The threads of her story, though, were apparent in the Black world: In childhood, America had been kind and welcoming to her and her gifts. But in adulthood, like many Black artists of the 1950s and 1960s, she was nearly forgotten and forced to carve out a living abroad. She had even had to change her name, assume another identity! Blacks were aware, more than any other race of people, of the difficult journey, but her journey had had an even darker element, given that her confused parents had believed in "hybrid vigor." She was not so much a child to them as a creation, an experiment.

Vietnam was a place of numbers (body counts, troop totals) and dates of battles and surprise attacks. But there were so many riddles inside the riddles. There was most certainly never any accounting of Black soldiers who were so light-complexioned that they could pass themselves off as white—and did so to get far more favorable assignments. After all, the trick of "passing" was to go undetected. Army Colonel Andrew Chambers, a Black officer, was involved in investigating incidents of racial abuse in Europe during the Vietnam War. A fellow Black soldier felt that Chambers had been "passing for white down in Atlanta Georgia" during his previous postings.

The Black GIs of Vietnam who had gotten to know Philippa Schuyler saw fragility in her, saw how she cared about the napalm-scarred children who haunted her waking hours. She, of course, carried invisible scars, which burned as deep. And she so appreciated the nonjudgmental aspect of children. To the children she rescued, she was only the willowy lady in the colorful dress and sandals coming to help them, with her arms extended and a smile on her face.

Amidst war, the Black GIs saw Philippa Schuyler reaching for clarity in her life. She had begun to question why America was in Vietnam. The racism heaped upon Blacks and Vietnamese stung her. She now felt the two were somehow connected. Her mind, at long last, seemed to be opening up. "I am sure Philippa matured in Vietnam," one Black soldier wrote to her parents after she had dropped from the sky into the waters of Da Nang Bay.

Chapter Six

Wallace Terry's Special Saigon Assignment

The American military force that landed in Vietnam may have been racially integrated, but the press corps that followed certainly was not. In the early 1960s, American newsrooms were more than 97 percent white. Journalism was a profession that pulled its reporters and editors either from a rough-hewn crowd of World War II–era veterans, or from the more recent graduates of an elite pipeline of academic institutions that were overwhelmingly white: Hotchkiss or Exeter prep school, then off to Yale, Princeton, or Columbia.

The configuration of a newsroom consisted of a top editor and, under that person, multiple other editors who were assigned to oversee particular departments—state news, metro, sports, national, and foreign news. When editing positions were broken down racially, fewer than 1 percent of those editors were Black, and most of the figures from the studies conducted at the time were culled from the Black press. The percentages for Blacks in print and TV media were so low they were simply numbing. Little wonder that the racial imbalance produced a skewed and unbalanced angle of reporting.

Deep into the 1960s, the editors of *Newsweek* magazine realized

The reporter Wallace Terry was sent to Vietnam to be one of Time *magazine's correspondents. Black soldiers confided to him that they felt they were fighting the war on two fronts. The stories he heard haunted him, and he later used them for his bestselling oral history,* Bloods.

that the racial divisions of the nation seemed to be getting worse and worse, so they assigned a team of reporters to study the pains and rhythms of Black America. On November 20, 1967, the magazine published a special edition, "The Negro in America: What Must Be Done." Osborn Elliott, *Newsweek*'s top editor, believed that new ways of writing and reporting about Black problems must be incorporated into newsrooms. *Newsweek* acknowledged the sacredness of objective journalism, but now cautioned that the mere recitation of numbers and statistics often showed those suffering from the ravages of systemic racism in a bad and skewed light. There was a need, *Newsweek* pointed out in its special edition, for "advocacy journalism"—looking at inner-city problems from different viewpoints, not just from that of the white middle-class reporters who were assigned to cover inner-city America. "The problem is urgent—as the exploding cities and the incendiary rhetoric make inescapably plain," stated the

Newsweek editorial opinion. The Kerner Commission report, initiated by the White House, followed closely behind *Newsweek*'s issue, and there were warnings about the state of journalism. The report was highly praised and widely read. "The journalistic profession has been shockingly backward in seeking out, hiring, training, and promoting Negroes," the commission declared. "Even today, there are virtually no Negroes in positions of editorial or executive responsibility and there is only one Negro newsman with a nationally syndicated column."

A newspaper that sent a reporter or two into Vietnam had to be in muscular shape financially. Setting up shop in a foreign country was an expensive endeavor for any media outlet. Once on the ground in a new country, the reporters had to hire a technical crew and a driver. And often a translator and a "fixer"—someone who could cut through the red tape of foreign bureaucracy. Some reporters even had the luxury of hiring a cook. Among the organizations that had the clout to set early footprints in Vietnam were *The New York Times, The Washington Post, The Boston Globe,* the Associated Press, UPI, *Life* magazine, and *Time* magazine.

If any organization could be expected to practice a form of "advocacy journalism," it was the Black press. But they did not have the kind of financial resources it took to set up a full-time bureau in Vietnam. However, two Black reporters, Ethel Payne of the *Chicago Defender* and Simeon Booker of *Jet* magazine, arrived on the scene in the early years of the conflict. Both of them had to parachute in and out of the country. One advantage they did have, however, was that the Vietnam War was the first American war in which stories filed by reporters were not filtered by military censors, save when it came to military plans and troop numbers. Payne and Booker thus were free to angle their stories along racial fault lines if they wished to. And they did, inasmuch as they were writing for Black-oriented publications back in America.

Ethel Payne was a Chicago native. She dreamed of going to college after high school, but her father's death cut that goal short. Instead, she got a job with the Chicago Public Library. At night, she managed to take writing classes at Northwestern University. In 1948,

Payne accepted a job with the United States Army Special Services division, and was shipped to Japan, where she was given the job of managing a club for Black GIs in Yokohama. Payne was intrigued with the romantic relationships between Black GIs and Japanese women. She became curious about the introduction of multiracial children into conservative Japanese society, and suggested to editors at the *Chicago Defender* that she be allowed to write stories on the hardships encountered by both the GIs and Japanese women. The editors were very impressed with the stories she filed. When she finally returned Stateside, she was interviewed by the *Defender* for a full-time job; she was not above talking about her high-school teacher Margaret Dixon, who had once taught Ernest Hemingway. The *Defender* hired her in 1951, and she began her rise. She became the first Black woman to become a member of the White House Press Corps, and covered the Army-McCarthy hearings, as well as some of the early dramas of the civil rights movement. In 1963, she left the *Defender* and took a job with the Democratic National Committee. Three years later, John Sengstacke, publisher of the *Defender*, reached out to Payne and asked her if she'd be willing to make a short reporting trip into Vietnam for his newspaper. Payne thought about the offer and concluded the assignment would be "a gamble and an adventure."

Payne landed in Vietnam in December 1966. The *Chicago Defender* wasted no time heralding her in their ads as the first Black female correspondent to cover the war. Her stay, however, lasted only nine weeks. She was told to give particular attention to the Black troops, since Chicago boasted a large Black population and she was working for a Black newspaper. She visited villages, chatted with soldiers, saw a Bob Hope performance. Years before, while in Japan, she had noticed there were no Black officers on General Douglas MacArthur's staff. She took note of a similar reality in Vietnam: there were no Black officers on the staff of General William Westmoreland, the supreme commander. The Black soldiers were happy to see Payne, a brassy Black woman sent all the way from America to glean their opinions about the war. "I'm all for the civil rights demonstrations because it's just as important to clean house at home as it is to be fighting the Communists over here," Specialist Carl Wheatly, from Chicago, told her. "I wish I was there to take part in them." Ernest Lavender of Atlanta was eager to express his opinion: "We shouldn't have to go back and accept second-class citizenship like our forefathers did in World War II," he told Payne. "I don't believe we will either." When she returned to American soil, Payne could feel the churning antiwar movement all around her. She began wondering if she had missed an opportunity to discuss the "immorality" of the war in her reporting.

Simeon Booker of *Jet* magazine, the other Black reporter who trekked into Vietnam, had, in 1951, gotten noticed for being only the second Black chosen as a Nieman Fellow at Harvard. He had gone on to cover many of the civil rights clashes of the late 1950s and early 1960s—Emmett Till, Little Rock, the March on Washington—all as a lead reporter for *Jet* and *Ebony.* Tall and slim, he was an elegant dresser, with horn-rimmed glasses and lovely suits. He was the first Black reporter to join the staff of *The Washington Post.* But he really made his mark with the Negro press, with *Jet* and *Ebony.* Once, in Mississippi, a white woman approached Booker and, eyeing his dress and his expensive horn-rimmed glasses, declared, "You're not from around here. Niggers from around here don't wear glasses like that." In Vietnam, Booker wanted to report on the topic that he knew his readers would care most about—the status of the Black soldier in the first racially integrated war. In an article for *Ebony* titled "Negroes in Vietnam: 'We, Too, Are Americans,'" this was his first paragraph:

> In Vietnam, a Negro GI can walk through downtown Saigon with virtual immunity, or he can go to the suburbs where Viet Cong informers assure him: "There'll be no bombs or gunfights, because you are our friends." Few grenades are thrown at dark skinned Americans . . . But GI Joe doesn't fall for the propaganda.

Booker spent only two weeks in Vietnam, less time than Ethel Payne. Neither of them was there long enough to leave a footprint. They simply were not given enough time by their cash-conscious publications to amass a body of work that would have garnered wide attention. They did, however, bring the Black GI into the media orbit of Black popular publications. But those were not publications with a wide readership in the white community. To the white community, the Black GI was just another soldier, viewed so often from the lens through which they had been viewed in other recent wars—as second-class citizens. The white reporters in Vietnam—Bob Poos, Homer Bigart, David Halberstam, Charles Mohr among them—were gifted, but they did not angle any of their reporting in the direction of Black GIs, or the unique challenges those soldiers faced.

There needed to be a reporter in Vietnam who possessed another antenna and was not only covering the war but focusing on the Black GI, who was engaged not only in fighting the enemy but also in fighting to earn respect unto his cultural lineage. After all, until President Lincoln turned the cannons loose, the American military had all but accepted the "peculiar institution"—a term that had been uttered by John C. Calhoun, a slave owner and onetime vice-president, seemingly to diminish the savagery of slavery. It would greatly help if that aforementioned reporter had a media powerhouse behind them, so that there would be no griping about expense reports, about traveling where one needed to go, about when it was time to pack up and come home because of financial worries. And that person needed to convince their editors—their white editors—that the story of the Black GI was worth paying attention to, and that mainstream America needed to read such a story. Plus, they needed the stamina and determination to stay in Vietnam for months and months on end.

In early 1967, *Time* editors began thinking of doing something special on the Negro soldier in the war. Wallace Terry, a *Time* reporter based in Washington, D.C., wanted in on the story, and the editors were happy to get him on a plane.

—

Born in New York City in 1938, Wallace Terry would spend many of his youthful years in Indianapolis. As a kid, he loved going to the local library. "I'd buy Smith Brothers cough drops, or Ludens or something, because I didn't want to be caught with a bag of candy, and I'd live in there among the books," he said. He acquired a reverence for history, and how it affected Black people. In elementary school, he was disciplined because he would not stand up while they were playing "Dixie," the musical ode to Southern segregation. At Shortridge High School, Terry thought that, despite his slight frame, he might become a football star. But a serious wrist injury derailed him. A teacher noticed his writing talent and steered young Terry toward *The Daily Echo,* the student newspaper advertised as the first high-school newspaper in the country. For a high-school paper, the *Echo* had an enthusiastic following. Terry's work habits propelled him into being named editor of the paper. Girls were eager to date Terry, but he let them know he was too busy: he was always hanging out in the offices of the *Echo.*

Word leaked out about Wallace Terry's industriousness. William Dyer, the general manager of the *Indianapolis News-Star,* heard about him. Dyer, a graduate of Brown University, thought a young man like Wallace Terry would be a fine candidate for admission to Brown. He recommended Terry to the school, and Terry was accepted.

It was possible in the 1950s to step onto the grounds of any Ivy League university in America and not see a single Black student. Wallace Terry's family knew it was a special opportunity for him to be attending Brown, an all-male school at the time. They also cautioned him about the likely added pressures he would face because of his race. Terry enrolled in the fall of 1955, just a little over a year and a half after the Thurgood Marshall–launched public-school desegregation victory at the U.S. Supreme Court. Many in civil rights hoped the case would propel higher-education institutions to follow suit, but they did not. Not long after arriving on campus, Terry joined the staff of *The Brown Daily Herald,* Brown's student newspaper. He went after stories with an aggressive mindset. When Arkansas Governor Orval Faubus came to Rhode Island in 1957 to meet with President Eisenhower, Terry talked his way past security and knocked on Faubus's hotel-room door. He wanted an interview, and Faubus obliged. As the young Black student reporter and the segregationist governor interacted in the hotel room, the flash of cameras popped. The photograph—given the rigid segregation of America and the two worlds the reporter and governor represented—ended up in newspapers all around the country, even on some front pages. Wallace Terry had gotten quite a scoop, and also made a name for himself. Not long thereafter, he was named editor-in-chief of *The Brown Daily Herald,* the first Black named to that position, or to any editorship of an Ivy League newspaper. Again, he made national news, especially in Black communities around the country: news of his appointment appeared in the February 6, 1958, issue of *Jet* magazine.

After college, Wallace Terry went to work full-time at *The Washington Post.* Like other big-city newsrooms, the *Post* could be a lonely place for Black employees. Terry went out of his way to befriend the Black janitors and cafeteria workers. At a Washington party in 1960, he met Janice Jessup, a college student studying to become a teacher. She was beautiful and sophisticated. "When he would say to prospective brides that he worked at *The Post,* they didn't know that he meant *The Post* newspaper, because no Black people worked there," recalled Janice, who married Wallace in 1963. "They thought he meant the post office, and for educated women in Washington, that wasn't good enough. But *The Washington Post* was cool with me." Terry was only the second Black reporter at the *Post,* Simeon Booker having been the first. Neither Booker nor Terry remained there very long. For Wallace Terry, *Time* came calling.

In the middle of the twentieth century, there was arguably no more powerful organ of journalistic muscle than *Time* magazine. First published in 1923 in a weekly format, it proceeded to establish itself as required reading from country club to White House. Henry Luce and Briton Hadden, its cofounders, had both been Yale men. The magazine's signature was its conservatism. As the years rolled out, profits grew; bureaus were opened around the globe. *Time* had a man in Rome, in Paris, in Los Angeles, in Atlanta, in Houston—everywhere, it seemed. When it came to communism, its editorial position was loud and clear: *Time* loathed communism and the world leaders who espoused it.

Despite its conservative bent, the magazine was certainly not going to ignore the civil rights revolution unfolding across America. In 1963, they had named Martin Luther King, Jr., as Man of the Year, the first Black American given that news-making honor.

Time was selective and peculiar about whom they hired. Wallace Terry's Ivy League pedigree helped get him in the door. He came aboard in 1963 and soon was assigned the civil rights beat. He traveled the country, stopping in most of segregation's hot spots—the small towns and big cities of Alabama, Virginia, Michigan, Mississippi, Georgia. He got to know Martin Luther King, Jr. He was in Jackson, Mississippi, on June 11, 1963, talking with the voting rights activist Medgar Evers. The next evening, June 12, Evers was assassinated. "One night, Wally called me and he was crying. I had never heard a man crying before," says his wife, Janice. "And he said, 'They killed Medgar.' "

At *Time,* Wallace Terry, over the course of several years as a correspondent out of their D.C. bureau, experienced the deep pockets and resources of the magazine. *Time* had reporters, researchers, photographers; they even had a company plane! Reporters could take background sources—individuals who did not want to be quoted by name because of the sensitivity of a story—out for lunch and not worry about the expense tab. Simeon Booker and Ethel Payne had been crippled by the parsimonious Black press, but Wallace Terry did not have such problems.

Terry landed in Saigon in 1967, ostensibly sent to help put together the magazine's special edition about "the Negro soldier." He met

John Cantwell, an Australian and fellow *Time* reporter, and they became fast friends. Cantwell had plenty of pointers to offer about being in a war zone. Terry went and met military officials as well as U.S. Embassy officials. Then he set out to meet Black GIs. In war zones, a common question—between reporter and soldier—was always "Where are you from?" When the Black soldiers heard of Terry's background—Harlem, traveling the deep South, having met Medgar and Martin Luther King, Jr.—they half-joked with him that Vietnam might be safer for him than America. He was able to detect a brewing anger among the Black soldiers. They were fighting for America—the very nation that had seemingly unleashed a law-and-order net around Black America. And a nation that had witnessed the murders of so many civil rights martyrs: Emmett Till in 1955 in Mississippi; Mack Charles Parker in 1959 in Mississippi; Herbert Lee in 1961 in Mississippi; the four young Black girls in the Birmingham, Alabama, church bombing in 1963; James Chaney, Andrew Goodman, and Michael Schwerner in 1964 in Mississippi. The litany of names—ongoing as it was—proved painful to the psychic disposition of the Black soldier.

In its usual manner, *Time* unleashed a cadre of reporters and researchers to report the Negro and Vietnam story. Their photographers took pictures of Negro soldiers in the field. Sergeant Clide Brown graced the cover. The special edition of the red-rimmed magazine—"The Negro in Vietnam"—was dated May 26, 1967, when it hit the newsstands in America. *Time,* of course, shipped copies into Saigon. On the inside pages was another headline: "Democracy in the Foxhole." The story was written in straight-on prose, sending the reader into Vietnam and its racial issues. There was a pro-war tone to the piece, and it included expressions of patriotism from the Negro troops. It was impossible—because of the *Time* style, which combined reporting and other writing from various journalists working on a big story—to determine which parts of the story Terry himself wrote. But in the magazine's "A letter from the Publisher" column in this edition, Terry was able to comment: "In the course of my interviews I came across a Negro Navy radio man who was in grade school with me in Indianapolis, a helicopter pilot who belonged to my college fraternity at Brown, and an infantry officer who lived in my old Harlem neighborhood." Terry added: "The tank I rode on had a Negro commander and an all-white crew."

The response to the *Time* issue—both Stateside and in Vietnam—went in several directions. Some Blacks thought it buried the real and raw issues of race in the armed services. Some whites thought Blacks were complaining too much about the way they were treated. And there was, of course, that cross burning in front of Sergeant Clide Brown's tent, which had inflamed race relations. Since the culprits were never caught, tensions became even more inflamed. Other cross burnings in other locations followed.

Janice Terry was delighted with the *Time* cover story: "*Time* had never done a story like that!," she says, excitement still in her voice all these years later. "Wally took the Black brothers—and their fierce courage—and put them on the front pages of *Time* magazine."

The last paragraph of the *Time* cover story, however, seemed less like a reporting team's summary and more like an editorial wish: "By channeling the energies and accommodating the ambitions of the returning Negro veteran, the nation can only enrich its own life and demonstrate that democracy can work as well in the cities and fields of America as in the foxholes of Vietnam."

Wallace Terry benefited from his work on *Time*'s special issue: editors asked him if he wanted to join the Saigon bureau for a long-term stay. He talked it over with Janice and both agreed it was an opportunity not to pass up.

Janice, however, decided she was not going to remain in America alone with the three children. She went about making phone calls and found a place to live in Singapore. She'd be close enough to her husband to fly over every month or so, and he could visit her from his Saigon posting. "I had a sense of fear," she says about the move out of America, "but I wasn't frightened." Some people Stateside warned her about the dangers. "When I was thinking about going, I had to wonder: 'Are you gonna be another Philippa Schuyler?' But then I just went."

—

After his trip back to America, Wallace Terry returned to Vietnam, now to stay on a long-term assignment. It took only a few weeks of being in-country for his antennae to go up: There was a big story here, and its dimensions were far, far larger than one edition of a magazine like *Time* could even fathom. That story was race, how it was rearing its head as it had not in any other war. How it needed to be understood. Terry heard about the Confederate flags, and about soldiers who preached the gospel of the Ku Klux Klan. The more he got away from the base camps, out into the bush, where the soldiers were more willing to talk openly, the more he heard about the fierceness of Black anger—and the Blacks' political awareness. There was an advantage to working for a weekly: he had no daily deadlines. He could move about Vietnam as long as he made plans in advance with drivers and pilots. "These travels were often unofficially discouraged," he said. "In many places, white officers and sergeants looked on suspiciously as I drank, ate or talked with black Marines, soldiers and sailors in their barracks, mess halls, tanks and foxholes."

What Wallace Terry came to realize—and to witness—was that in Vietnam there was, as he put it, "a war within a war," and that this other war was between Black soldiers and the attitudes held by many whites. They were clashing, even as both groups kept fighting to the best of their abilities. At times Terry wondered about his own treatment by white helicopter pilots. He was once dropped off in the middle of a combat area; though he had arranged a pickup time from the pilot who dropped him off, that pilot never returned, and Terry had to scramble to get another ride—"but I think they just didn't care if they happened to lose that Black reporter from *Time* out there . . ." He kept going back out into the field to "rap" with the Black soldiers—engage them in conversation. The Black soldiers began to trust him. He wanted to hear as many of their stories as they would share with him. Another reporter, Joseph Galloway, who had so memorably been at the Battle of Ia Drang, realized how important it was for reporters like himself and Terry to be out in the field. "There's a certain honesty," Galloway said, "that operates out there on the cutting edge . . . If you're there, you're sharing the risk, and you share the truth of it."

When she began popping into Saigon to visit her husband—it was, after all, a city with decent Vietnamese and French restaurants, even amidst war—Janice Terry started to see the camaraderie between her husband and the Black soldiers he introduced her to. Her visits became frequent enough so the soldiers began calling her "Soul Sister No. 1." "It was exciting to see Vietnam, and it felt like an early valve had opened up: the hidden history of Black men," she says. "It was amazing to see these brave Black men fighting for their country—and being so angry. Some of them called generals 'Whitey.' "

Wallace Terry began to sense a palpable change in the racial climate of Vietnam in the months following the special-edition cover story. Many of the newly arrived Black soldiers were fresh from the other war—the one being played out on the streets of America. And just as they had questions for authorities back in America—about inequality and police brutality—they had questions in Vietnam about American brutality against Vietnamese civilians. "The black soldier brings certain sensitivities to the situation when he brings his poverty to the poverty around him," Terry felt. "He sees the dominant culture imposing itself or damaging the other. He sees the Vietnam woman being humiliatingly searched when she comes on the base, and he thinks about his own mother, who works for the white woman but is given 'totin' privileges.' "

Wallace Terry was in a Singapore barbershop when the news came that Martin Luther King, Jr., had been murdered. He was devastated; his Chinese barber began crying. King had been godfather to one of Terry's children. It didn't take him long at all to see the increased defiance among the Black troops: "The younger generation was mostly drafted, and they were beginning to identify with the black militancy they'd experienced at home. And of course, to have King killed—by white people . . . devastated them."

The roiling racial tensions in Vietnam, exacerbated by King's death, seemed relentless. Newman Jackson, a Navy seaman from Charleston, West Virginia, found himself on land, in Saigon, and working a security detail. Upon news of King's death, he and some other Black soldiers gathered together. They needed to talk, to commiserate, to shed tears. They didn't know what they were going to do as a form of protest. All they knew was that King had been murdered, and that America was on fire, and that they themselves were in the blaze of war fire. One thing they did was to surreptitiously remove rebel flags wherever they saw them. Military officials became aware of the brewing anger, and they took action. "Some of us were restricted to base," Jackson recalls all these years later, talking about those deemed responsible for removing the rebel flags. "You also weren't allowed at the time to take weapons off base, because they were afraid of a race war." Jackson was always worried about the civilian Vietnamese who worked at his base camp. Many had come over from the Viet Cong forces, having abandoned their communist ideology and now vowing allegiance to the South Vietnamese and Americans. Jackson thought of double agents, even of triple agents. "A lot of the Vietnamese had equated themselves to the Black experience in America," he says. "They talked about having been oppressed by the French. They would put that out there as propaganda to get into the minds of Black soldiers."

Reporters never felt completely comfortable in Vietnam. Spies seemed to be everywhere. The cook or housemaid for an American news bureau, needing money, might have been bribed or pressured to reveal information about the news bureau's reporters to North Vietnamese insurgents. Desperation was always in the air. Reporters had to trust their guts, and they had to get out there in the field. They had to board those rattling helicopters, which so often drew enemy fire or encountered mechanical problems.

In the early morning of May 5, 1968, five reporters—John Cantwell, age twenty-nine, working for *Time* magazine; Bruce Pigott, twenty-three, and Ronald Laramy, thirty-one, working for Reuters; Michael Birch, twenty-four, from Australian Associated Press; and Frank Palmos, a freelance Australian journalist—all hopped in a jeep in Saigon and drove toward Cholon, a suburb. They had spotted plumes of smoke and knew there must be some kind of story there. As they reached Cholon, they noticed a stream of panic-stricken civilian Vietnamese—men, women, children—flowing toward them. They also could spot American bombers in the sky over the area, firing. The civilians began yelling at the reporters, telling them Viet Cong soldiers were in the area and that they must turn around. But these were war correspondents; this was a story; they kept going. Then shots rang out in the direction of the jeep. A band of young Viet Cong soldiers had risen up from behind some petroleum cans, and kept firing. One of the reporters was hit, then another. Blood was squirting. Cantwell, driving, gunned the engine and turned into an alley, but it was a cul-de-sac. More bullets. More screaming from inside the jeep, which was now a bloody and horrific scene. The Viet Cong soldiers moseyed up to the idling jeep. One of the reporters cried out, "*Bao chi*"—newsman. It made no difference. A Viet Cong soldier began laughing; then they fired again. Frank Palmos, one of the reporters, had fallen out of the jeep before it came to a stop. He was playing dead. When the firing commenced, Palmos had hopped up off the ground and begun running. Bullets whizzed by him, but he made it into a crowd and started walking with the civilians who had just left the area. He finally made it to safety, and reported the ambush to authorities.

As soon as word of the attack reached Wallace Terry, he sprang into action. He and a fellow reporter, Zalin Grant, raced to track down Frank Palmos. They listened to his story, but quickly had suspicions that his retelling was not accurate. They believed that Palmos must have jumped out of the jeep as soon as he spotted the guerrillas—and fled. When Terry and Grant—in their own jeep now—got within a few blocks of the area where the shooting had taken place, their driver announced he could go no farther, because he felt it was too dangerous. They were forced to return to the center of Saigon. Not long after, they launched what they thought would be a second try at a rescue mission. As Terry recounted: "We are finally able to drive down Minh Phung. At road No. 46, we spot a demolition team. They tell us it is still too dangerous to go farther. When we say we are going to try anyway, they give us each a carbine. We walk down the dirt road. There, we find them. I am too overwhelmed to cry." Terry and Grant needed a bomb specialist on site to check the jeep for booby traps. No one moved; then a Black Army sergeant stepped up. When the sergeant deemed that it was safe to do so, Terry and Grant proceeded with the grim task of loading their fellow journalists into their jeep. They were all dead. The two reporters drove back into Saigon in shock.

Through the ensuing years, the ambush survivor, Frank Palmos, would find himself haunted by memories of what had happened to his fellow journalists. Twenty years later, in 1988, he returned to Vietnam with an Australian television crew and managed to track down some of those who had attacked the group. They largely confirmed Palmos's version of the story, disproving what Terry and Grant had originally felt.

Time's editorial position had always been pro-war, obliging the slant that McNamara and the Pentagon were doling out. And LBJ had established a nice friendship with Hedley Donovan, the magazine's editor-in-chief. Yet, early in 1968, things slowly started to change. *Time* began wondering when the war was going to end, began wondering if there was any kind of exit strategy in place. Lyndon Johnson grew frustrated with the magazine's more aggressive tone, which questioned America's war strategy.

Wallace Terry decided he needed to think of a different way to write about the Black soldier in Vietnam. There was that Black bomb expert who had stepped forward to search the jeep for bombs; there was the fact that Terry had covered the civil rights movement in America up close and now he was in another type of war, unable, yet again, to ignore the issue of civil rights. It wasn't that the Black soldiers hadn't encountered some good white military personnel, but the examples were too rare, and the soldiers let him know about it.

"What changed was not the white soldier, but the black soldier," Terry felt. "He wasn't going to take it anymore. Segregation, abuses, inequal treatment on promotions, assignments, decorations. The men took a new pride from Malcolm X and the student movement and the Great Society."

This is what a white psychiatrist said in *Time*'s special edition about the Black soldier: "Many times I have found that the complaint because of race is not really that, but that race has been used by some as a crutch." And Black soldiers—after the story had been published—wondered why *Time* didn't probe more deeply the question of why, out of 380 combat-battalion leaders in Vietnam, there were only 2 Blacks who held such positions.

As the year 1969 was unspooling, Wallace Terry, now deputy bureau chief of Saigon for *Time,* knew he was nearing the end of his two-year assignment. There were reporters who had parachuted in and out of the war, and then there were those, like Terry, who had become veterans of the conflict. He had covered the aftermath of the Tet Offensive, had gone on night patrols and combat missions, had been at the Battle of Hamburger Hill—there were too many bad dreams.

On June 27, 1969, the weekly issue of *Life* magazine began arriving on American porches and in mailboxes. The headline in the upper-right corner: "The Faces of the American Dead in Vietnam: One Week's Toll." Inside the magazine was a several-page spread of head shots of American soldiers, a total of 242. They were Black and white portraits, racially mixed. Some were still in their teens, but the average age was around twenty-two. They represented the Army, the Marines, and the Navy. These were the kinds of photos, posed head shots, that moms and dads put on the mantelpiece. But every one of the soldiers pictured was dead, killed in Vietnam. It took a few minutes to digest the devastation; it seemed surreal. One week—and so many families changed. I could imagine someone in

West Quincy, Massachusetts, or King City, Missouri, or Tucson, Arizona, or Manhattan, Kansas—among the places the soldiers hailed from—opening the layout and recognizing someone and suddenly crumbling against a wall or dining-room table. The inside headline: "Vietnam: One Week's Dead." "Yet in a time when the numbers of Americans," the *Life* editors wrote,

> killed in this war—36,000—though far less than the Vietnamese losses, have exceeded the dead in the Korean War, when the nation continues week after week to be numbed by a three-digit statistic which is translated to direct anguish in hundreds of homes all over the country, we must pause to look into the faces. More than we must know how many, we must know who. The faces of one week's dead, unknown but to families and friends, are suddenly recognized by all in this gallery of young American eyes.

Like everyone else in *Time*'s Saigon bureau, Wallace Terry saw that photo spread. It was impossible to shake the war, no matter how many times he slipped into Singapore to see his wife and kids. Months later, after two long and bloody years, he was on his way back to America.

LBJ was now convinced that *Time* had abandoned him. "Hedley Donovan betrayed me," he lamented.

Before Wallace Terry left Vietnam, he went to visit Army Captain Alexander Benjamin, a Black native of Alabama, now in Dong Tam. "The young black soldiers are much more hostile than ever before," Benjamin told Terry. "I think we are probably building a recruiting base for militant groups in America. It frightens me."

Not long after Terry landed back in America, he was hearing that thumping hit song "War" on the radio, especially on the urban radio stations listened to by Black America. It was sung by Edwin Starr, an Army vet:

Oh, war, has shattered many a young man's dreams
Made him disabled, bitter and mean

Wallace Terry found it difficult to ease back into America. When he landed in Washington, he got a room at the Washington Hilton. He wanted to call people—family, friends—and he'd pick up the phone receiver, start dialing, then stop and hang up. Finally, he got a call from his employer, *Time.* "Would you call your mother?" they asked him. As he recalled: "I just couldn't bring myself to call her and tell her I was home. It wasn't just the shock of being back in the U.S. . . . It was an inability to express what I'd been through." He wanted to tell people about Vietnam, the look and smell of the place. His brave wife. There were long walks in the evening, when he'd ponder what he had experienced. Finally he had summoned the resolve to talk. He'd get to talking about John Cantwell, one of the four journalists killed in that jeep by the Viet Cong, and he'd tell them that he—and others—had tried to get Cantwell to leave the country before that fateful day for a respite, because they felt he had been in the field too long. He'd tell them that one time Cantwell was interviewing someone and, bang, just like that, the person's head was blown off. Terry finally saw his mother. "She didn't ask a single question" about the war, he said. "It was as though we were all unclean somehow."

In 1970, Wallace Terry was awarded a Nieman Fellowship at Harvard University. He aimed to study international relations. He and Janice settled nicely into the environs of Cambridge, Massachusetts. But it was a fraught time on American campuses; the antiwar movement was a fierce presence. Janice was especially alarmed by the sight of so many antiwar demonstrators.

Terry had a cache of notebooks from Vietnam; during his last months there he had acquired enough vacation time to take time off, and he used it to search out Black soldiers and conduct more interviews. Away from the war, in Cambridge, he began writing. He submitted two long pieces to *The Harvard Crimson,* and the newspaper published them on October 8 and 9, both under the title "Bringing the War Home": "Black soldiers schooled in the violent arts of guerrilla war as no generation of blacks are returning home from Southeast Asia, fed up with dying in a war they believe is white man's folly and determined to earn their share of American opportunities even if that means becoming Black Panthers or turning to guns," Terry wrote with heat and emotion; his words didn't read as if they had been put through the grind of *Time* editors. He wrote of a study he had done of Black soldiers while in Vietnam: "A frightening number—45 per cent of black combat troops—say they would join riots and take up arms if necessary to get the rights they have been deprived of at home." He recalled: "A fight between black and white Marines at a tank battalion base near Danang almost ended disastrously when a dozen black Marines in black shirts and gloves showed up armed with rifles and grenades to help another black who was being beaten by whites." And he wrote of his interactions with two white soldiers as they expressed their feelings about race and war: "Percentage wise, I believe blacks do get more dangerous duty," Dennis Camire, a white soldier from Mississippi, had told Terry. From Dan Miller, a white soldier from Iowa: "I think you have to honestly say that the black man in our brigade receives less consideration than his white soldier. He has almost no chance of getting a support job."

Here are some of the voices he had recorded that kept ringing in Terry's ear:

> There was another guy in our unit who had made it known that he was a card-carrying Ku Klux Klan member . . . Well, we got out into a firefight, and Mr. Ku Klux Klan got his little ass trapped . . . So we laid down a base of fire to cover him. But he was just immobile. He froze. And a brother went out there and got him and dragged him back . . .
>
> Specialist 5 Harold (Light Bulb) Bryant

> The thing that really hurt me more than anything in the world was when I came back to the States and black people considered me as a part of the establishment. Because I am an officer . . .

> You see, blacks are not supposed to be officers. Blacks are supposed to be those guys that take orders.
>
> First Lieutenant Archie Biggers

> I think blacks got along better with the Vietnamese people, because they knew the hardships the Vietnamese went through. The majority of the people who came over there looked down on the Vietnamese. They considered them ragged, poor, stupid. They just didn't respect them. I could understand poverty. I had five brothers and three sisters.
>
> Specialist 5 Emmanuel J. Holloman

There was someone whom Wallace Terry had never actually met in Vietnam but who began to haunt him as well: Dan Bullock, a Marine who hailed from North Carolina. He arrived in Vietnam in May 1969, assigned as a rifleman. One night, while he was stationed at the An Hoa combat base, he was in his tent with two other Marines when enemy soldiers threw an explosive into the tent. All three Marines died. Terry heard that one of them was quite young, and he wanted to find out who he was and how young he had been. It was revealed that Dan Bullock had lied about his age to get into the Marines. He was, the reports said, only sixteen when he had joined up. Terry had gone to the site where Bullock and the other Marines were killed. He specifically wanted to find out as much as he could about Dan Bullock, aiming to write about him. But he couldn't find out much: Bullock had lost his mother when he was a child. He had left North Carolina and moved to Brooklyn, where his father lived. He liked lollipops. He had dreamed of being a Marine. It was later revealed that Dan Bullock wasn't sixteen when he forged paperwork to join the Marines. He was actually *fifteen years old* when he died, fourteen when he enlisted. A man-child and a red-blooded Marine. "He was mourned yesterday by a saddened and bewildered family in their hot, darkened railroad apartment in a dilapidated Brooklyn tenement," stated a *New York Times* account of the death.

The young soldier was thus memorialized for all time on the Vietnam Memorial:

Dan Bullock: December 21, 1953–June 7, 1969.

So many people—thousands upon thousands, then millions upon millions—had started to wonder: Why was America reeling in such a manner? Why were there so many fires across urban America? Why was life in the Black ghettos of the nation still so awful? And another question linked to those questions: Why were things going so hellishly in Vietnam?

Just after midnight on January 31, 1968, a combined force of North Vietnamese Army and Viet Cong forces launched a surprise attack against thirty-six of the forty-four provincial capitals in Vietnam. Dozens of American military bases were attacked. Hanoi had launched the so-called Tet Offensive. Three of the biggest cities in South Vietnam were hit—Da Nang, Hue, and Saigon. Communist leaders had told their commanders that they aimed to "split the sky and shake the earth." American officials were caught badly off guard. The communist military forces had dared to enter Saigon; it was a fist right to the gut of American military muscle. The walls of the U.S. Embassy were breached. In the end, 216 U.S. Marines and soldiers were killed and 1,609 wounded. It took American forces a week to secure Saigon again. American reporters had now started to report on the war in a more aggressive manner. President Johnson was outraged by the reporting. He had some choice words for Jack Horner, a reporter for *The Washington Star*. "Your press is lying like drunken sailors every day," LBJ told Horner in a phone call. "First thing I wake up this morning was trying to figure out after seeing CBS . . . watching the networks, reading the morning papers, was how can we win—possibly win—and survive as a nation and have to fight the press's lies."

Chapter Seven

The Gambler, the Segregationist, and the Withering of a Dream

They were linked by the American South, Lyndon Johnson and Richard Russell, two politicians who had known each other for decades. Johnson hailed from Texas and Russell from Georgia. They had such rapport that many of their acquaintances looked upon them as a kind of father-son tandem, with Russell offering Johnson advice in critical situations as both rose in politics. In the U.S. Senate, Johnson grew so fond of Russell—who never married—that he would have him over to his Washington, D.C., home on many a Sunday afternoon. Johnson's daughters called Russell Uncle Dick. It bewildered those who knew the men that they could remain so close while they differed so sharply over an issue causing convulsions throughout America—the issue of Blacks and their struggle for freedom.

Richard Russell led an ascetic life and, as a bachelor, seemed to enjoy his own company more than being around others. He lived in plain hotel suites or drab apartments. He read books on law and taxation and seemed to revel in the mysteries of mundane subjects. Born in 1897, he grew up listening to Confederate Civil War veter-

Segregationist senator Richard Russell of Georgia, chairman of the Senate Armed Services Committee, knew that the war would relocate a lot of Black youth to Vietnam, a reality he was hardly opposed to.

ans telling him how they hated the Yankees from up North. He was governor of Georgia from 1931 to 1933, when a special election sent him to the United States Senate. He belonged to that Southern bloc of conservative Democrats who loathed talk of civil rights. Other Dixiecrats—as they called themselves—may have yelled nastier language on the campaign stump, but he never let anyone doubt where he stood on the issue of Blacks and their quest for freedom. During his political rise, he refrained from socializing with his Senate staff. Now and then, he would attend baseball games in Washington with Lyndon Johnson, who had become his protégé. Russell was counted on as a fervent believer in white supremacy. "We believe the system of segregation is necessary to preserve peace and harmony between the states," he declared.

In the Senate, Russell began to accumulate power. And with power came other dreams: He had run twice, in 1948 and 1952, to be the Democratic candidate for the American presidency, on a white-supremacy platform, losing both times. In 1956, he was one of the signers of the so-called Southern Manifesto, along with many other Southern politicians who opposed integration. Lyndon Johnson did not sign. Johnson and Russell seemed to have reached an impasse in 1964, when LBJ was moving into high gear to pass his 1964 Civil Rights Act. "Dick, I love you and I owe you. But I'm going to tell you something. I'm going to run over you if you challenge me on this civil rights bill." Even with their filibustering, the cadre of Southern politicians couldn't derail LBJ's mission. But in those dramatic years of the mid-1960s, he had to adjust his sights to deal with two churning events: the explosive civil rights movement and the Vietnam War. Richard Russell would not assist him on the former, but on the latter—war—Russell, as chairman of the Senate Armed Services Committee, as a man who loathed the communists just as LBJ did, was his deeply wizened father figure once again. There were a good many military bases dotting the American South, and Russell was going to keep them well financed. He also knew the mindset of LBJ: "I am not going to lose Vietnam," LBJ vowed. "I am not going to be the President who saw Southeast Asia go the way China went." Russell made sure that the Johnson administration had all the funding it needed to keep dropping those bombs, to keep sending those boys off to war.

It wasn't long, though, before LBJ was crying the blues that the Democrats would likely lose the white vote in the South forevermore because of his civil rights programs. (On that premonition, he would prove correct.)

LBJ went through turmoil similar to that of the Lincoln presidency, when Black freedom and a war claimed the national discourse. All those kids howling outside the Johnson White House! "Hey, hey, LBJ! How many kids did you kill today?" In some quarters the quip became similar to a national refrain, part of a screeching soundtrack. LBJ—who had a notorious temper—wanted to wring their goddamn necks. He complained to the Secret Service about all that noise outside the White House gates. It was so embarrassing! He told the agents that Lady Bird couldn't get any sleep! And the agents would tell him that there was nothing they could do about the protesters, that it was a free country. The president continued to fume, and then he'd get to howling about sending even more Green Berets into Vietnam.

Like every other president before him, when it came to those two issues—race and the military—LBJ was bewitched. There had been racial clashes across the decades, presidents drawn into the fray, presidents turning their backs on Black servicemen who had suffered indignities. Sometimes, as well, there were courageous moments, in rhetoric and deed. In 1880, James A. Garfield, running for president, addressed a group of military veterans in New York City, with race and the military on his mind. "We have seen white men betray the flag and fight to kill the Union; but in all that long, dreary war we never saw a traitor in black skin." He received applause. Now, with President Kennedy's assassination, with flames flickering coast to coast, with civil rights workers being murdered, Lyndon Johnson was in a quagmire. "Everything I had ever learned in the history books taught me that martyrs have to die for causes," Johnson had said. "John Kennedy had died. But his 'cause' was not really clear. That was my job."

Could the gambler in Johnson—on a legislative winning streak—maintain his friendship with the wily segregationist who had propelled his political career? Yes, he could, because Richard Russell *was* Mr. Defense. He shaped military budgets. And the generals loved him.

First came the LBJ domestic agenda. He assigned Sargent Shriver the task of putting his War on Poverty into action. Shriver headed the Office of Economic Opportunity. The array of programs that began to flow out of his OEO were unique in their originality and sweep, from the very young to the aged. There was Head Start, which would feed and give poor children—starting at the age of three—a head start with education and nutrition. There was Medicare, which helped lower the costs of health care for senior citizens. A friend of Johnson's warned him that Southern hospital administrators and doctors were going to challenge him on Medicare. "Do you want to be responsible for closing St. Francis Hospital in Biloxi, Mississippi?" Johnson was privately asked. "That's what will happen if you put this thing [Medicare] into effect . . . Doctors won't treat the coloreds, and the nurses won't treat them." Johnson had no intention of relenting. "It was a great gamble" that paid off, Harry McPherson, a Johnson aide, remembered.

LBJ sat in the White House on November 3, 1965, and signed eight more pieces of War on Poverty legislation, totaling fifteen billion dollars. There were pre-college programs and antihunger programs and programs that placed Blacks in city-hall jobs across the country, literally integrating the city halls of America. Congressman Adam Clayton Powell, Jr., of Harlem—shrewd, slick, savvy, brilliant, and devilish when he had to be—was chairman of the Education and Labor Committee and helped spearhead many of the Johnson bills toward passage.

In hindsight, it was amazing that so much got done so fast. The rising buoyancy of MLK's "I Have a Dream" speech and the horror of JFK's death had created that palpable opening of goodwill. But when Vietnam came clashing into view, and the war kept lengthening, and defense budgets began to swallow antipoverty funds, Blacks began talking about "guns and butter"—too many guns and not enough butter, not enough food for the poor. Two centuries of inequality hadn't yet been defeated, and now, suddenly, that effort seemed to go wanting.

A war that was sapping young Blacks out of their communities, and a war that was also wrapped up in the gyrations of domestic politics and civil rights, began to make news from a variety of angles.

George Hamilton, a man-about-town in Hollywood and someone who was starting to get noticed in acting circles, received a wartime draft deferment. The explanation given was that he was the sole breadwinner for his mother, who lived with him in his Hollywood mansion, which boasted thirty-nine rooms. The prizefighter Muhammad Ali, citing his Muslim religion and antiwar beliefs, was not given such understanding: he had been indicted for refusing to be inducted into the Army. It didn't take Blacks long to express misgivings about how differently the white George Hamilton was treated from Muhammad Ali. Ali was fined and stripped of his title belt. The prizefighter was quite fond of metaphors. In his mind, white America lived in a burning house, all while mistreating Black Americans: "The house's been on fire for 300 years, and the whites have let the blacks sleep. The Negro's been lynched, killed, raped, burned, dragged around all through the city hanging on the chains of cars, alcohol and turpentine poured into his wounds. That's why Negroes are so full of fear today. Been put into him from the time he's a baby. Imagine! Twenty-two million Negroes in America, suffering, fought in the wars, got more worse treatment than any human being can even imagine, walking the streets of America . . ." Ali had such a following that Tom Wicker, the *New York Times* columnist, wondered if he might entice others to refuse the draft. "The fact is," Wicker opined, "he is taking the ultimate position of civil disobedience; he is refusing to obey the law of the majority on the grounds of his personal beliefs, with full knowledge of the consequence . . . What would happen if all young men of draft age took the same position!" Ali's case went all the way to the United States Supreme Court, where, in 1971, his conviction was overturned.

Senator Richard Russell didn't care about civil rights, or about the shenanigans of the overwhelmingly white draft boards across the country. He wanted to defeat communism. And he was going to give his boy, LBJ, everything he needed to fight this war.

During the latter part of the Kennedy administration—and the beginning of the Johnson administration—there had been plenty of geopolitical maneuvering going on in Vietnam. But it wasn't yet a "declared war"—meaning that Lyndon Johnson hadn't gone to Congress and the American public to announce that American security was under threat. That all changed on July 30, 1964. South Vietnamese forces fired upon the North Vietnamese while patrolling in the Gulf of Tonkin. The North Vietnamese, knowing the Americans had been directing South Vietnamese forces, took this as an affront from America. Days later, the USS *Maddox* was patrolling and noticed a North Vietnamese vessel moving into what they perceived to be an attack position. Firing commenced from both sides. Although there were no casualties, that was enough to get American planes roaring off from carriers and striking at the North Vietnamese. The White House warned that such North Vietnamese maneuvers would result in "grave consequences." Subsequent communications about North Vietnamese aggression became jumbled, and when word was conveyed to the White House it came out sounding as if the North Vietnamese had attacked. Bad communications or not, the moment would not go unanswered. On August 4, 1964, Johnson went on nationwide TV. "Aggression by terror against the peaceful villagers of South Vietnam has now been joined by open aggression on the high seas against the United States," he told the nation. "Yet our response, for the present, will be limited and fitting. We Americans know, although others appear to forget, the risk of spreading conflict. We still seek no wider war." But then Everett Alvarez, an American pilot, was shot down and taken prisoner by the North Vietnamese. He became the war's first aviator to be captured. On August 7, the U.S. Senate and House of Representatives both passed the Tonkin Gulf Resolution, authorizing war. Only two senators opposed it. In the House, no one opposed it.

America was "officially" going to war.

In Johnson's mind, the Tonkin Gulf Resolution was like "Grandma's nightshirt—it covers everything."

But "everything" did not necessarily take in the mindset or the psyche of the North Vietnamese. General Maxwell Taylor, burdened with worry, had returned from Vietnam in 1964 with a report for President Johnson. Among Taylor's assessments: "The ability of the Viet-Cong continuously to rebuild their units and to make good their losses is one of the mysteries of the guerrilla war . . . Not only do Viet-Cong units have the recuperative powers of the phoenix, but they have an amazing ability to maintain morale. Only in rare cases have we found evidence of bad morale among Viet-Cong prisoners or recorded in captured Viet-Cong documents . . ." And yet General Taylor well knew the position of the hawks inside the Pentagon. They were still squirming from the 1961 Bay of Pigs debacle. The attempted coup backfired and only strengthened Soviet support for Castro.

The American military's attitude: damn the guerrillas.

But the guerrillas in North Vietnam were doing what guerrillas do: moving down from the Central Highlands, traveling at night, getting help from local villagers, and ambushing American forces.

In late 1964, upward of two thousand North Vietnamese troops had slithered, at night, into South Vietnam undetected, carrying about forty tons of heavy weaponry, including machine guns and mortars. It was the largest incursion of soldiers and weaponry the communists had thus far made into South Vietnamese territory. On December 28, the communists took the village of Binh Gia in Phuoc Tuy Province. The Battle of Binh Gia was hellish. It stretched across several days. In the end, an estimated five hundred South Vietnamese troops either lay dead or wounded or were missing. A total of five American military advisers—who were *officially* not there—died. When word reached Hanoi and Ho Chi Minh about the huge victory, he was ecstatic. To him, the victory at Binh Gia was "a little Dien Bien Phu"—a reference to the humiliating 1954 defeat of the French by Ho's forces.

Grandma's nightshirt was being ripped apart.

America had long been transfixed by its heroic military figures, which is why World War II's General William Westmoreland was back in action, commanding the troops in Vietnam. Following the latest coup in South Vietnam, Westmoreland sent a cable to the White House saying he wanted American troop strength raised to 175,000. He also told them it was time to start planning to "deploy even greater forces if and when required." Secretary of Defense Robert McNamara referred to the Westmoreland cable as "a bombshell." "Of the thousands of cables I received during my seven years at the Department of Defense this one disturbed me the most . . . We could no longer postpone a choice about which path to take," McNamara said.

LBJ verbally twisted the arm of his mentor, Richard Russell: "I guess we've got no choice, but it scares the hell out of me. I think everybody's going to think, 'We're landing the Marines. We're off to battle.' " Russell confided to Johnson that he felt "there's no way out" of Vietnam.

Indeed, there did seem to be no way out, because Vietnam, rather quickly, turned into both a rabbit hole and a catch-22: fall deeper into the darkness, or stay and possibly risk defeat. For the LBJ administration, the lies and obfuscations and misinformation kept unspooling. The American public swallowed those lies, up to a point. The CBS television correspondent Morley Safer took a crew into Cam Ne, a village near Da Nang that had recently been attacked by U.S. Marines. He filed his report to the American TV audience on the evening news of August 5, 1965: "The day's operation burned down one hundred and fifty houses, wounded three women, killed one baby, wounded one Marine, and netted four prisoners," Safer said into the camera. "Four old men who could not answer questions put to them in English. Four old men who had no idea what an ID card was. Today's operation is the frustration of Vietnam in miniature. There is little doubt that American firepower can win a victory here. But to a Vietnamese peasant whose home . . . means a lifetime of backbreaking labor, it will take more than presidential promises to convince him that we are on his side."

Television was quite a powerful medium. Technology had much improved since the Korean War, and many Americans were seeing such battle imagery for the first time. The newsreel footage and Safer's report ricocheted throughout the White House and caused immediate anger. LBJ quickly got on the phone with Frank Stanton, the president of CBS News.

"Hello, Frank, this is your president."

"Yes, Mr. President."

"Frank, are you trying to fuck me?"

It went downhill from there, with Johnson telling Stanton he should fire Safer.

—

It wasn't just the soliloquies about race and the military offered by many returning Black soldiers that were having a negative effect on public perception about the war in Black communities; it was the drumbeat that was building up among various Black factions. The Student Nonviolent Coordinating Committee and the Black Panthers certainly did not see eye to eye on many issues, but when it came to castigating the war, they did. Malcolm X had started linking the war with the ravages of colonialism. His message seemed to resonate even more in the aftermath of his February 21, 1965, assassination by fellow Muslims inside a Harlem ballroom.

In 1965 Black Americans made up 12 percent of the population. Yet they constituted more than 30 percent of ground combat battalions. They were carrying the heavy end of the log. The Army paid fifty-five dollars a month more for those who volunteered for combat units; those units were being filled by greater numbers of Black soldiers because they needed the money, money that would be useful back home. It was also nearly impossible for a Black soldier in the early portion of the war to spot a Black officer, because less than 2 percent of the officers were Black. When the Southern Christian Leadership Conference became aware of these numbers, they broke precedent and weighed in about the war, announcing that Blacks should not "fight in Vietnam for the white man's freedom, until all the Negro people are free in Mississippi." But their statement, coming out of their Atlanta offices, did not get much traction in the press, and seemed more of a regional outburst than a national one.

College students—just as many of them had been doing on behalf of the civil rights movement—began voicing their disagreements with the war. On April 17, 1965, the largest antiwar protest in American history up to that point took place on the Mall in Washington. Accounts varied, with some estimates as high as twenty-five thousand; the administration preferred to limit the estimate to fifteen thousand. Despite this discrepancy, the March on Washington to End the War in Vietnam was certainly massive, and garnered nationwide news. The military draft had also recently been instituted, and some in the crowd were brazen enough to openly burn their draft cards.

—

In September 1965, the 1st Cavalry Division headed off to An Khe in Vietnam—sixteen thousand men and more than four hundred helicopters. The helicopter blades kept swirling over the tall grass of Vietnam and transporting American soldiers, and the number of casualties kept growing. "In the first two months of 1966, the United States suffered more than 4,300 casualties in the Vietnamese war," *The New York Times* reported on its front page. "American casualties for all of last year were under 7,000."

In 1966, the CIA wrote a memo about the futility of airstrikes in Vietnam: "Hundreds of bridges had been wrecked, but virtually all of them had been rebuilt or bypassed. Thousands of freight cars, trucks and other vehicles had been destroyed, but North Vietnamese traffic was moving smoothly. Roughly three quarters of the country's oil storage facilities had been eliminated, but there were no fuel shortages."

Given all of the dying and deaths, all of the attrition, all of the cruel math, Robert McNamara came up with an idea for how to get more young men into the military. He thought of all those Black youths he'd see on street corners while being driven back and forth from the White House. There must be scenes like this, he thought, in every inner city! He labeled them the "subterranean poor." The young Black men of that group were the most vulnerable and desperate. And McNamara wanted to get them into the Army. He wanted to get them over to Vietnam! Put them to work! Only the "work" would be fighting a war. He had read a report by Daniel Patrick Moynihan, then an assistant secretary of labor, who had studied the state of Blacks in America. Moynihan's report, *The Negro Family,* was a strange brew of statistics, stereotype, analysis, and critique. It said, in essence, that Black families suffered because so many of them were headed by women. It came desperately close to blaming the victims of poverty themselves for the inequality they suffered in America. And the boys, the young men, in those families needed a kind of overseer, and that overseer could be represented by the military, which, McNamara reasoned, held such opportunity for them! McNamara thought the Moynihan report was brilliant. He was well aware that not everyone who signed up for the military met the military's IQ requirements. So he set about having the IQ standards lowered! He changed the acceptable minimum test score, which was 31 out of 100, to 10 out of 100. This would get those poor Black men—and even some young white men—off the streets of America! McNamara and his aides put out the word: Send Black recruiters into the inner cities—the ghettos—with the news that the new test-score minimum would be more amenable to low achievers. And those recruiters would be given bonuses for higher induction rates as they went about encouraging the poor to join the Army—and see the world! They took special care to tell the recruits about the veteran benefits they'd get after their military service! For the coup de grâce, there was some winking about all the beautiful girls the recruits were going to see in those foreign locales. To a poor Black kid, who'd had learning difficulties in school, this might have sounded like they'd won big on a game show.

McNamara ran the whole new recruitment idea by LBJ. He told LBJ he planned to name the program Project 100,000 because that's how many soldiers he wanted the military to bring through the specially designed program every year. Johnson thought about it, then thought about all the Southern politicians who hated his civil rights bills, then thought about how such a program as Project 100,000 just might get some of those pesky politicians off his back. "Looks to me," LBJ told McNamara in a confidential chat, "like what it would do for Russell is move all these Nigra boys that are now rejects and sent back on his community, to move them [into the Army], clean them up, prepare them to do something . . ."

That was the unique thing about Lyndon Baines Johnson: Offstage, he could turn into the vulgar Texan. And then, on a church stage, or at a podium on one of those Negro college campuses, he could utter that phrase—"We shall overcome"—with such sincerity. And he possessed the singular ability to put muscle behind that overture.

Johnson realized that a program like Project 100,000 would keep those student deferments in place, and it would continue to acknowledge the strength of the middle-class vote—as he often put it—out there in America. He gave McNamara approval to proceed with the plan. McNamara stepped before an annual meeting of the Veterans of Foreign Wars in 1966 and told them, with such passion, about his Project 100,000, and how it was really an important program, actually an extension of President Johnson's Great Society program! And who didn't want to help the poor? McNamara neglected to tell his audience that those impoverished men were, for the most part, mentally challenged and unfit for battle; that most of them were headed straight for combat; that high numbers of them were young Black men.

In 1964, two years before Project 100,000 was launched—and as if he were fearing just such an idea—William Walsh, a military vet and an attorney, wrote an article for the *American Bar Association Journal.* "Warfare is steadily growing more complex," he wrote. "The day is past when an effective soldier needed only the intelligence to point a musket downhill and obey the order . . . Service in the Armed Forces today requires an alert, questioning mind simply to master the technology of weapons and tactics . . . There is likely to be no room for the low-IQ soldier, the 'warm body' who cannot—or will not—'cut the mustard.' That man . . . is going to get in the way of those who will have to do the job."

Once they were in Vietnam, many of the problems of those recruited under Project 100,000 quickly became exposed. There were literacy problems. There were problems about following directions, a grave issue when it came to reading battlefield instructions and maps. Promotions for those under the program were practically nonexistent. A slur became attached to the McNamara program: "McNamara's Morons." The racial aspect was devastating. Across all branches of the military Blacks accounted for 11 percent of the troops. Forty-one percent of those brought into the Army under Project 100,000 were Black. In combat, Black deaths were consistently higher, proportionately, than white deaths. In 1965, 23.5 percent of those killed in action in Vietnam were Black.

—

Complaints about the racial makeup of draft boards started arriving in government offices from Black families. In 1967, only 1.3 percent of the 16,632 draft board members across America were Black. These, of course, were the individuals who decided on draft decisions, on who would be granted deferments. In Indiana, Kansas, Arkansas, Louisiana, Mississippi, Alabama, and New Jersey—to cite a few of the states that reported their draft board racial makeup—there were zero Blacks on the boards. It was assumed that the states that refused to report the racial makeup of their draft boards did so because they wanted to hide their racial numbers.

It didn't take long for criticism of the Vietnam War that had been uttered by the SCLC to flow into other parts of the Black community. The younger members of the NAACP and SNCC and CORE all began seeing a direct link between the pain in Vietnam and the pain in a nation still bucking integration. Some were calling it—all the legislation that had been passed, and the pain still in the streets—the challenging "transition period" that America simply had to go through. Two hundred years of slavery–cum–Jim Crow–cum–second-class citizenship could not be overcome by six hundred days of legislation. Many theaters and restaurants in the South remained unwelcoming to Negroes.

This period of civil rights protests saw disagreements between some of the organizations on their respective strategies. Some advocated a continuation of nonviolence. Others were calling for outright confrontations. Stokely Carmichael was still making the rounds of civil rights protests, and possessed a fearless style when it came to interactions with whites. Some of the elders of the civil rights movement continued warning him that he risked getting lynched. He'd smile at them—and keep talking. He was talking up a storm in Greenwood, Mississippi, during the time of a march by the civil rights figure James Meredith. "We're asking Negroes not to go to Vietnam and fight but to stay in Greenwood and fight here," Carmichael told a gathering. Also, he refused to let up on that phrase that had lightning attached to it: Black Power. The phrase made its way into articles and conversations, unleashing waves of concern and fear among whites, many of whom were in constant confusion about Black demands for equality. "McNamara is trying to thin us out," Carmichael said on another occasion. "Calls it 'black urban renewal.' Well, I've got news for Mister Mac. Ain't no Vietcong ever called me nigger . . . and if I'm going to do any fighting it's gonna be right here at home. We will not fight in Vietnam and run in Georgia!"

Mostly healed from shotgun wounds he had received during his march from a white shooter—who was caught—James Meredith started thinking about the future. "Negroes are dying bravely alongside whites in Vietnam, and when that generation comes marching back to the small and large towns of America," he said, "they will not easily put up with the inequities they have suffered in the past."

Life magazine, long a handsome addition to newsstands, was one of the few national magazines in the early and mid-1960s to devote attention-grabbing space to the civil rights movement in its pages. One of its most renowned photographers was Gordon Parks, who was Black and had made a name for himself by virtue of his versatility. He photographed couture fashion shows in European capitals. He swung his camera around the urban ghettos of America. He spent time photographing Black and Puerto Rican families in Harlem, doing for them what James Agee and Walker Evans had done for the poor whites of Hale County, Alabama, in the late 1930s—garnering attention to their plight. Gordon Parks also had a son in Vietnam, a tank gunner. "I now have my fifth kill, dad," Parks's son, David, had recently written him. "We got the bastard sniper later that afternoon." Parks was afraid for his son, but also proud that he was defending the United States of America. Not long after that letter, the elder Parks found himself traveling around Los Angeles with Stokely Carmichael. Two Black cats, from the world of hipster Black America, one of them working inside the American system, the other trying to alter that system. Parks told Carmichael he felt he had been too harsh in criticizing the White House about its Vietnam policy. "They deserved every bit of it," Carmichael told him. "My words for them don't start to match the criminal acts they perpetrate against the Vietnamese people. How can McNamara deny racism when proportionately more black boys are dying every day in his stinking war?" Parks felt that Carmichael was confusing civil rights with international peace. Carmichael didn't agree: "The people who support the war in Vietnam are the same ones who keep their foot on the black man's neck in this country. Bigotry and death over here is no different from bigotry and death over there." The two men went back and forth, riding around the streets of Los Angeles, their interview turning into a kind of rap session as they talked about race and history, with soul music humming on the radio. "Remember," Carmichael told Parks, "we fought 300 years of American Negro history in a year and a half—organizing, bleeding, starving and educating at the same time. We gave a nation hope. If there is a future for us, we had better face it with hard political lines."

Racial uprisings kept sweeping across the land, from Newark to Harlem to Detroit. Whites called what was happening "riots." In the minds of many Blacks, they were rebellions. "It was as though the Viet Cong had infiltrated the riot blackened streets," a columnist wrote in *The Detroit News* of July 26, 1967, referring to the racial clashes that had happened in that city. Forty-three people died in Detroit, and more than a thousand were injured. One of the more ghastly events around the uprising took place inside the city's Algiers Motel. Three Black teens were murdered by a member of a riot task force. Charges were later filed against task-force members but all of the accused were eventually acquitted. The government's answer to the uprising was to send in the 82nd Airborne Division, along with the Michigan National Guard. To many of the young Blacks in Detroit, this was the Army in action: ready to destroy them.

Fighting a war cost money, and LBJ had to start cutting funding for his War on Poverty. In late 1966, Robert McNamara began, at times, talking with the kind of clarity he had never expressed before about the war. "I never thought it would go on like this," he said. "I didn't think these people had the capacity to fight this way." He was referring to the North Vietnamese, to the men and women who were fighting, some of them wearing rags and sandals and floppy hats.

In 1967, Sargent Shriver got only a third of what he asked for in the annual budget for his War on Poverty.

It went on and on, the protests, the troop deployments to Vietnam, the McNamara doublespeak press conferences. Project 100,000 added another hundred thousand ill-equipped soldiers to those being sent to Vietnam. Then another hundred thousand after that. Robert Marshall of Tulsa, Oklahoma, had no way of knowing if he had gotten into the Army by virtue of allowances under Project 100,000, but he met the qualifications for the program. "We were poor. I was running the streets, getting in all kinds of trouble," Marshall says of his Tulsa teenage years. "I came home from running around one day. My mother was crying. I said, 'Mama, what's wrong?' She said, 'I don't have any money to feed y'all kids.'" As soon as he turned seventeen years old, he sought out an Army recruiter. "My mother went from zero to eighty-two dollars a month," he says, meaning his first Army paychecks. "I lived off the other forty a month." He landed in Vietnam in early 1965 for a twelve-month stay. It wasn't just the ferociousness of the enemy that alarmed him; there were also leeches, red ants that could cut through ponchos, and wild monkeys that would sometimes attack soldiers. He received promotions and became a sergeant, which he attributed to his aggressiveness. He was shot by a sniper and got a Purple Heart medal. During his trips back to the States, he took note of the different reactions to his uniform. "In Oakland, California, I was hated because I was a soldier," he says, referring to the liberal environment there. "In Fayetteville, North Carolina, I was hated because I was Black."

A total of 354,000 soldiers from challenged backgrounds, with mental and physical deficiencies—again, 41 percent of them Black—landed in Vietnam. The best accounting of how many Black enlistees through Project 100,000 died in Vietnam was known to be "several thousand." The Army dared not single them out, for fear of a backlash about how they had gotten into the military. Herb DeBose was a Black Vietnam vet who worked with returning soldiers in New York City after the war. "I think McNamara should be shot" was his sentiment. "I saw him when he resigned from the World Bank, crying about the poor children of the world. But if he did not cry at all for any of those men he took in under Project 100,000, then he really doesn't know what crying is all about. Many weren't even on a fifth-grade level."

Lyndon Johnson had assumed office in a crisis. He had had to imagine a new national order. He had to express to white America the need to make a new, freer America, and give Black Americans the confidence that such a thing could happen. In those fast-moving early years of his presidency, he strode upon the stage like a colossus. He had demanded more from everyone around him. More than sixty domestic bills were passed in addition to the landmark civil rights bills. He did not hail from the moneyed class, as so many who worked in the White House did. Those staffers did not know poverty. But he had looked at poverty from the ground up. He had seen empty cupboards in his youth—those of friends, and relatives, and Blacks living in Texas. There was something almost romantic and egalitarian about his domestic agenda, which is why some of those poignant speeches written for him had a tinge of the gospel in them. But a domestic agenda was far different from a foreign-policy agenda, and all of LBJ's domestic dreams unfolded in the maelstrom of war, an unforgiving war from all angles. And the war certainly—and unevenly—depleted Black communities of too many sons, or tossed those Black sons right back into a fiery social order once they returned home.

The more the war droned on—and the deeper the quicksand became—the tighter the relationship between Richard Russell and Lyndon Johnson wound itself. They were now knotted to each other, tighter than ever. Johnson dismissed Russell's racial philosophy because he required his war-funding savvy. LBJ convinced himself he needed to show the Ivy Leaguers in the White House—that condescending crowd still worshipping so much about the late JFK—that he could win a war. Kennedy may have started the outlines of this war—and some of the seeds had been sown by earlier presidents—but LBJ convinced himself he was going to finish it.

Lyndon Johnson castigated other senators in and out of the White House when they didn't always agree with him, but such treatment did not land upon the segregationist Richard Russell. In depending on—and taking advantage of—Russell's outsized role in the continuation of the war, Johnson slowly allowed antipoverty funding to become less and less. In some circles, civil rights enforcement even began to wane. While underestimating the wall of white resistance to equality in America, Johnson prolonged a war. Half of his legacy—the domestic agenda—was righteous and honorable and often so very beautiful, lifting a whole race of people into finally experiencing full citizenship. But the other half of that legacy was being cuckolded by the machinery of war. No matter how much blood was being spilled, it never seemed enough to end the war.

There were so many questions: Was it year four of the war? Or year five? Or even year six? The ministers in the pulpits of the Black churches were getting more and more weary. All those crying mothers; all those funerals. There were even reports in the Black press of Black soldiers in Vietnam uniting to form self-defense groups, as a reaction to rising reports of Ku Klux Klan activity in Saigon.

Archie Biggers was quite proud to be a Marine officer in Vietnam. Especially a Black Marine officer. The Marines had been the last branch of the military service to integrate. Biggers returned to the States from his tour of duty in Vietnam in 1969 and became a Marine recruiter. One day, he got himself over to Howard University in Washington, D.C., the renowned Black school. "I thought I would feel at home," he recalled. "The guys poked fun at me, calling me Uncle Sam's flunky. They would say the Marine Corps sucks. The Army sucks. They would say their brother or uncle got killed, so why was I still in. They would see the Purple Heart [for having been injured] and ask me what was I trying to prove. The women wouldn't talk to you either. I felt bad. I felt cold. I felt like I was completely out of it."

Chapter Eight

A Murdered Minister and a Prison Revolt

For decades the old guard of the civil rights movement—and it was dominated by members of the Black clergy—avoided making any type of comments that might seem unpatriotic when it came to military matters. The churches had an acceptable lane, just as the state had an acceptable lane. And never, the sentiments went, should the entities of church and state meet. When Martin Luther King, Jr., began making subtle noises about the buildup of the war in 1964, he drew private rebukes from fellow ministers. The war was an anticommunist crusade, they reminded him, and warned him to steer clear of any utterances that might seem friendly to communism. In early March 1965, during a visit to Howard University that coincided with reports of more bombing in Vietnam, King felt determined to stop remaining silent about the war. "I know that President Johnson has a serious problem here, and naturally I am sympathetic to that," King said to the gathering, and proceeded to tell them he felt there was no way war could solve Vietnam's woes: "The war in Vietnam is accomplishing nothing." Now King was officially—if gently—on the record. In his mind, he had held his tongue too long. He had now gone where many other ministers had

The notorious Long Binh Jail (cryptically referred to as LBJ, given that the president's full name was Lyndon Baines Johnson) in Saigon disproportionately imprisoned Black soldiers. A bloody, racially ignited uprising there shocked military officials.

warned him not to go. His coming-out position, however, did not yet dominate the mainstream news.

Some in King's camp realized that to go against the war would be viewed as unpatriotic, anti-American. "You don't think I know what I'm doing when I talk about Vietnam, do you?" King had asked his aide C. T. Vivian, who angled King onto another subject rather than answer.

It wasn't easy to go up against LBJ, who had such currency and goodwill in Black households because he had passed a civil rights bill and a voting rights bill. "Lyndon Johnson, in fact, may be the best John Wayne part ever written," the *New York Times* columnist Tom Wicker wrote. "[He] seems 20 feet tall—when he really measures no more than 10."

During his visits to churches now, King began to notice the increased questioning from Black women who wondered if he had any idea when the war might end. They were worried about their sons. Some thought of him as a sage. The Black mothers were starting to hear alarming details about the death rate of Black soldiers. King offered up his handsome smile, then was forced to palm his questioners off gingerly on to nearby aides. He knew, however, that the questions flowing from mothers would not go away. He asked his wife, Coretta, to share her thoughts about the war during an SCLC retreat. "I talked about how it would continue to drain resources from education, housing, health, and other badly needed social programs," she recalled. "I said [to Martin], 'Why do you think we got the Nobel Prize? It was not just for civil rights . . . Peace and justice are indivisible.' "

Politicians of both stripes were unnerved by King's anti-Vietnam pronouncements. "He [King] is not your friend," Chicago's powerful Democratic mayor, Richard Daley, told President Johnson. "He's against you on Vietnam. He's a goddam faker." The clashing noise around King—Black Power militants, FBI wiretaps, Vietnam concerns—only served to embolden his critics. It was King's inching into the Vietnam War debate that encouraged LBJ to listen more and more to J. Edgar Hoover's rantings about the civil rights leader. A dutiful FBI agent, intent on impressing the boss, J. Edgar—and obviously having tapped into King's recent phone conversations—wrote a memo to agency higher-ups stating that King was aiming to "direct his entire efforts in opposition to the war in Vietnam."

All of it seemed a prelude to what loomed for King: an invitation to give a talk at the famed Riverside Baptist Church, which sat on the edge of Harlem near Columbia University. The event was organized by the group known as Clergymen and Laymen Concerned About Vietnam. The date was set as April 4, 1967. King told his aides he had no intention of dodging the invitation. An announcement was made presenting the title of his upcoming talk: "Beyond Vietnam."

No one, of course, could see the dark forces gathering.

Most entering the high-ceilinged neo-Gothic Riverside Church on April 4 were accustomed to hearing progressive speakers from all walks of life. The church's leaders were proud of their reputations and their identification with the community. The pews quickly filled with an overflow crowd of thirty-five hundred. Disappointed folks unable to get in remained lined up outside, gyrating in place against the chilly air. It was a given that FBI undercover agents were in attendance; national news outlets had been writing about government wiretaps of King. King was calm and deliberate as he began his speech, thanking attendees as well as the clergy who had joined him. He explained he had come to Riverside to give this address "because my conscience leaves me no other choice." And he proceeded to explain why, in his mind, Black freedom and Vietnam were inextricably linked, why those who vilified him really did not know him or the goals of the civil rights movement itself—and why so many questions had turned into veiled attacks on his patriotism. As always, he spoke slowly, enunciating perfectly in his Southern drawl. "As I have walked among the desperate, rejected, angry young men [of Northern ghettos] I have told them that Molotov cocktails and rifles will not solve their problems . . . But they asked—and rightly so—what about Vietnam? I knew that I could never again raise my voice against the violence of the oppressed in the ghettos without first having spoken clearly to the greatest purveyor of violence in the world today—my own government. For the sake of this government, for the sake of the hundreds of thousands trembling under our violence, I cannot be silent." He had now carved an unmistakable line in the sand, and gone where other Black ministers would not go. He continued: "It seemed as if there was a real promise of hope for the poor—both black and white—through the poverty program. There were experiments, hope, new beginnings. Then came the buildup in Vietnam and I watched the program broken and eviscerated as if it were some idle political plaything of a society gone mad on war, and I knew that America would never invest the necessary funds or energies in rehabilitation of its poor so long as adventures like Vietnam continued to drive men and skills and money like some demonic destructive suction tube." This was the fearless King, the visionary King. This was King in the North, away from the Southern newspapers and their editorial writers beholden to all things military. This was King delivering a sermon not only to Georgia Senator Richard Russell but to the president of the United States as well. He went on: "So I was increasingly compelled to see the war as an enemy of the poor and to attack it as such . . . This business of burning human beings with napalm, of filling our nation's homes with orphans and widows, of injecting poisonous drugs of hate into veins of people normally humane, of sending men home from dark and bloody battlefields physically handicapped and psychologically deranged, cannot be reconciled with wisdom, justice, and love."

For the next 365 days, he set about roaming the land, preaching. He was unable to turn back now, seized with his integral role in the momentum of the antiwar program and the ongoing war itself—and the plight of Black soldiers. King now gave their mothers a little more time when they wanted to confer with him about the war. Precious few in the U.S. House of Representatives or the U.S. Senate agreed with him. He had started talking about death, his time on earth, about mountaintops. And, exactly one year to the day after delivering his Riverside Church address, Martin Luther King, Jr., lay bleeding on a Memphis hotel balcony, shot to death by a white supremacist. Gone in a blink, like so many soldiers who had died in Vietnam.

News of his death circled the globe. When the news landed in Vietnam, Black soldiers were crestfallen. But the Black soldiers locked up inside the Long Binh Jail were more than just crestfallen; they were seething. And they began plotting.

The penalty for disobeying orders in Vietnam could quickly get a soldier sentenced to a stint in Long Binh, a prison that had been constructed outside of Saigon. Blacks constituted close to 25 percent of the Army population, but they often made up as much as 80 percent of the Long Binh population. The disparity in numbers between white and Black incarceration clearly meant Blacks were being punished more harshly than whites. The administrators of the prison and the guards were themselves overwhelmingly white. "I came to have a lot of respect for those young Black men in Long Binh who had taken the position of 'I don't want to be here,'" said the physician Elbert Nelson. "I had a friend of mine who was sent to Long Binh." The prison sentences could vary—a month, three months, five months. Because the confinement did not count toward any soldier's yearlong tour of duty, it only lengthened prisoners' stay in Vietnam. For the soldiers who served more than one stint in Long Binh, it could feel like a revolving door, like *Groundhog Day.* And those Black soldiers who had been sent to Long Binh would often emerge with an even bigger chip on the shoulder. They'd start their war regimen all over again: fighting and killing; trying to stay alive; struggling for some shut-eye when the bullets and grenades were not whizzing by. And there were those times—too many, they felt—when they'd catch a slice of demeaning racial chatter from white soldiers.

Soldiers had rituals, little superstitions they held on to in hopes of warding off bad luck. Black soldiers liked to lock eyes with one another—especially following a bloody fight against the enemy—and offer the "dap" handshake. Dapping had become particular to Black soldier life. But to the white soldiers who were flying Confederate flags atop their hooches—thatched tentlike huts—the gesture was viewed as downright subversive.

The makeshift prison sat twelve miles from the center of Saigon. The inmates mocked the fact that the initials of Long Binh Jail were LBJ, and they cursed Lyndon Baines Johnson in a myriad of ways, first and foremost for landing them in hot and wild and crazy Vietnam. The prison was surrounded by concertina wire and sandbags and featured tents to house prisoners. In time actual buildings were added. The food drew constant complaints. Guards had orders to shoot escapees. The MPs thought it was insane to try to escape. "No one ran away because we were out in [Viet Cong] country," said Military Police Brigade Commander Tom Guidera. Some structures of the prison had tin roofs; the noise from the rain made sleep difficult. One area of the jail complex was known as Silver City; it was where the silver conex containers sat. Inmates who caused repeated disciplinary problems were put inside one of the containers, where the temperatures could rise to more than a hundred degrees. The prison had a Devil's Island vibe: dangerous, sweltering, with insects everywhere. "We were the first ones to get suspected of anything,"

Dennis Wilson, a Black sergeant in Vietnam in 1969, says of his fellow Black soldiers. "And we were sometimes weak when it came to temptations, because we never had anything. I saw so many white guys get breaks. The brothers generally got no breaks for anything." Blacks had been using the term "soul brothers" since the dawn of the civil rights movement. It defined camaraderie.

Reveille was at 5:00 a.m. Fights were often quelled by the use of tear gas.

The work detail consisted of breaking red clay down into sand, and filling sandbags. These were then flown out to other base camps, where they were placed on the ground around the perimeter of the camps to stop enemy bullets.

Guard shifts could last up to twelve hours. Sergeant Sam Mullin had a routine for trouble-causing inmates at Long Binh: "I'll handcuff [a troublemaker] and drag his ass down and throw him into a conex container and I'm going to keep that sonofabitch on the driest fourteen-day diet I can get away with."

Jimmy Childress was not an atypical inmate inside the prison. He was a badass, and proud of it. The eighteen-year-old from Kansas City didn't really think about the consequences of stealing merchandise and racing across state lines to sell it. But in the springtime of 1967, he found himself locked up in a Kansas City jail for his misdeeds. Childress—a handsome young man with a sweet smile—walked into his court hearing imagining he'd get jail time, but not serious time, so he wasn't too worried. But the judge had his own solution: "Either go into the military or go to prison," the judge said, stunning Childress with such an offer—an offer he wished he had more time to contemplate. "Which is it going to be?" Childress had a feeling state prison might be a rough ordeal. He chose the military, and was swooped up into the parameters of Project 100,000. "I knew nothing about the war. I knew nothing about Vietnam," he later confessed.

The fighting in the war—the night patrols and day-after-day

shooting and killing—was numbing to Jimmy Childress. He grew angry. He commiserated with other Black soldiers, many of whom were just as angry. Childress made up his mind one day: He was going to stop killing the enemy, and was going to go AWOL. Just like that, he was in the Saigon wind. Black soldiers who had gone AWOL before had a kind of template: They'd usually meet up with a Vietnamese girlfriend on the outskirts of Saigon and reside with her and her family. Or they'd hide out in "Soul Alley," that popular area of bars and nightclubs often frequented by Black soldiers. The Black soldiers in good standing—and even patrons of Soul Alley—could be generous toward Black AWOL soldiers, even if such charity was risky, because MPs were on the lookout for deserters. "During that time, I was stealing from the military M-16s, grenade launchers," Childress recalled about his time on the run. "I even stole a couple jeeps."

The longer Jimmy Childress sat inside LBJ, the more he listened to the heated anger about the death of Martin Luther King, Jr. And the more he listened to the escape plans—no matter how byzantine they sounded—the more he convinced himself he had to be part of one. "Why am I even over here?" he wondered. "When you can't even go back to America and sit at a lunch counter, you know?" Many, at first, refused to believe King was dead, but then radio news reporters—and the letters from back home—confirmed the horror of it. Word seeped inside the facility that some white soldiers on the outside were celebrating King's murder. More anger. The Blacks began vowing revenge: "A new burst of anger was afoot in the prison," the inmate Scott Riley admitted, referring to King's death. Riley was doing time on a dope charge. Jimmy Childress was more than ready for something to happen. "We were hot, and crazy, we were fed up. So we decided, we're going to tear this Motherfucker down."

The legal system set up by the American military in Vietnam was quite different from what Americans were accustomed to Stateside. The Army did not use lawyers to prosecute or defend; instead, they used randomly selected officers. Leonard Powell, a Black junior

Army officer, was at the Chu Lai Air Base when he was selected to prosecute another soldier. He knew he had a job to do, but he was stunned by the workings of the "court": "There was a limited opportunity to go gather evidence, or do any type of real investigation. It was the worst legal system you can imagine," he says. "The legal system was damn near a joke."

In the three months leading up to King's assassination, the inmate population at Long Binh was 30 percent beyond capacity, and Blacks now constituted a whopping 90 percent of the inmates as the numbers had increased.

Gregg Payton became the first crucial player in the plot. "They had a little caucus meeting and I sat in on a couple of them. Clandestine. Lights out. People sneaking around the barracks," he said of his fellow inmates. Since Payton had gotten a job driving off the grounds a short distance to retrieve kerosene, which was used to burn waste, it was decided that he should steal a little extra kerosene on every trip, which he did. It was hidden in the facility.

Near midnight on August 29, 1968—over four months after King's assassination—the plot unfolded. Matches were lit. "In Vietnam they got a lot of tunnels . . . and we were going to try to go underground . . . hit a water drain or something," the LBJ inmate Nathaniel Fort, Jr., recalled about the feverish planning. "That was the route we were goin' to take. It wasn't goin' over any walls." The kerosene-based fires started in several of the structures. Heat was applied to cell locks, popping them open, freeing inmates. They had confiscated a shovel, and also pieces of rope and flashlights. One of the inmates had also acquired a pair of pliers, which they were going to use to cut through the fencing once they reached the planned exit points. Rousted MPs woke to see fire and hear yelling and rising mayhem. Confusion quickly set in among the inmates, because they couldn't reach the location where weapons were held. Gerald Stovall, an inmate, recalled that a lot of the Black inmates had sat around reading Black Panther literature brought over from the States by other Black soldiers. And the literature was more than enough to keep their ardor up about either escaping or seizing LBJ. "A lot of blacks were perceiving the war as a white man's war," Stovall said. Frank Troutman, an inmate, was leery of another inmate, Charles Planter. "There was a group that called themselves the syndicate," according to Troutman. "Planter was head of the group . . . The group had people shining shoes, doing their laundry, and everything else for them . . . This group controlled the stockade as far as marijuana, any type pills, narcotics, and the stealing. This group used to talk practically daily that someday they would burn the place down." It was determined later that Planter's "syndicate" consisted of Private James Anthony, Private David Coppege, Private Samuel Farmer, Private Richard Cleveland, and Kansas City's own Jimmy Childress. About twelve hours before the riotous mayhem started, David Zeller, a white inmate, had noticed something: "It was approximately 1300 hours [1 p.m.] 28 August, 1968, when I observed several Negroes that sleep in the same tent leave and go out by the fence near the guard tower. I saw the tower guard throw two packages of cigarettes, one syringe and needle and a package of Binoctal tablets over to the Negroes standing by the fence."

The clockwork timing of inmates fleeing out of cells seemed impressive. The general siren was going off. In the chaos and fear, several guards were attacked. "The synchronization of the riot was great," the inmate Gregg Payton confessed. "I was asleep and half high when it went off." It was in the facility's B Compound that the ruckus started. Two guards were overwhelmed, and their keys were taken. The rampaging inmates rolled up pages of newspaper and lit them to make instant torches. Howling inmates ripped metal bars from bunks as makeshift weapons; more inmates bounded into the kitchen and grabbed knives. LBJ suddenly became a scene of all-out revenge and riot. MPs scrambled to the exercise yard and began securing the front gate, because they imagined inmates would try to flee through that particular gate first. "We saw guards running for their lives out through the main gate," recalled Mike Doherty, a clerk inside the compound. "Some guards climbed the fence and through the roll of concertina wire at the top to . . . save their lives." As in any riot situation, bedlam quickly reigned. Louis Zarrelli, a guard, was knocked about: "I was kicked and punched," he said. "The two ring leaders who were trying to break open the Maximum gate were prisoner Coppege and prisoner Beauchamps. They were the two who stood out . . . They were yelling at the prisoners inside to 'kill those white mother-fucking guards.' I made it a point to remember those two."

Inmates from A Compound made their way to B Compound, and, once there, started freeing other inmates, with a focus on the Black prisoners, which wasn't difficult given how many inmates were Black. Some Blacks were so disturbed by the racial vengeance that they began protecting some of the white inmates. The destination of the Black rioters: the administration building. "So when the riot hopped off," Gerald Stovall recalled, "you had guys, some combat soldiers, who still tried to keep up camaraderie and at the same time you had blacks from rear areas caught up in the belief it was us against them . . . For some it was a black-white, get-anything-you-can thing. For others it was us against them. Prisoners against those in power. It went both ways." Black inmates wielded baseball bats, and swung them on MPs, both Black and white. "About 15 or 20 of us white prisoners took refuge in parolee tent #1," said the inmate Donald Albertson. Amidst the screams and fleeing, several white inmates made it to the outside, feeling they were safer in the open air, where there was a better chance of rescue. "We went outside," the white inmate Donald Bass revealed, "and [were] assaulted by several Negroes who beat and kicked us. A man I know by the name of CanTu [Ronald Cureton] beat me and held a razor blade at my throat." John Fanning, a white MP, thought the unspooling violence had a *Day of the Locusts* vibe: "Both Negro and white prisoners were like a human wave—everyone trying to get out." The swinging baseball bats clutched by Black hands kept sending shrieks of terror throughout LBJ. Jimmy Childress turned into an arsonist. As the prisoner Samuel Farmer later testified: "Childress, he helped start the fires, he burned the following places: mess hall, admin[istration] building and the finance building . . ." MPs not only had to try to corral the rampaging inmates, they had to try to put out fires.

The sounds of whistles being blown by MPs pierced the smoky surroundings. Vietnam had its own language in the minds of American soldiers; "chucks" became the term for whites. "Kill the chucks!" echoed throughout the compound as whites kept fleeing in various directions with—and for good reason—cold fear in their eyes. Leonard Thurmes, a white inmate, bolted for a fence with other white prisoners, all of them figuring that if they could get to the top of the fence, they'd risk jumping over to the other side, damn the possibility of broken bones. "We saw the Negroes coming toward us with sticks, razors, boards and bunk adaptors . . . We began trying to climb over the fence . . . so that no one could come after us. As we climbed to the top of the fence, we were told by the tower guard to get down off of the fence or that he would shoot."

Black inmates were screaming at the MPs that if any Blacks were bayoneted or shot, they would begin taking it out on white prisoners, meting out similar punishments to them.

Mattresses were burning; the air was fetid.

Jeremiah James, another Black inmate, had befriended Edward Haskett, a white private from St. Petersburg, Florida. "He was nice to me. They killed him that night," James recalled. "They covered his head with a blanket and beat him with sticks from the cots. He never said a word. They beat him to death simply because he was white."

The bacchanal of violence seemed ceaseless.

Two white guards were seen running from the mob. They climbed atop a structure, out of breath, looking around for the cavalry. Black inmates closed in, yelling, "Kill the guards."

There are times, throughout the annals of prison riots, when something happens that defies the bloodshed and horror of the riot itself. Inside Long Binh on the August night of the bloody riot, the inmate Charles Planter, one of the leaders of the uprising, saw those two white guards atop the structure. He knew they were going to be killed. And men who obeyed his orders were going to kill them.

But Planter walked in the direction of the two guards and called up to them, telling them to come on down, promising them he'd personally escort them to the front gate and safety. The guards came down, though they wondered if it was a ruse. Planter began walking, past hardened Black inmates, past staring eyes, strutting like a Roman general, and, finally, the trio reached the gate, and the men were freed into the waiting arms of a military response force. Who knows why Planter decided to save the two men? Sometimes in prisons, there comes a time to reward friendship. Perhaps one of the white guards—or both—had extended kindness and courtesies toward Planter at some point. Prisoners tend to have long memories.

Lieutenant Colonel Vernon Johnson, in charge of LBJ, had ordered his response force to form a ring around the prison during the early period of the riot. He held his team back from storming the complex, fearing widespread deaths.

As time passed, through the night and into the next morning, the fact remained that the riotous inmates simply had nowhere to go. They were not going to get past the well-armed response force. And even if by some miracle they did, the equally well-armed Viet Cong would surely be awaiting them in the mountains. Lieutenant Colonel Johnson made up his mind to walk into the compound and try to reason with the inmates. Another officer went with him. It did not go well; Johnson and his accompanying officer were both attacked. "He was bleeding about the head," Ernest Talps, another officer, said of Johnson. "I helped him out the gate and had some MPs rush him to the hospital." Next to go in was Major Joshua Williams, a Black Army officer. When Williams entered the compound, there was immediate debate about whether to attack him or to let him talk. They let him talk. One inmate recalled the scene: "They wouldn't listen to him and I tried to get them to listen . . . I told them I had known [him] back on the block and he was OK. They listened for two to maybe four minutes but it didn't do any good . . . When they wouldn't listen, the Major left." The Black inmate Frank

Troutman, who had gotten worked up into a maniacal rage, grabbed a white inmate and dragged him over near the fence—just like a hunter dragging a shot deer. "Do you want all your guys to look like this?" Troutman brazenly asked the MPs. At one point Troutman himself was seen beating a white prisoner with a thick piece of wood.

A supply building that had been torched collapsed to the ground. Tents were only rubble now. The fires illuminated the stockade. This was what an insurrection looked like. "On the night of the riot the records room was burned down and there was a guy trapped in there and we pulled away the boards on the side of the building to help him get out," the Black inmate Gregg Payton recalled. "Some guys escaped. They beat up some MPs and took their uniforms, dressed up, and walked out. I saw them later in Saigon. They were downtown still masquerading as MPs."

Some of the inmates who didn't have gas masks began coughing badly, and the ones who did have gas masks realized at some point they'd have to remove them. Their endurance was going to be compromised.

Finally, the military officials had had enough. They ordered an assault upon the rioters. The MPs had bayonets, grenades, and M-14 rifles; they meant business. "We bayoneted a lot of them," said MP Private First Class Thomas McKeon. "We *stuck* them; we impaled them with the bayonet. In the body."

General Frank Mildren witnessed a scene he couldn't quite comprehend. A group of Black inmates—most of the riot leaders among them—were now wearing turbans and robes, their homage to the sartorial splendor of Black Power on display back in America. Mildren was not impressed: "After one day . . . these people had turbans on their heads and homemade robes, and it looked like somebody out of Africa in there." The authorities, thinking of any gesture that might hasten the end of the ordeal, had thrown blankets over the fence as a gesture of goodwill. Inmates used those blankets to fashion quickly what looked like—at least to them—African robes. The spears the inmates carried had been fashioned from tent poles. Jeremiah James, another inmate, said of the makeshift clothing choices: "Guys went back completely to African customs and dress. They used sheets and tore headbands to wear and took off their clothes and made African clothes out of sheets. They took some other sheets, wet them, and stretched them over barrels and drummed on them. It was nuts." Military Policeman Eugene Murdock said of the newfound dress decisions, "Those blacks turned native. They wore blankets and put chicken bones in their hair and tied them in their nose."

After two days of the most energetic rioting, things began to ebb. Black inmates who hadn't slept were growing wearier as they came to the realization they were outnumbered and had nowhere to escape to. "None of the prisoners had gotten out because the outer enclosures still held," General Mildren said.

By the early morning of August 30, reporters, along with a crew from CBS News, began raising their voices to gain access to the jail. The Army wouldn't allow it. As days passed, more and more inmates gave up and walked out through the gates. They were immediately put into a different part of the stockade. More days passed—six, seven, eight, nine. "At any point the military could have overwhelmed this group of resisting black prisoners," the AP reporter Peter Arnett figured. "The decisions were made not to do it. The high command realized the story could grow much bigger. And with the resistance to the war growing, they just didn't want to start drawing even greater attention to the whole racial issue in Vietnam."

MP Eugene Murdock—known as Big Gene—finally made a decision to get brutally honest with the inmates. He let them know he had an airplane waiting, and that they were going to be getting on that plane one way or another. Those who refused the order to come out would suffer dire consequences: "I said, 'Now, if you don't come out [when your name is called] then we're going to court martial you for escape and you're going to get twenty more years' . . . We just waited them out. They'd see 'Frank' go out. And 'Frank' gets on an airplane . . . Then 'Bill' goes. Then 'Joe' would shout, 'I'm not going. Piss on you people.' Then they'd call out his name and he'd say, 'Here, sir.' And he'd come up front and center." MP Murdock was quite proud of his final tactic: "We never had one person refuse to come out . . . It must have taken a month or so."

The longest racial riot during the Vietnam War finally ended several weeks after it started. The American press was largely kept in the dark about the story, which is the way President Johnson's Pentagon, which had been closely monitoring the situation, wanted it. Seven buildings at Long Binh had been destroyed. And a total of nineteen tents had been shredded.

There was confusion about whom to punish, and that could be traced to Mr. Badass himself, Kansas City's Jimmy Childress. Childress had come up with the idea in the early hours of the riot to head for the administration building. "I figured the records were the key for causing more confusion for the military" is how he put it.

Childress had years to think about what happened inside LBJ, and his role in it. "After the riot, I felt bad about it. I had regrets," he said. "And I felt disappointed because we didn't accomplish anything, other than tearing something up. Like a child would tear up a toy. We just blew off steam. And we only made our bed harder than it was before."

It was reported that the main demand by Blacks involved in the riot had been that they be allowed to leave the fighting in Vietnam. In their minds, LBJ—both the president and the jail—had gotten them into this epic mess. Uncle Sam, of course, did not go for blackmail tactics. A later report and study of the LBJ riot called it "planned and unbridled violence by blacks against Caucasians."

It was amazing that the LBJ racial clash didn't claim major headlines in America. In the end, fifty-two inmates were injured, sixty-three MPs were injured, and one soldier was murdered. Unquestionably, it was the patience of Army officials that had prevented more deaths. A variety of military-prison sentences and punishments were handed out to those who had participated in the riot.

The Army had herded Black soldiers into Long Binh in such high numbers that even some whites pointed to the inequality in military justice. American prisons at the time were experiencing similar racial clashes. The Army—through its quadrupled Project 100,000—had plucked tens of thousands of Black soldiers from inner cities. Rushed through boot camp and into war, some of those soldiers clearly lacked the mindset for soldiering and taking orders. They were emerging from recently desegregated environments, and had not just chips on their shoulders but boulders. Dropped into a foreign jungle, asked to hew to a long-standing military code of justice, asked to kill, they sometimes committed criminal acts that demanded punishment. "I'm still angry about the way the military treated its own citizens," Jimmy Childress said years later. "I still feel that something had to be done. I guess I was just trying to prove that I was a human being."

In the fall of 1970—two years after the Long Binh uprising, with the war droning on and on—the status of race relations in Vietnam showed no signs of easing. Robert F. Froehlke, assistant secretary of defense at the Pentagon, received a letter from an Army officer who was expressing frustration about the direction of the war:

> It is the total lack of satisfaction that I now have. The feeling that we don't know what we're doing—that our role is now purposeless. I am tired of troops that refuse orders to go to the field; fed up with the Army's new judicial system that stacks the deck against the commander and adversely affects good order and discipline. I am tired of arrogant blacks who feel they can violate every regulation with impunity and do. Most of all, I am fed up with senior commanders who never question our reason for being, our mission, or the changing nature of [the] environment both socially and tactically . . . Well, I have had it.

The deterioration of race relations was significant enough to worry General Walter T. Kerwin, the Army's deputy chief of staff for personnel. "In the past year racial discord has surfaced as one of the most serious problems facing Army leadership," he said.

One of the immediate reactions by the Army after the Long Binh uprising was to pay more attention to racial inequality in all walks of military life—from its military academies to its base camps in foreign lands. Military recruitment budgets were increased, and more money was geared toward Black communities. One such advertisement was a direct takeoff of the 1969 Nina Simone song "To Be Young, Gifted and Black." The Army ad featured a picture of a Black man in a soldier's uniform with the wording "Young. Gifted. And in charge."

Yet, just three and a half months after Long Binh, a clash between Black and white soldiers erupted at Camp Baxter in Da Nang. A Black soldier was being held in pretrial detainment, and a group of Black soldiers, believing in his innocence, protested to such a degree that he was released. Camp Baxter military leaders acknowledged that racial tensions on the base had been intensifying for six straight months. The mounting racial incidents were enough to get the attention of General Westmoreland, the Army commander, who in 1970—more than six years after the official start of America's first fully fought integrated war—ordered the creation of a course on race relations for all military officers.

But racial incidents across the military—and across its various branches—persisted. From May 21 to May 25, 1971, there was a racial uprising at Travis Air Force Base in Fairfield, a small town in Northern California. The Black-white clash began with a dapping scene. Some white airmen who witnessed the scene demanded that the Blacks stop it, which they refused to do. Two Blacks were arrested, shocking other Blacks on the base. Word quickly spread, and a mêlée erupted, moving from the base to a Black nightclub, then to the environs of a nearby baseball field. The local police were summoned, and they came with dogs, creating scenes reminiscent of Selma and Birmingham in the 1960s. In later testimony, Blacks testified that they were repeatedly called "niggers" during the clashes. Gregory Price, a Black airman, stated that the cause of the rioting was that two Black airmen had been arrested for their dapping. "The problem was we wanted Airman Mays and Airman Byes released because they were arrested, as far as we know, for their political beliefs." This incident, in which dozens were arrested and a fireman died of a heart attack while fighting a blaze linked to the conflict, was so worrisome that California Congressman Ron Dellums, himself Black, traveled to the base to hold hearings.

> RON DELLUMS: This was an incident on Travis Air Force Base back in May. This is now November. Can you tell me whether the conditions that gave rise to this situation have been corrected, whether the programs that have been instituted over the past few months have been operable or realistic?
>
> AIRMAN [GREGORY] PRICE: Today you could look at it and actually say nothing has come of it. Because to this very day the young Black airman has no way of voicing his opinion that he's being crucified for his beliefs.

Captain Jeffrey Carter, a Black legal officer, also offered testimony at the Dellums hearing. "As things stand," Carter said, "a black airman could be cited on three occasions for such a minor offense as having a non-regulation haircut, and learn that his commander has recommended an undesirable discharge."

Chapter Nine

Dorothy Harris Would Like Another Coca-Cola, Please

She grew up in Cincinnati, cocooned from the world of 1940s segregation by a protective family. Her dad kept her away from the areas of the city where racial strife had taken place. In the 1950s, Cincinnati experienced several racial clashes, the cause so often traced to disagreements between white transplanted Kentuckians—from just across the bridge—and local Blacks. "I also had older brothers and sisters who made sure I went only to certain areas of Cincinnati," Dorothy Harris says. "I learned later how prejudiced the city was."

As a kid, she was a committed tomboy, running and playing games with boys and disregarding the prospect of injury. She climbed fences and trees. She dared other kids to follow her lead. Then, when she was eight years old, she received a gift: a doctor-and-nurse kit. And she was hooked. "I decided I wanted to be a nurse," she says. Family members played along with her as she dabbed ointments on them, and peered hard at their scratches and cuts. "I was like a little nurse!" She attended Cincinnati's Hughes High School, and graduated in 1959. She had a brother who had been in the Navy, and that inspired her, after graduation, to join the Navy, too. She became

Dorothy Harris had a tomboyish childhood before becoming a nurse in Vietnam. At Cu Chi, she befriended Captain Leroy Pitts, who was stuck at a desk job.

Captain Leroy Pitts told anyone who would listen that he wanted battlefield experience. He got his wish.

a Navy Corps nurse, stationed at St. Albans, New York. "I loved the military. It was teamwork. And I was away from home." When she emerged from the Navy, after three years, she still dreamed of becoming a nurse, and enrolled in nursing school. Her on-the-job training took place at the Jewish Hospital in Cincinnati, which had opened in 1850 to handle a cholera epidemic in the city, and was advertised as the first Jewish hospital in the nation. Because of an Army scholarship she received for nursing school, Dorothy Harris had a three-year commitment to the Army after her training. In 1966, full of patriotic fervor, she volunteered to go to Vietnam. "I wanted to take care of our soldiers. And I was adventurous," she says.

At the outset of World War II, young Black women who had trained as nurses wanted to show how patriotic they were, and applied to join the Army. They received a letter back in the mail:

> Your application to the Army Nurse Corps cannot be given favorable consideration as there are no provisions in Army regulations for the appointment of colored nurses in the Corps.

Some women wrote letters to First Lady Eleanor Roosevelt asking for her help; the Black press also went into action on behalf of the Black nurse applicants. In 1941, the U.S. Army Nurse Corps finally admitted fifty-six Black nurses, a number that would swell tenfold by war's end. The Black nurses were dispatched to segregated Army bases, among them Fort Livingston in Louisiana and Fort Bragg in North Carolina. When the women ventured off their bases, they were often refused service in restaurants: the uniform did not matter. Black families began inviting them into their homes for social gatherings. Reports came out of Camp Florence in Arizona that white nurses were becoming too friendly with German POWs, who had been held there after being sent to America to perform various forms of labor (with so many American men away at war, there was a labor shortage). Black nurses were not allowed to administer care to white American enlisted men, but the Army decided to send them to Camp Florence, where they were ordered to help care for the Nazis. At Camp Papago Park, which was near Phoenix, a German POW had blurted—in front of Army personnel—that he hated "niggers." The Black nurses complained, but nothing was done. One of them wrote a letter about the incident to a group known as the National Association of Colored Graduate Nurses: "That is the worst insult an army officer should ever have to take. I think it is insult enough to be here taking care of them when we volunteered to come into the army to nurse military personnel . . . All of this is making us very bitter."

When she landed in Vietnam in January 1967, Dorothy Harris thought she'd be stationed at a base camp in Saigon. But after an interview with one of the chief nurses, she was told she'd be going to Cu Chi. Everyone knew Cu Chi was extremely dangerous, a location that played host to a lot of enemy attacks. "It was one of the most isolated places! About twenty miles outside of Saigon. And it was a Viet Cong area."

A lot of Black nurses requested to work in evacuation hospitals, close to the battle. Army officials were a bit confused, but then began realizing why: since a good many Black soldiers were in infantry units, where the rate of injuries was always high, the Black nurses figured that those soldiers, traumatized by their injuries, might receive a psychological boost from seeing a Black nurse.

There were upward of ten thousand nurses who came to serve in Vietnam. More than 95 percent of them were white. There were so few Black nurses that nursing organizations never bothered to keep an accounting of them. During her entire stay in Vietnam, Harris saw only three other Black nurses.

In and around Cu Chi, she heard a lot of mortar fire. Harris was told about the myriad tunnels in which Viet Cong soldiers hid out and from which they launched attacks. "We knew about the tunnels but we didn't know that they came right up to our perimeter," she says. The tunnels were small, and the American soldiers were often too big to get down into them. Those enemy soldiers who did squeeze into them were called "tunnel rats."

One American soldier, Second Lieutenant Vincent Okamoto, recalled walking into a small South Vietnamese home not far from the Cu Chi base where Harris was stationed. The rice inside the home smelled good, and he offered to exchange a pack of his cigarettes and some American rations for some rice. But not long after being inside the small home, Okamoto and his radio-telephone operator began chatting, and realized there was enough visible rice to feed many men. "And then," Okamoto recalled, "it dawned on me: they did have enough rice to feed a dozen men . . . So we started looking around again, and we found a tunnel mouth. I was given a phosphorus grenade. After the smoke cleared, we pulled, I think, seven or eight bodies to the town square. You couldn't identify these charred bodies. So we wanted to see who would cry over these people. Then we'd have more people to question. The women that lived in that house, whose rice I had eaten, they're all squatting down, wailing. I think that was the first time I knew that I personally had killed people. I got an 'Attaboy' from the supervisor. But it wasn't something that had any glory in it, or made you feel a real sense of accomplishment."

—

When Dorothy Harris first arrived at Cu Chi, she couldn't help but notice the paucity of Black soldiers. Then she was told: "The Blacks were always in the combat zone. They were always on the front lines." When she was answering the letters from family back home in Cincinnati, she reassured them that she was fine, even though the mortar fire was often constant. "You're young and invincible. You don't worry," she says.

The nurses all slept on cots. For the patients there were mattresses, of course, and nurses were instructed to toss the mattresses on the floor inside the makeshift hospital and get as many patients as possible underneath them when the mortar fire was incoming. Nurses ate two hot meals a day. They considered nothing better at the end of a twelve-hour shift than a cold Coca-Cola. The Cokes cost a nickel. Sometimes the base ran out of Cokes, and the complaints were as loud as flapping geese. "We had a little Vietnamese worker in our compound," Harris says. "We would give him anything—but not a Coke! That was a coveted item in Vietnam." Sometimes—after the miracle of pulling a young soldier back from death during a medical procedure—a Coke and a smoke made Cu Chi bearable. The cigarettes cost eleven cents a pack. As nurses, they worked six days a week. Instead of nurse whites, they wore fatigues. Military officers often stopped by the outside of their hooches, to check on them. "Most of the officers were white." She thought they were all unbelievably brave.

Many times, Dorothy Harris and her fellow nurses had to turn and give assistance to a captured Vietnamese soldier being operated on. MPs would be standing near the gathered doctors, nurses, and enemy soldier. When the enemy soldiers awoke from surgery, there'd be thrashing and yelling amidst their new surroundings. "I never saw such hate," Harris says. "I saw hate in their eyes. Even though they were badly injured, there was hatred there. It was understandable. After all, we were in their country."

The hospital was a mélange of hanging wires attached to bulky medical machines, beeping monitors, lights, wheelchairs, crutches, fans. No one truly knew if the newcomer hired to clean the place, a Vietnamese, was a dutiful and honest worker stuck in a desperate situation inside his own country—or someone apt to pass along information to a Viet Cong regiment in the bush.

Dorothy Harris spent a lot of time beyond the perimeter of Cu Chi, tending to Vietnamese children who had been wounded in battles. Many were suffering from malnutrition and other diseases. Their suffering broke her heart. They'd rub her skin, then they'd rub their own skin. "Same! Same!" they'd say. Her light black skin was close enough to their yellow-hued skin so that the Vietnamese children saw kinship. When it was time to leave the children and get back to Cu Chi, she and the other nurses who had gone out into the bush felt sad that they could leave only a limited supply of medicines behind. "We could not leave a lot of medicine there, because we knew the Viet Cong would come and take the medicine after we left."

Everyone was acutely aware of the dangers of being away from the fence-fortified base camp. All of the nurses had been trained on how to fire a .45 pistol.

Harris wasn't the only nurse who smiled when Leroy Pitts, a Black officer, dropped by one of the nurses' hooches inside the compound to visit with them. They all did. Pitts had the friendliest disposition. "And he was handsome," Harris says of the married captain. Pitts wanted to keep morale high, even in such a stressful environment, so he'd glide through the hospital doors smiling, carting some Coca-Colas to pass around. Sometimes Pitts was accompanied by commanders coming to the hospital to visit their wounded soldiers.

Riley Leroy Pitts—everyone called him Leroy—was born in 1937 in Fallis, Oklahoma, a small railroad town that had suffered mightily during the Dust Bowl days. He attended Douglas High School, and from there went on to Wichita State University, where he joined ROTC and decided to major in journalism. He graduated in 1960. He got married—he met his wife, Eula, in college—and, because of his ROTC enrollment, was off to Uncle Sam's Army. He became a public-information officer at Fort Sill, near Lawton, Oklahoma. Army life agreed with Eula Pitts, though she wasn't one to complain anyway. Both were delighted with their next posting—Orléans, France. Once settled in Orléans—now with two little kids, a boy and a girl—they made it to Paris, sixty miles away, whenever they could, to enjoy the sights and scenery. They'd stroll the long boulevards. While in France, they listened to the radio and heard the tumultuous news coming out of America regarding Blacks and civil uprisings.

In December 1966, Pitts received new orders: Vietnam.

In Saigon, Leroy Pitts settled into the familiar role of public-information officer. Besides plenty of press releases to write, the job also involved chaperoning visiting dignitaries from Stateside around the base, as well as commanders who came to check on their wounded men. And he always tried to make time to bring Coca-Colas to the nurses. "He also brought Wallace Terry around," Dorothy Harris says, referring to the *Time* magazine journalist—"the only Black journalist I saw in Vietnam." But the more Dorothy Harris got to know Leroy Pitts, the more she sensed something restless in him. His wife, back in the States, sensed it, too. "He used to tell me, 'I'm going to be a general,'" recalls Eula Pitts. "He knew you had to have combat experience in your background. You couldn't get to be a general by sitting in an office."

When Captain Leroy Pitts was nearing the end of his first six months of duty, and could make a decision about what he wished to do for the next six months, he asked to leave his public-information posting and join a combat unit. It wasn't just any combat unit Pitts joined. It was the "Wolfhounds." The Wolfhounds—2nd Battalion of the 27th Infantry Regiment—were a storied military outfit, and Pitts soon became a commander of their C Company. They had fought in many battles across wars going back decades. They were feared, and they were relentless on the battlefield. James Jones had been a Wolfhound and wrote about some of his experiences in his acclaimed novels *From Here to Eternity* and *The Thin Red Line*. "We all said, 'Why do you want to join *them*!'" Dorothy Harris recalls about the moment when Pitts told the nurses he was joining the

Wolfhounds. "They were one of the toughest outfits we knew of." Though the nurses tried to conceal it, they were afraid for him.

On October 31, 1967, the Wolfhounds, deep in the dense jungle of Vietnam, received an order to reinforce an Army unit that was drawing heavy enemy fire. Captain Pitts led an air-mobile assault team to the area, landing under heavy Viet Cong fire. Pitts successfully led his men to overrun the Viet Cong forces. But, just as a lull came in the battle, he received a radio transmission stating that another American outfit, to the north, had also come under fire and needed immediate help. Pitts and his Wolfhound team raced to the area. As soon as they neared it, they were blindsided by fire coming from enemy bunkers. The foliage was thick. Pitts zeroed in on one of the bunkers, inching his way to within fifteen yards of it. He gripped a grenade and threw it at the bunker now in front of him. But the grenade smacked up against a tree trunk. And then it ping-ponged right back in the direction of Pitts. It lay there on the ground. This was the moment of death for some Wolfhounds. It was the fate of war. Things happened so quick. There was not a damn thing anyone could do. From here to eternity. Captain Leroy Pitts, however, chose then and there to die for his men: he heaved himself onto the grenade. In a millisecond, his body would be ripped apart and going in all directions, spraying blood. Only the most miraculous thing happened: the grenade didn't go off! Everyone wondered what had happened. Was this some kind of collective ghoulish dream? It was not. Pitts rolled over and off the malfunctioning grenade—and began anew barking orders to his men. They had to keep firing. They had to fortify this position. They had to kill the Viet Cong, which they commenced to do. And they kept moving, taking ground all around them. And happy as hell that their captain was very much alive.

Back at base camp at Cu Chi, no one knew of Captain Leroy Pitts's act of searing bravery out in the bush. They were expecting him and his air-mobile unit to return on the evening of October 31.

The nurses had planned a Halloween party. Everyone had gotten into their costumes. They all made their way over to the officers' club, where the party would take place. The sun had set. But once they were all inside the officers' club, as the mingling and laughter began rising about whose costume looked the most eye-catching, an announcement was made. "We were told we had to suddenly leave right away," Dorothy Harris remembers of the evening. "We had to get back to our barracks and hooches. We didn't know what was going on." They suspected a possible looming attack.

As he was advancing his men out into a swampy area of Ap Dong in the aftermath of the recent assault—all of them still processing the sight of Captain Pitts lying atop that grenade—the Wolfhounds came under fire again. And again Pitts was directing fire. In one fluid motion, he took aim at the enemy. It was right then that a mortar round from the Viet Cong tore into his body. His life was over in seconds—memories of running along the railroad tracks back in Fallis, Oklahoma; his wedding day; hearing the sound of his kids over telephone wires while he was away on assignment; seeing Paris for the first time; the goal of becoming a general—now over, and all receding in split seconds. His horrified men saw his torn-apart body twisting to the ground.

Back at Cu Chi, the Halloween revelers were standing around, eager for some kind of news. "That's when the chaplain came and told us Leroy was dead," says Dorothy Harris, pain still in her voice all these decades later.

In Oklahoma, Eula Pitts went to answer her front door. There were two men in military uniform. "One of them was Black, the other one white." She knew the Black officer, because he was a local. The news they delivered was crushing. She wondered how to tell the children. Her minister came and sat with her. The house filled with relatives and friends of both her family and her late husband's. Weeks and months rolled over into bone-deep sadness. She mumbled to people that she desperately wanted to "go to heaven" to be with Leroy. She told visitors to her home how Leroy had sent money to extended family members, how he was just about the most generous man she had ever met. There were stories in the newspaper about criminals who had committed dastardly deeds and were still out there walking around, free. And she wondered about decisions the good Lord had made to take good people like her Leroy away from this earth. Someone suggested she talk to her minister about the turns and twists of fate. "And my minister finally told me, he said, 'Eula, the good Lord doesn't only want bad people to keep him company. He wants good ones, too!' "

A year later, the telegram and phone calls came from the White House. Captain Riley Leroy Pitts had been chosen to receive the Medal of Honor, the nation's highest award for bravery in battle. The news release mentioned the grenade he had fallen on, that last battle he had led in front of the enemy bunkers. The whole Pitts family ventured to Washington. Lyndon Johnson presided over the White House ceremony. The moment, judging from the photos, seemed to weigh heavily on LBJ, who stared down at the two small Pitts children, five-year-old Mark and seven-year-old Stacie. "What this man did in an hour of incredible courage will live in the story of America as long as America endures—and he will live in the hearts and memories of those who loved him," Johnson said. "He was a brave man and a leader of men. No greater thing could be said of any man." The family all returned to Oklahoma, where more letters and cards awaited them, from members of the Wolfhounds. A large number of Black soldiers and Marines had been recipients of the Medal of Honor, but never a Black *officer.* "First Negro Officer Gets Medal of Honor," proclaimed a December 11, 1968, *New York Times* headline.

Dorothy Harris was back in America in 1969 when she heard the news about her fellow nurse Sharon Lane. On the morning of

June 8, 1969, having been in-country less than eight weeks, Lane, stationed at the 312th Evacuation Hospital in Chu Lai, died in a mortar attack. Though several nurses in Vietnam died from illnesses, Lane was the first and only nurse reported to have died from a direct enemy attack. Dorothy Harris found it difficult to sleep in the days after she got this news.

Part Two

CHAPTER TEN

FRED CHERRY PARACHUTES INTO HELL

In grade schools all throughout America, little boys and girls heard the true tales of Wilbur and Orville Wright, who built their contraption in Dayton, Ohio, transported it to Kitty Hawk, North Carolina, and first flew their airplane in 1903. The world began to change; flying had become a reality. Other much-talked-about events unfurled in subsequent generations: commercial flights began in 1914; Charles Lindbergh took his transatlantic solo flight in 1927. By the time of World War II, pictures of zooming airplanes and their pilots were dominating magazine layouts as well as movie screens around the world. Wartime pilots had become mythic; they were brave, and they became heroes.

At the outset of World War II, little Fred Cherry of Suffolk, Virginia, was living near a naval auxiliary base. There were eight Cherry children. His parents, John and Leolia, worked at farming and labor, as did many other Blacks in the area. Of all the Cherry children, Fred was the one most excited about living near the naval base, about seeing things zooming in the sky above area rooftops. "All day long these aircraft would be flying at very low altitudes," he recalled. "You could see the pilot, and we would wave to him." Young Fred, upon

Military branches ignored Fred Cherry and his dream of becoming a pilot until the Air Force finally welcomed him. His bombing missions earned him medals. Then he found himself chained to a wall inside a North Vietnamese prison.

hearing the planes, would rush out the front door of his house and watch as the pilots engaged in combat maneuvers and exercises. He turned his arms into airplane wings and allowed his imagination to lift him off. As he grew older, Fred began reading the Black newspapers that he came across—*The Pittsburgh Courier,* the *Baltimore Afro-American,* the *New York Amsterdam News,* the Norfolk *Journal.* And those newspapers were carrying numerous stories about the all-Black Tuskegee Airmen.

It was during World War II, amidst relentless pressure from the NAACP and the Negro press—and even First Lady Eleanor Roosevelt—that the War Department authorized establishment of the 66th Air Force Flying School. The school was headquartered in Tuskegee, Alabama, and its aim was to train Black military pilots. There were two principal reasons Tuskegee was chosen as the site: it featured good year-round weather and it was home to the Tuskegee Institute, a Negro college with a storied reputation situated in a town that boasted a Black middle class. The training was rigorous, and the dropout rate was high in the beginning. Flying, of course, depended on exactness; infractions or mistakes were judged harshly. Those who successfully emerged from the training school were toughened and smart men. They were well aware of what some were calling them: "Eleanor's Niggers," in reference to Eleanor Roosevelt's support of them.

When they landed in the European theater for their first flying missions, some of the Tuskegee pilots stenciled the initials "EN" on the sides of their planes: they gleefully wanted to mock the slur, and also wanted the world to know that Eleanor's Niggers were coming at full speed. The Tuskegee Airmen may not have been featured in the wartime movies following the war, but they certainly distinguished themselves. From their perch in North Africa during World War II, they flew 1,578 missions. The military credited them with destroying more than four hundred enemy planes. No group of wartime pilots had ever been under such social scrutiny—and performed so ably—as the Tuskegee Airmen had done. Their record of success proved to be one of the reasons President Truman was convinced in 1948 that it was time to desegregate the military.

Fred Cherry wanted to be like the Tuskegee Airmen. He wanted to fly jets. He wanted to be like Lucky Lester, whose exploits, during World War II, had been showing up in the Black press.

Clarence Lester acquired his nickname in the military. There was a reason "Lucky" stuck: The Tuskegee Airman had whirred away from countless tight aerial situations in the skies of Italy during the war with nary a nick or bullet making a dent in his plane. He described the kind of encounter that solidified his nickname: "We were flying in a loose formation, about 200 feet apart and zig-zagging. The flight leader commanded 'hard right and punch tanks' (drop the external fuel tanks). I saw a formation of Messerschmitt Bf 109s straight ahead, but slightly lower. I closed to about 200 feet and started to fire. Smoke began to pour out of the 109 and the aircraft exploded. I was going so fast I was sure I would hit some of the debris from the explosion, but luckily I didn't." In one military-confirmed account, Lucky Lester had downed three Nazi planes—in a single day. (In later years, he would find himself working alongside the assembled

"Whiz Kids" in the office of Defense Secretary Robert McNamara during the buildup of the Vietnam War.)

When Fred Cherry was eleven years old, his father, John, suddenly died. Fred's mother, Leolia, thought it would lessen some of the family hardship if Fred went to live with Beulah, one of his sisters. No matter the family heartache, Beulah wasn't going to coddle her little brother. She pushed him hard in high school, and was proud to see him off to Virginia Union University, a historically Black school. But though he was majoring in biology, Fred's mind wandered to those machines flying up in the sky, which claimed more of his attention than his classes. He decided to quit college to become a Navy pilot, and moseyed over to the naval recruitment office in Portsmouth. When he told the recruiter he wanted to be a pilot, he was advised to come back, because he'd have to see a different recruiter. He found this odd, but returned, actually twice, and each time was given a similar excuse. Fred Cherry did not realize that the United States Navy had no Black pilots, nor were they looking for any. On his fourth try, when he got another painful runaround, heated words were exchanged, and a scuffle ensued. Cherry finally left of his own accord, cursing as he backed out the door; those in the office eyeballed the short, slight young man as he retreated down the street.

Back in school, time rolled on for Fred Cherry. He tilted his head to the sky when he heard planes overhead, and continued reading magazine stories about aviators. He vowed to family and friends that, no matter the odds, he was going to become a military pilot.

In 1951, now a senior in college, Cherry got a better reception at Langley Air Force Base, over in Norfolk, where he told the recruiter he wanted to become an Air Force pilot. His eagerness paid off: he was invited to take the series of mental and physical tests required by the Air Force for entry to flight school. Twenty individuals were in his group, and Cherry was the only Black among them. He scored the highest of everyone in the group. The Air Force did not want to let Fred Cherry get away. That fall, he entered the Aviation Cadet Training Program. During his time there, he performed very well. When he graduated, the four other graduates, all of whom were white, refused to walk alongside him in the procession. He walked alone.

Fred Cherry was commissioned a second lieutenant in 1952, whereupon he received his pilot wings. Soon he was dispatched to South Korea, where he was assigned to the 58th Fighter-Bomber Wing at Taegu Air Base.

It was the Korean War that, ostensibly, provided evidence of President Truman's executive order to integrate the military. But, with few exceptions, the military's ground leaders—white men who had come of age in a world of segregation and were still holding tight to certain attitudes about race and the military—were downright sluggish in executing Truman's orders. The Navy sent more than 60 percent of its new Black recruits to their Steward's Branch, which meant they were destined to become cooks and waiters. For the most part, the Marines handled their integration edict by sending their new Black recruits into athletic divisions, in which it was hoped that they would win sports-related medals. It took the Army nearly two years following Truman's order to stop using racial quotas during recruitment drives. The reluctance by many inside the military to integrate demanded further action, especially with the sudden onset of the Korean War.

In March 1951, a group of social scientists came together to study the military's integration efforts. Their report, titled Project Clear, clearly showed that there were fewer racial incidents in integrated units than in segregated units, and that integration in itself seemed to boost morale. A good deal of military intransigence when it came to integration had flowed from General Douglas MacArthur, who was leader of the combined United States–United Nations forces in Korea. In order to add momentum to the integration efforts, Truman was forced to replace MacArthur with General Matthew B. Ridgway, a more agreeable figure in the social experiment of integration.

North Korea's invasion of South Korea certainly rattled American military leaders. It was seen as a blistering assault to promote communism. Because an American military response was—albeit cautious—all but assured, it was bound to cast a light upon Truman's executive order for desegregation: Korea, then, would be a testing ground. And this caused civil rights leaders to wonder: could Blacks receive fair treatment—as well as promotions—in the newly integrated military? Blacks in the military had a long history of being consistently diminished and overlooked. Neither white nor Black schoolchildren read about the history of Blacks in the military.

The pursuit of racial realignments in Korea did not go well. In 1950, the majority of Blacks in the United States Army were still assigned to either supply or service units. And many units still had a racial identity. By the summer of 1950, the Army's all-Black 24th Infantry Regiment was actually in Korea, along with several other Black units—the 512th Military Police Company, the 77th Engineer Combat Company, and the 159th Field Artillery Battalion. "I can assure you by 1952 [desegregation] did not get down to the troops at all," said Charlie Rangel, a product of Harlem in New York City, who would later become a notable congressman. And yet one of the earliest American victories in Korea was won by the all-Black men of the 24th Infantry. They were hailed in the *Congressional Record*—"First United States Victory in Korea Won by Negro GIs."

Colonel Fred Cherry—like everyone else in the American military—had no hesitation about going to war in Korea in the battle against communism. But he found that his fellow officers did not want to fraternize with him inside the officers' clubs on military bases. Up high off the ground, the skies were friendlier and freer. When he was in the cockpit of his F-84 Thunderjet, Fred Cherry pictured himself back in Suffolk, Virginia, the little Black boy waving to those Tuskegee Airmen when they flew low enough to see him on the ground. Now he was one of them, an airman in the cockpit of his own jet. And during hours and hours of practice maneuvers, Cherry had begun to set himself apart from other pilots, all of whom were white. He seemed to outperform many of them in drills. They begrudgingly gave him respect and began calling him "the Chief," all because he was so knowledgeable about flying. He flew more than a hundred missions during the Korean War. His targets were bridges and dams, and any railroads behind enemy lines. "We were carrying 1,000-pound bombs, napalm, 5-inch rockets, and .50-caliber machine guns," Cherry recalled. He was so skilled in the air that he only got hit once, and that time he made it safely back to the base despite the damage done to his tailpipe.

It was hardly the aim of the American press at the time of the Korean engagement to delineate the racial conflagrations of the war. But an encounter took place in 1951—in Mississippi, of all places—that prodded the newspaper editor Hodding Carter to consider what was happening in Korea amidst America's racial tensions. Carter was a progressive-minded white figure in Mississippi journalism. A Black woman had come into his Greenville office, where he ran the *Delta Democrat-Times.* "She was a well-dressed woman in her thirties and not too much at ease," Carter recalled. The woman requested that Black women be properly identified just as white women were in the newspaper; she wanted the proper "Mrs." to appear in front of the names of married Black women. Carter pondered this woman and her insistence on a new policy. The question ultimately got him thinking about Korea and the war, and what America had asked of its minority citizens. The newspaper came to change its policy; local Blacks gained a small measure of long-sought-after respect. "That demand, I thought, is part and parcel of the tangled reasons why Americans and Englishmen and Turks and Filipinos and Puerto Ricans are dying in Korea; dying in battle against an Oriental people to whom face was paramount and in whom the social condescension and racial vindication of imperialism had aroused murderous hatred of the Westerner, a hatred fanned by the Communist incitement into a will to destroy all the good which had at least partly offset the mistakes and the evils of Western exploitation of the Orient."

Not until 1953, however, were the all-Black units in the U.S. Army finally, top to bottom, disbanded.

After Korea, Fred Cherry returned to a still-segregated America. By 1957, he and his family had settled into Dover, Delaware, and

Cherry was assigned to Dover Air Force Base. Cherry's wife, Shirley, gave birth to their first child, Debbie, at the public hospital in Dover. But both parents came to realize that while the baby was being cared for in the hospital during her mother's recovery, the white nurses refused to change the infant's diapers. Fred Cherry wasted no time in removing both his wife and daughter from the hospital and, before exiting, he left some choice words hanging in the air about the staff's inhumane conduct.

In the fall of 1964, Fred Cherry received new military orders. He was on his way to Thailand, where he became a member of the 35th Tactical Fighter Squadron based at Korat Royal Thai Air Force Base. (His wife set up housing for the family in Japan.) Cherry's squadron had a simple mission: fly over and bomb North Vietnam. "I had no problems with the orders to go to Vietnam," Cherry said, believing, like so many others, that "the Commies were trying to take over." By now, his reputation as a combat pilot was secure: he was highly respected across racial lines. Though he predated by a few years the origin of the term "top gun," Fred Cherry was clearly a top gunner. He was now flying an F-105 jet, and he felt comfortable with it: "It was fast. Mach 2.5. Had good range. Dependable. Comfortable. Good weapons. Good navigational systems." He could load more weaponry on the F-105 than he could on the jets he had flown during the Korean conflict. "On a normal flight," he would recall, "we'd have 10, then 2.5-inch rockets, and a 20-millimeter cannon, which was a real jewel." It was important for Cherry and his fellow pilots in 1964 to hit supply lines and those caravans of soldiers scooting up and down the Ho Chi Minh Trail in Laos. By 1965, they were also focusing on other bombing targets—military barracks and bridges.

There were a few noticeable things as preparations began for Fred Cherry's flying mission on the morning of October 22, 1965. The major factor was that he and the other fliers were not allotted the usual time to plan the day's mission. Usually, they'd put at least five hours into figuring out the specifics of a particular mission, but on this morning, the time was greatly reduced, because of the gloomy weather: rain was forecast, and they needed to get up into the air. Something else also concerned Cherry: Often, he would be given an array of photographs of his intended targets; on this morning, there was only a single photo. He was given a code name—the Ironhand—for the site of the enemy's military installations (surface-to-air missles had been spied) where the bombs were to be dropped. "We have to knock it out as soon as we can," Cherry was told. It was 10:00 a.m. when he took off, accompanied by several other planes, which were flying nearby. As Cherry recalled: "I had to keep the wingman and everybody else higher than me. You gotta watch what's gonna be in the way of the wingman, 'cause he's not watching. He's watchin' the lead, and everybody's watchin' him."

This was the life Fred Cherry wanted to live—flying, earning respect, and cognizant that others knew he was a damn good pilot.

His family had been living in Japan for the past several years, and he was happy he had gotten them out of Jim Crow America. He had won distinguished flying medals. His performance evaluations were always very impressive. One commander commented that Fred Cherry moved "like an eel" through the air. "I consider Captain Cherry one of the most effective officers of his rank that I have worked with during my entire Air Force career," Major Bobby J. Mead wrote in a 1964 evaluation of Cherry. During his years in the military, Cherry had flown from segregation into integration; he had flown in two wars, gotten medals, and become a near legend in the eyes of many. He was thirty-seven years old now, and realized Vietnam would doubtless be his last mission. He had obviously been responsible for a lot of killing. During his rare moments of introspection about having unleashed so much deadly firepower from the skies, Cherry would justify it by telling himself there was only one way to end war: by annihilating the enemy and bringing a stop to it. The bombing missions, of course, were dangerous. Just consider the career of Air Force Captain Richard Keirn. Keirn had been shot down by the Nazis during World War II and taken prisoner. He later found himself flying missions in Vietnam. Just three months before Cherry's October mission, Keirn was shot down over Vietnam—and taken prisoner once again.

In the cockpit on that morning of October 25, 1965, Fred Cherry looked cool, as he always did: his visor was down; his blue-and-white helmet was fixed; his .38 revolver was fastened; his snug antigravity suit felt fine; the parachute check was completed. His F-105 was a lethal weapon, equipped with a 20-millimeter cannon, and it was carrying cluster bombs. "You're loaded to the teeth, sir," an Air Force corporal who had made a final check of the plane told Cherry before takeoff. And, with that, Fred Cherry roared off. Soon he was clocking six hundred miles per hour. Thirty minutes into his flight, nearing his target area, he dipped low—falling to one hundred feet aboveground—and could now see North Vietnamese who began taking rifle shots at his jet. He flew until he reached his target and began dropping his bombs. Then came a distinct kind of noise. "I felt my aircraft take a very definite hit," Cherry recalled. But this was what he had trained for—unpredictability, chaos, danger. He saw fit to pass along a quick message to his fellow fliers: "Let's get the F[uck] out of here." But it only took seconds for Cherry to realize that his plane had been too damaged to make it back to base. He'd have to zoom out into the Tonkin Gulf, where naval personnel could pick him up after he parachuted. But the damaged plane began filling with smoke, which meant that that idea was no longer possible. Then came the plane's explosion. "Just blew up," Cherry recalled. "The smoke was so dense, I couldn't see outside the cockpit." The plane went topsy-turvy, and he didn't know if it was upside down or right side up. He angled the nose of the plane upward as best he could, and ejected; he went in one direction, the plane in another. He was now zooming toward the ground, in the direction of the Vietnamese who were firing at him, and kept firing. Their aims were bad; they kept missing. He cursed, lamenting that if the plane had held up for just two more minutes he would have made it out to the coast and to safety. But he was descending to the ground now, to definite danger. At about two hundred feet aboveground, he opened his chute. He had opened it a bit later than he normally would have, and was falling too fast, and knew it. Then came an awkward thud as he hit the ground. It was hardly a textbook landing, and the pain was excruciating, from a broken wrist, shoulder, and ankle. He was surrounded not by soldiers, but by local villagers. A little disoriented, he heard laughter and saw men and young boys, some with crude farm tools, who removed his parachute and took his weapon. They tied his arms with nylon cord. Then they began marching him to their village. During the walk, Cherry could hear jets overhead: his fellow pilots were looking for him. Soon enough, Fred Cherry was deposited at Hoa Lo Prison in Hanoi. He became the forty-third American prisoner of war, but the first Black to be captured in the war.

At Hoa Lo Prison, there were rats the size of small cats. The food—mostly rice—was served in very meager portions. The leg irons hurt like hell. And there was plenty of torture—heads banged against walls, arms tied behind backs while bodies were being beaten, legs bound by rope and stretched. Men screamed and howled. But Fred Cherry, no matter the pain, only gave what was required by the Geneva Convention—name, rank, and serial number. His fellow POWs, with rare exceptions, followed those same orders. The Vietnamese laughed at their resolve. The prisoners were just happy to be alive. A few weeks after his capture, Cherry was taken to another location, Cu Loc Prison, also in Hanoi. It was known as "the Zoo." And it was at the Zoo that Cherry met Porter Halyburton.

Halyburton was a white Southerner. The Vietnamese, knowing America's racial history, hoped the Black Southerner and the white Southerner—while sharing the same cell—would destroy each other.

These two cellmates inside Cu Loc Prison represented the divided history of America: a man of white privilege (high school at a white military academy, on to all-white Davidson College), then becoming a naval pilot, and a Black born into segregated America who went to a Black college because of segregation and who proved he was as talented as many white pilots, earning his chance to fly. But war had now bloodied and imprisoned both men and left them in a rat-infested cell surrounded by brutal guards, half a world away from home. Cherry was convinced that Halyburton was a spy, perhaps a French spy, and that he was supposed to get spy secrets from Cherry and relay them to the Vietnamese. As for Halyburton, he scoffed at believing Cherry was an Air Force officer when Cherry told him he was a pilot. In the Navy, Halyburton had never seen a Black pilot. Matter of fact, he was informed in the Navy that Blacks didn't become pilots, because they had depth-perception problems. Neither man trusted the other. "For days we played games with each other," Cherry remembered. "Feelin' each other out. We would ask each other a question. And we both would lie. He would change the name of the ship he came from. I didn't tell him much more than I told the Vietnamese, like I had flown out of South Vietnam. I figured he went back and told them the same lies I told him." Cherry had bad injuries that were not healing. The surgical procedures performed by the Vietnamese left incisions that became infected. By spring, without the necessary medicine, Cherry's health had worsened, and he could hardly move his limbs: "I was an invalid." Military rank, of course, is quite important in the relationships between soldiers. In their cell, the Black man outranked the white man, something Halyburton had never experienced before. He finally began believing everything Cherry told him about himself, since it was impossible to fake genuine knowledge about planes and flight patterns and military protocols. Halyburton and Cherry came to realize they needed each other: Cherry because he needed physical help, Halyburton because he relied on Cherry's optimism and steely defiance against his tormentors. Halyburton fed and bathed Cherry, who was convinced he was dying. Sores spread over his body. He coughed up blood. That spring, his weight dropped to 80 pounds; his normal weight was around 135 pounds.

That summer, in July 1966, a group of American POWs were taken from various locations and paraded in their prison pajamas through the streets of Hanoi. In handcuffs, they all looked ragged and malnourished. They were pelted and spat upon; some of the gaunt POWs had their teeth knocked out by onlookers who screamed about how their homes and families had been bombed. The prisoners were shown pictures of North Vietnamese babies who had died from American attacks. And while they were glancing at those pictures, they'd be spat upon and kicked some more. Cherry was spared that march, because he was undergoing another surgical procedure, having flesh scraped from his bones so the sores could go away. The prison medical staff did not want a POW to die if they could prevent it. He had to endure this procedure without anesthesia. The pain was brutal. When he returned to his cell, Halyburton was there, having returned from being beaten during the march. They fell into each other's arms. Cherry's surgeries may have been crude, but he did seem to be recuperating.

The North Vietnamese had a general routine: Prisoners would be taken for torture—twice a day. The more America bombed the North Vietnamese, the harsher the torture became. James Stockdale was a celebrated naval commander and flier—now turned POW. "Our country has no capability to defeat you on the battlefield," a Vietnamese official told Stockdale. "But war is not decided by weapons so much as national will. Once the American people understand this war, they will have no interest in pursuing it . . . We will win this war on the streets of New York."

After eight months of imprisonment, Halyburton was transferred to another prison. The separation was crushing for both him and Cherry. Cherry had no doubt that Halyburton had literally saved his life by feeding and washing him while he was recuperating. And Halyburton was continuously inspired by Cherry's will to survive, which increased his own determination to endure the repeated beatings. Their alliance proved, again, that it was a war in which white couldn't survive without Black, and Black couldn't survive without white.

As the highest-ranking Black at the prison, Fred Cherry constantly stood out. He knew the strategy of the North Vietnamese: "Now they want me to make tapes, write statements, denouncing the war, denouncing our government, and telling young GIs, especially black ones, they don't have any business in Vietnam fightin' for the American imperialists." He remained resolute, which only led to more torture. There were also daily interrogations, which would sometimes last up to five hours. "They never got to home plate," Cherry would recall about his captors' attempts to get information from him. "Just like when they beat me, I always kept in mind I was representing [twenty-two] million black Americans. If they are going to kill me, they are going to have to kill me."

It was natural to think of escaping. Even in their weakened condition—physically and mentally—the prisoners plotted. But there were just too many guards. And even if they made it beyond the gates, they had no idea how they'd summon American help. Meanwhile, the beatings and interrogations continued.

One evening, against all odds, and after a year of planning, two POWs, John Dramesi and Ed Atterbury, launched an escape attempt. They had decided they could not take the torture any longer. After squishing some iodine pills and making a liquid to darken their pale faces, they managed to make it up onto a roof, and then to disable the electrical wiring so they wouldn't be shocked. Outside the prison, they slogged and sloshed through weeds and bamboo. They made it about twelve miles before being captured. The other POWs caught sight of them the very next morning, blindfolded and being paraded back into camp. A new round of torture began for them. Atterbury was taken away from the prison shortly after being recaptured, never to be seen again. (It was later revealed that he died in captivity in 1969.) The guards had imagined that Cherry and the other prisoners had helped with the escape plan, so they increased the torture for the whole lot of them.

Not all of the torture was physical. Guards enjoyed playing recordings of the American actress Jane Fonda denigrating the war effort. In 1967, the North Vietnamese released two Black POWs, neither of them Fred Cherry. A message from the North Vietnamese accompanied the release of the Black men, stating that they supported "solidarity and support for the just struggle of the U.S. Negroes . . . for basic national rights."

Diane Nash Bevel was a heroine of the American civil rights movement. She had participated in protests throughout the South in the early 1960s and managed to stand out amidst the patriarchal world of civil rights decision making. But she was aggrieved about the American presence in Vietnam and made a trip to North Vietnam—at the invitation of Ho Chi Minh—while Cherry was imprisoned. After she departed, the North Vietnamese delighted in playing some of her taped comments over loudspeakers to American prisoners, realizing her words would infuriate them. "The Vietnam War is a colonialist war," Bevel had said. "If you fight it, you are fighting Asian brothers who are determined to prevent their country from becoming owned and managed by racist capitalist white men." Fred Cherry became so incensed while listening to such recordings that he frantically yanked his leg and wrist irons, causing deep welt marks.

Because of his intransigence and refusal to give in to his tormentors, Cherry was dragged off at one point to spend fifty-three days in solitary confinement. The window was boarded up, blocking outside light. Footsteps outside the cell often signaled the arrival of a Vietnamese soldier and impending torture. Terror always seemed to be seconds or minutes away. His fellow POWs were in awe of Cherry's endurance. "The V were demanding all would write a biography which would lead to confessions of crimes," Air Force Captain Bob Lilly, also a POW, recalled about the interrogators. "All eventually wrote something, except Fred. To my knowledge, he never gave in and wrote what the V wanted. [When] the V finally realized he was going to die before he would write, they let him off the hook. This is the only time that I know of that anyone outlasted the V . . ." Whenever Fred Cherry returned from an interrogation-torture session, he'd wait awhile and then, still in pain, begin banging his head on the cell walls. The POWs had devised a code delivery system. Through the banging—a certain number of bangs for each letter of the alphabet, and prisoners would have to connect the letters mentally into words—Cherry would tell the others what the Vietnamese had just asked him, so they could prepare themselves and plot answers. Bob Lilly would never forget Cherry's continued defiance: "He became a legend to the POWs." There were times when Cherry used humor in his tapping code: "The Vietnamese are very democratic," he tapped in one message. "They're treating us all like niggers."

Like Fred Cherry, Air Force Second Lieutenant Lloyd "Fig" Newton was proud to be a pilot. And he knew how proud it made his family and relatives back in his native South Carolina, who knew how rare it was to see a Black pilot like their Fig. He was praised in the Black community of his hometown. Photos of him in his pilot gear were shared among many. Even though he had just received orders to go to Vietnam, the first couple of days of April 1968 were good days for Newton. Headquartered at Travis Air Force Base in Northern California, he was given some downtime before heading to war. Like every pilot, he had a solid understanding of what his mission would be. Newton made time to enjoy a few hours with friends before leaving for Southeast Asia. Then, on April 4, came the news—dizzying at first, then, within hours, confirmed and stultifying—that Martin Luther King, Jr., had been shot dead. Newton was furious, and bewildered. America seemed bent on extending its hatred of Black leadership: Malcolm, then Medgar, now Martin. "My whole day, my whole life changed at that point," Newton recalled. He was so angry he asked his friends to give him some time alone: "What was really going through my mind, of course, was why should I be going to Vietnam to fight an enemy when I have an enemy right here in the United States." Realizing the grave consequences he'd face if he refused an official order, Newton decided he had to honor the oath he had taken as a soldier. From April 1968 to April 1969, Fig Newton flew seventy-nine missions over North Vietnam, dropping cluster bombs and napalm. Sometimes the bombs he dropped weighed a thousand pounds. These were very dangerous missions, and he knew it. "You begin to calculate real quick: If we lost five airplanes in a week, there's a very good chance I could get shot down out here." But Fig Newton was far luckier than Fred Cherry: he completed his Vietnam assignment unscathed and earned numerous medals.

The family of Fred Cherry—having returned from Japan to Virginia—had to adjust itself to the rhythms of being Black and back in America. The scars of the many Virginia schools that had been shuttered in 1958 and 1959—rather than obey court-ordered school desegregation orders—still hung in the air.

Now and then—his captivity having reached a fifth year and counting—Fred Cherry would be given a Red Cross package. Then, in 1970, he received his first letter from a family member. It took sheer faith for Cherry's family members to write to him, because, for all they knew, they were writing to a ghost: Shirley Cherry had long been telling her children and her friends that her husband had died in Vietnam. She had even begun dating. Leolia Cherry, Fred's mother, held out hope her son was alive. And whenever she was in her small garden and a jet flew above her home, she'd wonder if her son had gotten free and was flying home to a local military base. But he was still in captivity when his mother died. "She died," he said, "believin' I was comin' home."

Dreams went a long way to helping sustain many of the POWs. They dreamed about girlfriends and wives and sex parties and bacchanal weekends in beautiful cities. They dreamed about horse racing and racing cars and sailing boats. They dreamed of being rescued. Fred Cherry prayed that the Blacks of America knew he was holding on, not just for his country but for them as well. "I know how some white Americans feel about blacks," Cherry said. "If I do one little thing wrong, they're going to multiply that and you'll hear the same old thing: blacks aren't capable of doing this or that, they can't stand up under pressure, and they're not loyal to their country, which is the damnedest thing I've ever heard. Well, it wasn't going to happen on my watch. I was fighting for [twenty-two] million black folks. That was my battle."

So Fred Cherry kept dreaming. Dreaming that he and his fellow POWs might be rescued. Dreaming that some fierce American soldiers were out there, right now, cutting through the tall grass to free all of them.

Chapter Eleven

Some Badass Marines Are Humping the Hills Around Da Nang

There was a period during the Revolutionary War, in 1776, when a few Blacks—former slaves and free men—were allowed to fight with the Continental Marines. Some were at the Valley Forge encampment with George Washington. They were quite proud of the opportunity to be involved in the forging of a new nation. Reports of their prowess and commitment spread throughout Black communities and villages. Young Black kids heard about them and conjured up songs in tribute. But their service in the Marines would end in due time. The Militia Act of 1796 altered their involvement going forward when it came to matters of war and the military branch of the Marines: "No Negro, Mulatto, or Indian is to be recruited [in the Marine Corps]." It took more than a century and a half for that policy to be altered.

Everyone in Beaufort County, South Carolina, seemed to know the Reed family, who were connected to the military surroundings of the area with pride and passion. They lived inside the county in the small enclave of Burton. Henry Reed had served in World War II, and his

Having grown up at the doorstep of South Carolina's Parris Island, site of a Marine Corps boot camp, Henry Reed knew his destiny.

Robert Stewart was superstitious about reading letters from home; he thought they weakened resolve.

own father had been a World War I veteran. The steady paychecks of the military service seemed to lift the Reeds up from the raw poverty many Blacks experienced in the county and its surrounding areas. Whenever the Reed men returned home from the military—be it on leave or on completion of service—there'd be celebrations, dinner gatherings, and then extra prayers given over at First Jericho Baptist Church, where the family attended. Everyone was so grateful that they had returned home from their service safely.

Henry Reed and his wife, Leola, held jobs at the Marine Corps Recruit Depot at Parris Island, less than five minutes from their front door. They were so proud of the military life that surrounded them. The firstborn of Henry and Leola Reed was a son, also named Henry. Everyone called him Boy Blue; he seemed to like being around the water. "Because we lived so close to the base, on Fridays, when they had graduation, me and my brothers could listen to the band playing the music, and we would march to the music of the band," Henry Reed recalled.

The older Reeds—uncles and aunts and cousins—saw a natural

leadership ability in young Henry. He was disciplined; he didn't get into trouble; the teachers and classmates in his segregated world admired him. And he well understood the racial dynamics of the area: "I grew up knowing white kids; we'd pick pecans and all that stuff. But we were still separated from each other." Young Henry attended the local all-Black Robert Smalls High School. The school was named after a Black man who had gone down in the annals of Civil War heroism: Smalls, born a slave in Beaufort, South Carolina, in 1839, took an opportunity in 1862 to overpower and seize a Confederate ship. He stealthily guided the ship into Union-controlled territory. The daring act played a role in President Lincoln's decision to allow Blacks, finally, to join the Union Army.

There were two bits of local history that the elder Reed had taken time to share about military life with his son Henry. Both incidents concerned the Marines, which young Henry was intent on joining someday.

The first story the elder Reed wanted his son to know and appreciate was about the Montford Point Marines.

The United States Marines were never less than blunt about not wanting Blacks to join their modern force. At the beginning of World War II, there were no Black Marines that anyone knew of. Much of the Marines' leadership believed Blacks were not disciplined enough to take the rigid Marine instruction. They simply believed Blacks unworthy to penetrate and navigate the Marine way of life. The Marines' commandant, Lieutenant General Thomas Holcomb, had testified, "There would be a definite loss of efficiency in the Marine Corps if we have to take Negroes . . ." But in 1942, Holcomb was forced to honor an executive order signed by President Roosevelt paving the way for Blacks to join. Most of the young Blacks who signed up and were accepted heard about the Marine recruiting efforts in local Black newspapers, on Black radio stations, or from their local church ministers.

A segregated Marine boot camp was created near Camp Lejeune, at Montford Point, in North Carolina. In the late summer of 1942, those Black recruits arrived. They were near Montford when they were told by white MPs that they'd have to get off the buses and walk the rest of the way. This angered them—white recruits never had to abandon the buses—but they began walking. From the beginning, Ernest Smith was bothered by the treatment he and other Black recruits were receiving: "The white Marines went into nice, beautiful, clean barracks. We went into huts, square huts." Edgar Cole, who hailed from Dallas, was proud to be at Montford Point, but "we were mistreated in every way possible," he recalled. "What bothered us was, they tried to pretend that we weren't Americans too. But we were young, courageous, and loved our country."

On June 15, 1944, the Black Marines who had trained at Montford Point had their first opportunities to engage in overseas battle. Here is an officer's report about those Black Marines at Saipan, in the Mariana Islands: "Mortar shells were still raining down as my boys unloaded ammunition, demolition material, and other supplies from amphibious trucks. They set up 'security' to keep out snipers as they helped load casualties aboard boats to go to hospital ships. Rifle fire was thick as they rode guard on trucks carrying high octane gasoline from the beach. A squad leader killed a Jap sniper that crawled into a foxhole next to his." On Saipan, Lieutenant Joe Grimes, a white officer, also took note of the Black Marines. "I watched those Negro boys carefully," he later said. "They were under intense mortar and artillery fire as well as rifle and machine-gun fire. They all kept on advancing until the counterattack was stopped." Kenneth Tibbs went from Ohio to Montford Point and then to Saipan. There were days when he thought it all some kind of strange dream. Tibbs was in the military in hopes of making life better for him and his pregnant girlfriend back home. But he would never see his little daughter, Helen; he died from an enemy bullet on Saipan. Helen's mother told her daughter that her father died fighting for freedom for everyone in America. The American press began taking note of the Black Marines on Saipan. "When the battle of Saipan is recorded for history it will not be complete unless these Negro marines are given full credit for their contributions to the victory," stated *The*

Chicago Defender. "The erroneous statement that 'they cannot master the intricacies of modern warfare,' has been disproved by the heroic deeds of untrained Negro messmen in the navy, shattered by the unparalleled success of Negro flyers in Europe and buried by the fighting quality of the Negro marines on Saipan."

The elder Henry Reed felt mighty proud when he strolled around Burton and introduced young Henry to the Montford Marines who were still in the area in the early 1950s. Young Henry had his first heroes in life. The Montford Marines may have been an experiment, but they had performed so well they could no longer be viewed as such. By 1949, the Marines had done away with the Montford Point training camp; all Marines, no matter their racial identification, went through training at Parris Island or in San Diego. The Montford Point Marine story passed down by the elder Reed to his young son was all about pride and respect—and how those Black Marines had proved so many wrong.

The other story Henry Reed wanted to pass along to his son was also about courage and resolve, and the kind of strength of mind he knew his son would need if he were to become a Marine.

In the early spring in 1956, when Henry Reed was all of thirteen years old, a busload of new Marine recruits arrived at Parris Island, and became members of Platoon 71. This was during the heyday of Cold War peacetime. Some of the recruits had joined the Marines because it meant a little extra money to send back home, and it meant one less mouth to feed at the dinner table. One of Platoon 71's drill instructors was Sergeant Matthew McKeon, a native of Worcester, Massachusetts, and a World War II vet who stood six feet four inches tall and had a stare as severe as his crewcut. He grinned when he saw the recruits bloodying one another during the football games, which he called "organized grab-ass." The new recruits came from all over the country. Joe Moran's mom was Thelma Ritter, a gifted character actress who had appeared in many motion pictures. One of her friends was Marilyn Monroe. Ritter got Monroe to write her son a letter at boot camp, which he showed off like it was the Hope Diamond.

It didn't take a lot of time for the recruits to realize that Sergeant McKeon was a hard man; he was going to drill, and drill hard. In the early evening of April 8, 1956, McKeon thought his recruits needed some extra discipline: there had been reports of their fooling around too much instead of doing what they were assigned to do, which was to clean their rifles. "Left column!" he shouted as the young recruits lined up outside their barracks. McKeon marched them all down toward Ribbon Creek, which flowed out into the Atlantic. As they marched, the dark began deepening, hanging around them like blankets. No one had been allowed to bring flashlights. They were holding on to one another or grabbing at tree branches. They couldn't wait to get back to the damn barracks. The temperature was cold, and so was the water they were trudging through. But as they finished this march, a tide came rushing in and overtook them, knocking them even more off balance. Tides can be like drains, pulling everyone down or sweeping them in various directions. Not everyone in the platoon could swim. Some Marines vanished beneath the water, as did their sergeant. This was the first platoon group McKeon had been assigned; now this, with young Marines hollering and kicking and going underwater, thrashing and looking for fellow Marines. Men riding in military jeeps soon arrived, along with a Catholic priest, who was seen praying. The scene was awful. Six Marines died. Sergeant McKeon was arrested and charged with six cases of negligent manslaughter, though the charges were later reduced to negligence, and his nine-month sentence reduced to three months. He was also busted down to private, and this demotion stood.

Because of those who had drowned at Parris Island, the Marines altered some of their training policies. Several members of Platoon 71 later served in Vietnam. Many of those who survived Vietnam came to say, were it not for their tough training by Drill Sergeant Matthew McKeon, they might not have made it out of Vietnam alive.

—

After the elder Henry Reed told his young son Henry about the Black Marines of Montford Point, and about what had happened on that dark night in 1956 at Parris Island, he felt he had readied his son as much as he could to face the rigors of life, manhood, and becoming a Marine.

When he entered the Hampton Institute in Virginia in 1961 and quickly joined ROTC, young Henry was wooed by Army recruiters. But he knew he was going to be joining the Marines, even if the word around campus within the college military community was that the Marines were inhospitable to Blacks. "I remember standing in front of the student union building, and my classmates, when they found out I was going to come in the Marine Corps, because at that time everybody went to the Army . . . they used to laugh at me," Reed recalled. "They'd say, 'Hey, you're going into the Marine Corps? All you gonna do, man, is shine shoes.'" Reed just laughed at his classmates. He was every bit a Parris Island boy; he was going to become a Marine. He got sent to Officer Candidate School after graduation. While there, he was summoned to meet with a couple of staff platoon commanders. They'd been eyeing him; they saw something special in Henry Reed, who seemed to outperform so many others, who already seemed to have the demeanor of a Marine. "Hey," one of the officers said to him, "most blacks are signing up for supply and everything else, but we've noticed how you've handled yourself with your assignments as a student and how you've led them through the various situations that we've provided . . . You should become an infantry officer."

Upon his college graduation in 1965 (with a degree in world history), Henry Reed had gotten married, having met his wife, Brenda, while at Hampton. His closest friends were now fellow Marine officers, white officers among them, "and they were all southerners," Reed said. And those Marines dominated the gathering at his wedding: Semper Fi. Always faithful. He and Brenda had emerged from the church after exchanging vows before an interracial mix of Marines standing at attention, their swords raised. This rare kind of interracial scene gave attendees hope about the future.

At the beginning of the 1960s, it remained difficult to find Black Marine officers. In 1962, out of a force of roughly twenty thousand Marines, there were a mere thirty-two.

When he completed Officer Candidate School, Reed was sent to the Basic School at Quantico, Virginia. If you were sent there—the place where top Marines trained to become platoon commanders—it had already been determined that you possessed admirable Marine talents. At the Basic School there was a special emphasis "on the duties, responsibilities, and warfighting skills required of a . . . platoon commander." When Henry Reed completed that assignment, in May 1966, he was assigned to the 1st Marine Division in Vietnam.

All of the predictions about Henry Reed—about his thinking, courage, strategic mind, boldness—came true during his two stints in Vietnam. An infantry officer, he was a man wired for combat. He went on reconnaissance missions. He became an adviser to the South Vietnamese Army, the only Black officer tasked with advising them, and disappeared into the jungle bush with them for days on end. He waded through swamps with the ease of an alligator in search of the enemy. The men under him revered him. He was wiry and thin. He wore a pistol, and he smoked cigars. During his two stints in Vietnam, he was a platoon commander in the 3rd Anti-Tank Battalion; he served with the 5th Special Forces Group; he was sent off to the Amphibious Warfare School, and also to the Army War College.

Marines went in first abroad, and that's what Henry Reed loved about the Corps: if you put the mass safety of Americans at risk because of political upheaval in a foreign land, if you committed acts of atrocity against Americans, then the Marines were coming. It didn't take a lot of paperwork and mind-numbing hearings on Capitol Hill, like it did to move the Army across an ocean. Marines were a rapid response force and they trained for the moment: Boots on the ground. Oorah!

President Johnson meant to calm the nation in 1965 in his speech at Johns Hopkins University when he laid out why Marines had landed in Vietnam. Their presence was a prelude to military action abroad. They were the first shadows in the jungles.

Here is LBJ at Johns Hopkins, sounding bold and confident:

> The task is nothing less than to enrich the hopes and the existence of more than a hundred million people. And there is so much to be done. The vast Mekong River can provide food and water and power on a scale to dwarf even our own TVA. The wonders of modern medicine can be spread through villages where thousands die every year from lack of care . . . We hope the peace will come swiftly. But that is in the hands of others than ourselves. We will use our power with restraint and with all the wisdom that we can command. But we will use it.

Henry Reed was either in Da Nang, or moving like a ghost along the Mekong River, or in Saigon strategizing, puffing on a cigar while poring over maps. He was helping orchestrate his commander-in-chief's war. He'd tell soldiers not only to remember their training, but also to be nimble enough to improvise. Word kept spreading about Reed.

Reynolds Peele went into the Marines from the Black community of Baltimore in 1968. He arrived at Parris Island that summer. By early 1969, he was in Vietnam, a Marine rifleman. He had heard of Henry Reed. "If the Marines promoted you to full-bird colonel, like they did Henry Reed, then you must have been walking on water," Peele says. Andrew Perkins was an Army man who'd been a classmate of Henry Reed's at the Hampton Institute. Even then Perkins sensed something special. "His tenacity was to be the best he could be. The Marines are Semper Fi; they go in first. They are leather-tough," Perkins says. "Henry knew he had to fight on the battlefield to rise in the ranks."

Many began bestowing upon Henry Reed the ultimate compliment: he was a Marine's Marine, a true leatherneck. He loved the Marines; this was becoming his career. But the longer Reed stayed in the Marines, the more he realized there were issues about retaining Black officers, and that bothered him. The Marines also realized they had a problem concerning race and upward mobility, so they decided to take Reed out of Vietnam and send him back to the States with a directive to help Blacks stay in the Marines. Reed reported to General Lou Wilson, Jr. "At that time," Reed recalled, "I used to always tell him, the Marine Corps, and black officers in particular, it seems like it was a bucket with a hole in the bottom. We were just putting guys in, but three years later, they were out. A lot of them just didn't have the desire to stay in."

Anthony Zinni, a decorated Marine who served in Vietnam and became a general, formed a close friendship with Reed during the war. "It was a calm, quiet fearlessness that he had," Zinni says of Reed. "He just seemed to have this built-in sense of courage. If you were around him, you just felt you were going to be okay."

Many could at least point to the fact that the Marines didn't seem to experience the kind of racial clashes other military branches were having during the Vietnam era. That is, until the eruption that took place at Camp Lejeune in North Carolina on the night of July 20, 1969.

Tensions between Blacks and whites on the base had been building since the death of Martin Luther King, Jr., a year earlier. The July mêlée began at an NCO dance. Two Marines, one white and one Black, were dancing together. When a Black Marine attempted to cut in on the white Marine, heated words were exchanged. And then fisticuffs. From ten-thirty onward that night, the clash seemed unstoppable, white against Black, Black against white. "There were four or five of us walking back from the enlisted men's club, back to our barracks," Marine Robert Jeannotte recalled. "And about 40 black Marines came around the corner. And all hell broke loose, so to speak." Fifteen Marines were injured. Corporal Edward E. Blankston, who suffered head injuries, died a week later. Blankston was at Camp Lejeune recovering from injuries he'd received in Vietnam, a war in which he had been decorated. A Marine investigation cited the role that Black "militant" Marines had played in the uprising, while also concluding, "The Marine Corps are returning Marines, both black and white, to civilian society with more deeply seated prejudices than were individually possessed upon entrance to service." The news about what had happened at Camp Lejeune leaked out slowly into the media. It was nearly four weeks after it happened before NBC News sent Robert Goralski, one of their correspondents, to the base to file a story. "Large secluded areas have been illuminated with flood lights and all outside lights are kept on until dawn," Goralski said in his report. Willie Robertson, a Black Marine who had been wounded in Vietnam, was at Camp Lejeune recovering when the riot broke out. "Most of them were on edge," he said about fellow Blacks at Lejeune. "After Martin Luther King got killed, they just took it out on whites because it was a white man that killed Martin Luther King." Reports from Vietnam reached Blacks at Camp Lejeune that whites had been waltzing around carrying Confederate flags following King's assassination. Robertson sensed the Marines were out of step with reality. "The Marines, they weren't too cool with blacks especially being in leadership positions," he said. "They didn't want any blacks to be able to tell a white soldier . . . what to do."

In the months ahead, it meant a lot to Black soldiers across all branches that they could notice changes the Pentagon instituted: Black hair-care products began showing up at stores on bases, as did Black magazines such as *Ebony, Jet,* and *Black Enterprise.* As well, race-relations training became a mandatory feature of military life. "The one thing about the Armed Forces, they can't change the way you think," believed Robertson, "but they certainly can change the way you act."

At the end of his second tour in Vietnam, Henry Reed and a handful of other Black Marine officers were able to convince the high command to rethink the way Black Marines were being judged on evaluation reports; these reports had often been negative, convincing many Black Marines that they were not wanted. "One of the real things that bothered me," Reed said, "was that I noticed that black officers were getting marked low in loyalty . . ." It struck many Black Marines—Reed among them—as rather ironic that their loyalty was being questioned when it had long been a sense of loyalty—from the days of the Continental Marines to present recruiting in urban neighborhoods across America—that had propelled many Blacks to want to swear allegiance to the armed services.

One day, in his hometown of East St. Louis, Illinois, Robert Stewart was casually glancing up and down the street. He hoped to spy a buddy who'd want to go see the Cardinals play! As a seventeen-year-old high-school student, Stewart had the same passion a lot of other teenagers in East St. Louis did at the time: he loved Bob Gibson, the fiery Black pitcher, loved how he'd whip his fastball past the startled player in the batter's box. He saw someone coming closer. "It was this kid who I knew from the neighborhood. He always used to look raggedy, but now he was in a shiny uniform. He had his hat on. He was really squared away. Walking tall!" The closer the soldier got to Stewart, the more in awe he became of the image. This was a military man, and he cut such an impressive figure. Young Robert couldn't shake the memory of the transformation his neighborhood acquaintance had made. "This guy impressed me!"

A lot of people in that East St. Louis neighborhood were talking about the war. It was 1967; talk about Vietnam flowed across kitchen tables, on backyard porches, in barbershops, and even in county jails, where some inmates were being given the option of going to prison or heading to Vietnam. After graduating from high school that year, Robert Stewart decided he was going to enlist in the military. Not because he was gung-ho, but because he figured he needed to be proactive and choose the branch of the military that might afford him the best chance to survive in Vietnam. The neighborhood soldier Stewart had seen was in the Army, but Stewart's research convinced him that the Marines could train him better than any other branch of the military. He found something reassuring in their tough-as-hell image. He saw all those slogans on billboards: THE FEW. THE PROUD. THE MARINES. And another one: ASK A MARINE. And yet another one: WE DON'T PROMISE YOU A ROSE GARDEN. He watched the recruitment TV commercials with wide eyes. "Those commercials really worked," he says.

In 1967, East St. Louis—because of zoning codes and gerrymandering and other features of real-estate discrimination—remained an all-Black community. But the mayor was a white man.

All through high school, the future was a concern for Stewart and his classmates. When he looked around East St. Louis—situated on the Missouri border—he did not see plentiful opportunities for young Black men. The city had endured an explosive race riot in 1917 and even after all these years, it was hard to say there was still not a residue lingering: housing segregation, an income gap between Black and white, mistrust between law enforcement and the Black community. Simply put, urban renewal had hastened destruction of parts of the city. Robert's father, Charlie, worked at Granite City Steel, over in Granite City, Illinois. His mother, Alice, worked for the Veterans Administration at the Jefferson Barracks in St. Louis. Alice Stewart was not opposed to the military, but that did not stop her from trying to talk her son out of joining the Marines after he had made up his mind to do so.

Because her son was only seventeen years old, Alice Stewart had to sign his consent form to go into the Marines. Not long after he took his date, Lillian, to the high-school prom, Robert Stewart was bound for San Diego and Marine boot camp.

Everyone kept reminding Stewart that the Marine boot camp he'd be attending was "near Hollywood," which seemed to be their way of saying, "How bad could it be?" But Stewart found the place hellish, with its nonstop exercise regimen—the push-ups, the screaming from drill instructors, the sleep deprivation, the physical training, the classroom work, all of it coming as if on a constant loop. There were drill instructors who'd call you "pussy," "maggot," "lunatic," "coward," "asshole." They'd tell you they were going to kill you—and make you believe it. "Boot camp was a nightmare," Stewart said years later. "They wanted to get you ready for a combat zone." There were sixty-four Marines in his class. Of that total, including Stewart, there were only four Blacks.

Deployment to Vietnam for Marines meant a thirteen-month assignment, one month longer than the twelve-month Army rotation. The difference was a holdover from World War II, when

Marines went overseas on ships. Their journey accounted for one month of duty, but it wasn't subtracted from the yearlong assignment they were going into.

In January 1968, Robert Stewart landed in Vietnam. A few weeks later came the Tet Offensive, that bombardment that began at midnight on January 31 when North Vietnamese Army troops and the Viet Cong attacked thirty-six of the forty-four provincial capitals. Stewart himself felt ready—and confident that the Marines had trained him well. "I'd rather be feared than to be fearful" was his attitude at the time. He was a rifleman. The Marines overall were a smaller force than the Army units. In Vietnam, they'd go on stealth missions up into the jungle. He began to understand why the Marines liked to recruit the young. "The Marines liked you young because you can hump the hills all day long and not get heat stroke. Forty-year-old guys wouldn't want to do that."

Sometimes it seemed as if the jungle was playing tricks: Stewart and his men would be fired upon by the enemy. They'd give chase, but, just that quick—poof—the Vietnamese soldiers disappeared. "They were gone, hiding in tunnels."

Robert Stewart turned eighteen in Vietnam, and by the time of his birthday he had been promoted to sergeant. Word reached him and his fellow Marines about Martin Luther King, Jr.'s April 4, 1968, assassination. As painful as the news was, he couldn't really reconfigure his mind to focus on anything happening back in the States. "At the time, I was concerned about staying alive, day to day. There was no TV to watch anything. Your thinking was: 'How can I make it past the next day?' " The racial turmoil in the aftermath of King's killing didn't seem to affect his Marine unit. Marines were careful about not antagonizing one another, at least in the war zone. "First of all," Stewart says about racial harassment, "I got three to four grenades, a bayonet. You didn't need to be picking on someone carrying a machine gun and hand grenades. I mean, accidents could happen. You just didn't have that mindset. You knew what training other Marines got. You weren't challenging people."

Sometimes, however, the dynamics of race were so complex that they would linger in Stewart's mind and come to haunt him decades later. "We had to go up into a valley one day," he recalls. "I had been walking point. The captain looks toward two of us, myself and another Marine, who was white. The captain had to choose who to go into that valley first. If he'd've chosen me, I wonder if some in the unit would have wondered if it was because I was Black. He chose the white guy. He went in, and he went down. It was suicide, walking point in Vietnam."

Now and then, they'd write letters home. "You'd be writing about your experiences with villagers, the food, the children. Or you'd tell your mom you couldn't wait to get home and get some of her sweet-potato pie. But I remember a sergeant telling us, 'When you get letters from home, don't get wrapped up in what's in them, because you put that letter up and see how many bullets it's gonna stop. So get back to the business at hand.'" From that day on he had another attitude about receiving letters. "If I got a letter, fine; if not, fine. I survived another day in Vietnam."

There were days when Robert Stewart grew weary, days when he wondered about the mission. Then he'd brush the weariness away. He could lean on fellow Marines, and they could lean on him. "We followed orders. We were there for each other. We indeed felt the frustration of the war, because we would attack the same hills month after month. We didn't appreciate the police-type action we were involved in. But we were patriots."

With every hill they took, every hill they humped, Stewart and his fellow Marines couldn't help but realize they were fighting a formidable and underestimated foe. "The will of the North Vietnamese was a lot better than the will of the South Vietnamese. But, again, we couldn't dwell on why we were there. You counted your days to stay alive. You had a target date of when you were going home."

When Robert Stewart returned to America at the beginning of 1969, his war tour over, he began noticing that some of the recruitment posters he was seeing were quite different. Beginning in 1968, and for the first time in its history, a photo of a Black Marine was used on posters. That Marine was James Capers, Jr., and he was right from Central Casting: handsome, square-jawed, and bedecked with medals on the chest of his blue uniform. Capers had become a legend with a harrowing Vietnam story. Toward the end of March 1967, Capers was on a foot patrol near Phu Loc. He and his fellow Marines were in search of a North Vietnamese regimental base camp. They were caught in a surprise attack, from both enemy fire and exploding mines. Capers, suddenly bloodied, suffered two broken legs. He still managed to direct his men, even though he was taking morphine to dull the pain of his bloody wounds. "While struggling to maintain consciousness and still under attack, Major Capers demanded continuous situation and status reports from his Marines and ensured the entire team was evacuated before himself," his award citation read. "Barely able to stand, Major Capers finally boarded the helicopter and was evacuated." Capers—who had also led recon missions to look for POW camps—received a Silver Star, three Purple Hearts, and two Bronze Stars with insignias of "V" for valor during his Vietnam service.

Capers had joined the Marines in 1956. His father—who had once served time on a Southern chain gang—drove the recruit to the train station and saw him off to boot camp. It was a tough separation: the elder Capers confided to his son that he didn't think he was making the right decision by joining the Marines. But now, in 1968, the photo of Major James Capers, Jr., had immediately become historic and iconic. It was seen in libraries and schools, on college campuses, in magazines. Teens from Los Angeles to Omaha to East St. Louis saw it. There were just three enlarged words accompanying the photo: ASK A MARINE.

Oorah!

CHAPTER TWELVE

A DANCING MOTOWN COMES TO SEE THE BLOOD ON THE WALL

It was one of the more explosive cultural movements of the early and mid-1960s. In 1959, Berry Gordy was a going-nowhere singer, a sometime factory worker, a Korean War vet, and a young-man-about-Detroit when he bummed some seed money with the aim of starting a music company. When he had a nest egg of twenty-five thousand dollars, he purchased a house on West Grand Boulevard. It was the beginning of Motown. Gordy amassed a cavalcade of singers—soloists, duos, trios, quartets—and sent them out across the country as their songs were climbing and often landing at the very top of the Billboard charts. It was impossible not to rush to the dance floor in some nightclub while listening to Martha & the Vandellas ("Heat Wave"), Smokey Robinson & the Miracles ("The Tracks of My Tears"), Stevie Wonder ("I Was Made to Love Her"), the Temptations ("Get Ready"), the Supremes ("Back in My Arms Again"), the Four Tops ("Baby I Need Your Loving"), or Marvin Gaye ("I Heard It Through the Grapevine"). It was the most profound infusion of Black music across the airwaves in one concentrated time period in the history of America.

The Motown acts swept out across the country. If they didn't fly,

At an impasse with Motown, his record label, Marvin Gaye demanded they let him record a sociopolitical album that had antiwar lyrics. What's Going On *proved to be the soundtrack to both the war and the civil rights movement.*

they traveled in custom buses. Fans mobbed them at hotels. White nightclubs, like the Copacabana in Manhattan, began welcoming Motown's Black acts onto their stages. Ed Sullivan booked them on his popular Sunday-night television show. Hardly a month went by when one of Motown's acts wasn't featured on the cover of either *Jet* or *Ebony,* magazines that were viewed as musical bibles throughout urban communities. The Motown groups and their hit songs quickly became crossover hits, drawing the dollars and emotional attention of whites, goals that had always been one of the aims of the label's founder.

But as the months and years began turning over, the calendar rolling into the mid-1960s, it was difficult to ignore the urban chaos happening beyond the windows of Motown's music offices. Vietnam kept creeping into conversations. Backup singers and employees of the company were coming into the offices and talking about sons and nephews and relatives in Vietnam, about their injuries—and their deaths. Marvin Gaye's brother, Frankie, was off serving in Vietnam. He wrote long letters to Marvin about the death and dying he

Dwight Johnson's heroic actions in Vietnam earned him the Medal of Honor and saw him feted in his hometown of Detroit, at an event attended by General William C. Westmoreland, commander of the U.S. forces in Vietnam. His bizarre death inside a Detroit convenience store stunned the nation.

saw, about the racism. Martha, of Martha Reeves & the Vandellas, had a brother who served in Vietnam and returned Stateside with health issues, which Martha admitted led to the cause of his early death. Coupled with the bloody urban unrest on Detroit's streets and around America, Motown could not avoid the daily headlines of war much longer. Lyrical love songs and pleadings were one thing; trying to explain Vietnam to Detroit's Black teenagers who were fleeing rifle-wielding, bayonet-carrying—and mostly white—National Guardsmen quite another. Gordy was always nervous about putting out so-called protest music, worried it might sound unpatriotic to his listeners, especially white listeners. A few years earlier, however, he did decide it was a good decision to record Martin Luther King, Jr.'s June 23, 1963, speech, given before twenty-five thousand at Detroit's Cobo Arena. Many passages in the speech would be repeated at King's famous "I Have a Dream" address two months later. The synchronicity struck many inside the company as another shrewd move on Gordy's part and an ode to his acumen. Gordy and King became friendly acquaintances; King was always careful to take note of Black businessmen who had ready access to cash they might donate to his causes. The King album was released to very modest sales; spoken-word albums tended to reach only niche buyers.

No one inside Motown could keep from being attentive to the war. Stories about Vietnam were beginning to appear frequently in the *Detroit Free Press, The Detroit News,* and the *Michigan Chronicle,* a Black newspaper. Detroit, dotted with large, mostly Black low-income housing projects around the city, became a hub of military recruitment. The Detroit neighborhood Corktown was home to the housing project known as the E. J. Jefferies Homes. Draft letters were showing up in the project's mailboxes, and one of them landed in the hands of Dwight Johnson. He lived with his single mom. They were on public welfare. His mom was proud that he'd never gotten in trouble. Dwight Johnson was about to make his mom prouder than she thought she'd ever be—and the rest of Detroit as well.

He was drafted into the Army in the summer of 1966, and sent off to basic training at Fort Knox, Kentucky. When he reached Vietnam, he became a tank driver. The guys in his tank became very close. By early January 1967, Johnson was counting the days until he'd be going home. On January 14, he was sitting in his tank and wondering why he had received orders the night before to leave his platoon and join this new tank platoon. He thought it was odd, but this was war, and he complied. Maybe the officers in his new platoon admired his tank skills; he couldn't come up with an answer. Johnson's new platoon, and the one with his old buddies, found themselves up near Dak To, near the Cambodian border, arrayed inside several tanks. North Vietnamese forces began an assault with rocket-propelled antitank grenades. Johnson was close enough to another tank, one with his close buddies in it, to witness the direct and surely lethal hit they took. Their tank became a fireball. Johnson popped out of his Patton tank and began firing his .45-caliber automatic pistol until no more bullets were left. He ducked back into his tank, climbed out again with a submachine gun, and commenced firing. When the submachine gun ran out of ammunition, Johnson came face-to-face with an enemy soldier; he bashed him with the stock of his gun and killed him. Another soldier crept up on Johnson and fired, but that soldier's gun jammed, and Johnson killed him, too. Johnson heard screaming; it was an American soldier who was on fire. Johnson went and rescued him. Then he went to the tank that had shielded his close buddies, and found that none of them had survived. Johnson made his way back to his own tank and commandeered a .50-caliber machine gun. He seemed seized by something otherworldly—heroism, courage, anger at seeing his good buddies burned beyond recognition. This spate of killing went on for thirty minutes, and later estimates would attribute upward of twenty kills to Sergeant Dwight Johnson. "I don't know how many I killed," he would later say. "I wasn't thinking, I wasn't counting. I was just shooting." Stan Enders had been on the ground at Dak To with Dwight Johnson that day: "No one who was there could ever forget the sight of this guy taking on a whole battalion of North Vietnamese soldiers," Enders would come to say. When the firing stopped and the ambush had been repelled, fellow soldiers reached Dwight Johnson. He collapsed, and woke up a day later in a hospital in Pleiku. His fellow soldiers couldn't stop calling him a hero. "He was really close to those guys in that tank," said Enders, by way of trying to explain Johnson's exploits. "He just couldn't sit still and watch it burn with them inside."

Not long thereafter, Dwight Johnson was back home in Detroit. No one knew what he had done at Dak To. He was now just another poor young Black man in Detroit. He couldn't find a job. The folks at the state employment office told him to come back next week, then the next, then the next. The rare job interviews he got didn't pan out. He met a girl, Katrina, and was soon swaying and slow-dancing with her while listening to the sweet sounds of Motown in smoky nightclubs. He worried about money, having come home with just six hundred dollars. No one recognized any notable changes in the old

Dwight after Vietnam, save for the fact that he almost never talked about Vietnam. Well, actually, there was one notable thing: He carried a stack of color slides around with him. They were pictures of dead Vietnamese soldiers.

Months began to pass. Then, one day in early November, there was a knock at his mom's apartment door. She saw two military policemen when she looked out the window, and hurriedly asked her son if he had done something illegal. He told her absolutely not. The policemen were welcomed inside the home. They asked Dwight a few questions—namely, if he had done anything to embarrass the military since he had been home. He told them he had not. Then the men asked him to remain inside the home for the next fifteen minutes. They left. The phone rang. It was an officer from the Department of Defense, telling Dwight Johnson he had been recommended and approved for the Medal of Honor, the nation's highest award for valor.

A week later, Dwight Johnson and some family members stood in the White House as President Johnson draped the Medal of Honor around his neck and bestowed the award on four other soldiers.

Back in Detroit, Dwight Johnson suddenly became the toast of the town. A huge ten-dollars-a-plate dinner was held at Cobo Hall to honor him. Fifteen hundred people showed, and among them was General William C. Westmoreland, the architect of the American buildup in the war. People nearly knocked themselves over to get close to the bigshot general. And to Dwight Johnson as well.

In the weeks to come, restaurants wouldn't accept Johnson's money. Bank presidents and Motown executives and high-school teachers and neighbors were all so proud of him. He was celebrated at Tiger Stadium before a baseball game. He and Katrina got married. The Army lured him back into service, as a recruiter. "The brass wanted him in the Detroit recruiting office because—let's face it—here was a black Medal of Honor winner, and Blacks are our biggest manpower pool in Detroit," an Army official said.

Dwight Johnson had become the first Black Medal of Honor winner from the state of Michigan. Detroit had a genuine hero.

During the celebrations, and the speaking engagements, the

damn nightmares resurfaced. He started staring at those color slides of dead Vietnamese again. Bills piled up. He started having stomach cramps. The Army sent him to local high schools, and some of the kids wondered why he was advocating for Blacks to join the military when so many Blacks had been expressing doubts about the war effort. He started missing days at the recruiting office. He was sent to an Army hospital. The diagnosis: "depression caused by post Vietnam adjustment problem." His mother asked him if he was on any kind of drugs, and even checked his arm for needle marks. She found nothing. He was sent back to the Army hospital, where he received another psychiatric evaluation: "Subject expressed doubts over his decision to re-enter the Army as a recruiter. He felt the Army didn't honor its commitment to him. The public affairs were satisfactory to him at first, but he started to feel inadequate."

And from another psychiatric report:

> [Johnson] didn't confide in his mother or wife, but entertained a lot of moral judgement as to what happened at Dak To. Why had he been ordered to switch tanks the night before? Why was he spared and not the others? He experienced guilt about his survival. He wondered if he was sane.

On April 29, 1971, Dwight Johnson, back home from the hospital and all the mental evaluations, phoned Eddie Wright, a friend from the housing projects he had grown up in, and told him there was someone who owed him money and he needed a ride to go collect it. It was late at night, and Wright, for a second, wondered why Dwight needed to go at this hour. But Dwight said it was important. Wright was sensitive to the challenges his friend Dwight was going through, and even though the request to go pick him up at such a late hour seemed odd, he wanted to help. About a block before they reached the destination Dwight had described, he told his friend to stop the car. "This guy lives down the street and I don't want him to see me coming," Dwight said. By now, strange behavior no longer surprised Dwight's family members; out of love, they tolerated it. Dwight wasn't going to meet any friend. He walked into a grocery store. He had a gun. He announced he was going to rob the place. A tussle ensued. Then the store owner got hold of his own gun and fired several times, striking Dwight in the chest and once in the face. Before he was rushed to the hospital, the detectives who had arrived searched Johnson's wallet for identification. They came across a small card: "Congressional Medal of Honor Society—United States of America. This certifies that Dwight H. Johnson is a member of this society." The war hero was pronounced dead a few hours after arriving at the hospital.

"He was exposed to a white middle-class society and used by it—exploited," James Pellegrini would later say. Pellegrini, who worked in the Detroit office of the Disabled American Veterans, waged a two-year battle, ultimately successful, to get Dwight's widow full-benefit pay. Bruce Danto, a Detroit psychiatrist, wrote testimony stating that he believed Johnson's attempted robbery "was an effort to get himself killed."

When he was buried at Arlington National Cemetery, Dwight Johnson was given full military honors. Just as would have happened if he had died on the battlefield.

Martin Luther King, Jr.'s assassination devastated Berry Gordy. That moment was the beginning of Gordy's decision to take a more aggressive stand in the fight for equal rights.

In 1969, Gordy created the Black Forum label under his Motown umbrella. He didn't expect to protest through his musical output—he'd leave that to the folksingers. But his new imprint did have a clear aim:

> Black Forum is a medium for the preservation of ideas and voices of the worldwide struggle of Black people to create a new era. Black Forum also serves to provide authentic materials for use in schools and colleges and for the home study of Black history and culture. Black Forum is a permanent record of the sound of struggle and the sound of the new era.

By "struggle," Gordy meant the civil rights struggle. In October 1970, the Black Forum label posthumously released the album *Why I Oppose the War in Vietnam,* Martin Luther King, Jr.'s 1967 speech. No one expected the album to reach more than the usual niche audience, but at least the label could say it had planted some kind of a flag. That same month, the label released *Stokely Carmichael: Free Huey!,* Carmichael's 1968 speech. This album also bored right into the ongoing civil rights struggle in America. Given that Carmichael was one of the country's most vocal antiwar critics, Gordy seemed to be showcasing that he was quite concerned with the social and political fate of the nation.

For several years, Gordy's brother-in-law, none other than Marvin Gaye—who had married Gordy's sister, Anna—had been chafing at Motown's unwillingness to allow him to sing edgier songs. Gaye couldn't shake his brother's searing stories about Vietnam and wanted to put something into song. He also was quite depressed about the death of Tammi Terrell, his sometime singing partner, who had died from a brain tumor. Gaye began going through periods of depression and experienced mood swings. He often limited his contact with the outside world, even refusing entreaties to perform. But he was struck by a conversation he had with Renaldo Benson, another Motown singer. Benson told Gaye about his recent trip to Berkeley, California, where he came upon a scene in which antiwar protesters were being beaten by law enforcement. Gaye told Benson that such stories made him think anew about what had happened during the Watts riots a few years earlier. Gaye pushed himself back into the studio and began recording some singles. He thought they might make an album. The tunes consisted of searing ballads, songs about ecological destruction, hungry children, police brutality—and the Vietnam War. Motown executives sat and listened to the tunes and were confused: they had no idea how to market an album that seemed so blatantly political. Gordy himself was downright apoplectic. Believing that the songs would be seen as unpatriotic, even dangerous, he told Gaye he would not release them. "I'm angry . . . I have to protest," Gaye complained to Gordy. Gordy told Gaye he was "taking things too far" in expressing his anger about police brutality and Vietnam. Gaye thought both were intertwined, right along with racism and poverty. This became a battle of the wills between the mogul and one of his most valued singers. "For months they wouldn't release it," Gaye said about his unreleased album. "My attitude had to be firm. Basically, I said, 'Put it out or I'll never record for you again.' That was my ace in the hole, and I had to play it."

There are pop-culture moments in Black America that seem to stop the clock of time dramatically, to put motion on hold, to force an immediate reevaluation of things throughout the culture. They are moments that invite conversation—and will prove to last and inspire for decades to come. For a people searching for and demanding freedom, the moments tumble forth from the calendar. Among them: Jesse Owens blowing past the competition on the track in Nazi Germany in 1936 to bring home four Olympic gold medals; Marian Anderson's 1939 concert at the Lincoln Memorial, which took place there because, as a Black woman, she was denied the opportunity to sing at Constitution Hall; publication of Richard Wright's novel *Native Son* in 1940, marking him as the first Black bestselling author; the first issues of *Jet* magazine in the early 1950s; and the whole decade of the 1960s, which saw Sidney Poitier's Best Actor Oscar win, the legal dismantling of Jim Crow, the nation-rattling defiance of protesting Black athletes at the 1968 Olympics, Thurgood Marshall's ascendancy to the United States Supreme Court. And, in May 1971, the release of Marvin Gaye's *What's Going On* album. It landed like slow and rolling thunder. Part symphony, part ballad, part stream of consciousness, it was an album that boldly captured the zeitgeist like few albums had ever done before. It was lush and gritty, poetic and provocative. By the time it was released, after having built momentum with the release of some of its singles, Gaye's fans were in a frenzy. The album consisted of nine tracks, all of which flowed from a Vietnam veteran's sojourn looking around and assessing America, from abroad and at home. It was an album that was both a plea and a cry. The feature song, "What's Going On," alluded to the war itself and all the killings. Its opening: "There's too many of you crying; / Brother, brother, brother, / There's far too many of you dying."

Those who knew Gaye realized the songs were a response to his brother's service in Vietnam, to the harm it had done to Frankie Gaye as well as to so many others. Another title, "Inner City Blues (Makes Me Wanna Holler)," lamented poverty and racism, decried injustice and the fires throughout urban America.

Politicians, mothers at funerals, and antiwar activists all were being ushered into the church of Marvin. He wanted them to think about war and peace and the dimensions of love.

Another song, "Mercy Mercy Me," told of ecological devastation. "What's Happening Brother" presents a soldier back from Vietnam and lamenting: "War is hell, when will it end?"

Deejays in urban areas around the country went wild over Gaye's album. Black record stores—Doris Records in Buffalo, Snoopy's Records in Durham, North Carolina, Reid's Records in Berkeley, Happy House Records in Harlem, the Miami Record Shop in Columbus, Ohio, the very record stores the Black Vietnam vets were strolling in and out of once they got back from the war—couldn't keep the album in stock. It quickly crossed over, drawing white listeners as well. *Time* magazine hailed the album as a "vast, melodically deft symphonic pop suite." Gaye's album broke various sales records, becoming the number-one album on Billboard's Soul Chart, staying there for several weeks. Three of the album's singles hit the Top 10 on the Hot 100, the first time one album had performed such a feat. In its first year of release, the album sold more than two million copies. It became a pop-culture sensation, both enlarging and igniting discussions about the war in Vietnam.

In 1971, American music critics were, by and large, white. Feature writers on Black publications—such as *Ebony, Jet,* and *Sepia*—were grateful for interviews with stars and often wrote adulatory pieces with only minor allowances for criticism. And so the terrain of Black music criticism was left to white writers. And though some were certainly culturally hip—particularly on avant-garde and underground publications—most were not. In any event, they simply could not ignore the success of Gaye's album; the word "masterpiece" was quickly being uttered. The critics expressed a collective surprise that Motown, renowned for all those love songs and ballads, had released such a so-called radical album as *What's Going On.* Radical and political. But they might not have been so surprised if they had paid attention to Motown's Black Forum label, which had released spoken-word albums by Langston Hughes, as well as Stokely Carmichael and Martin Luther King, Jr. Those albums garnered little attention in the press.

With the phenomenal success of Gaye's album, the spirits of company executives within Motown, especially Gordy himself, were lifted. The album was on its way to becoming the label's highest-selling album ever. The fanfare propelled Gordy to start thinking of another idea for his Black Forum label.

During the years when Marvin Gaye was thinking about and working on his album, America seemed to be a land turning toward the apocalyptic: LBJ was gone, though few missed him save for Blacks and victims of civil rights abuses. Richard Nixon had come into the White House, slow-walking his vow to end the war—and telling outright lies to the American public. Vietnam vets were returning home, flooding drug rehab centers as they tried to kick heroin addictions. Black veterans—just as many of them had done before the war—were still trying to find their footing in an integrated society. On May 4, 1970, National Guardsmen shot and killed four antiwar protesting students on the campus of Kent State University in Ohio, and injured nine others. Eleven days later, two students (one from the college and one a local high-school student) were shot dead by law enforcement on the all-Black campus of Jackson State University in Mississippi, where antiwar demonstrations had also been taking place. Things felt scary and out of focus across the nation; blood seemed to be spilling from so many directions.

On the morning of June 13, 1971, Americans awoke to a *New York Times* front-page story titled: "Vietnam Archive: Pentagon Study Traces Three Decades of Growing U.S. Involvement." From the initial story and subsequent reporting came blockbuster revelations about the endless lies and treachery employed by the U.S. government to maintain American support for the war in Vietnam. Secretary of Defense Robert McNamara had ordered the report, with a directive that it would remain secret. But Daniel Ellsberg, who worked as a policy analyst for the Defense Department, got hold of the papers and gave them to Neil Sheehan of *The New York Times.* The report—exposing fateful decisions leading up to and in promoting the war—boomeranged between the Kennedy and Johnson administrations, indicting both and their enablers for the ongoing war. Not long after the first rush of *New York Times* reporting, other media giants also began investigating. On June 28, 1971, a *Time* magazine cover story appeared: "The Pentagon Papers: The Secret War."

It was as if America had been participating in a war game within a political game, as if the nation had gone through one big trapdoor and could never find a way out. American corporations were making napalm and weapons and profiting from the war. The makers of Coca-Cola were profiting handsomely by shipping all those soft drinks to Vietnam! It would have made a great if very crazy movie. Historians not yet born would have feasted upon it. "To see the conflict and our part in it as a tragedy without villains, war crimes without criminals, lies without liars," Ellsberg said, "espouses and promulgates a view of process, roles and motives that is not only grossly mistaken but which underwrites deceits that have served a succession of Presidents."

People throughout Black America, particularly Black soldiers, didn't really need the Pentagon Papers to fortify many of their feelings about the war, about fighting and returning home. Confederate flags still flew, and racial slurs abounded. There were, to be sure, wonderful white leaders, men who didn't seem to have a racist bone in their bodies. But the match that fueled racial anger could be so easily lit. Returning soldiers, back home from tours, had started complaining to job counselors and local politicians about job discrimination and mistreatment. There was less money for social services under the Nixon administration. The rightward shift of America was apparent. Some of the young Black vets were nodding out on sofas while marijuana joints were passed around in apartments in their riot-scarred neighborhoods. Hell, turn on some Marvin Gaye and lean back and listen to his plaintive pleas:

Picket lines and picket signs
Don't punish me with brutality
Talk to me
So you can see
Oh, what's going on

Gaye's album title may not have had a question mark at the end of it, but queries from every direction about the state of America demanded one: What's going on?

Berry Gordy's new idea on the heels of Marvin Gaye's album got him thinking about Vietnam as never before. He heard about some interviews that had been recorded with Black soldiers in Vietnam by the journalist Wallace Terry, and produced them as an album. Even Motown execs were surprised at how hard and real and angry the voices were. The 1972 album was titled *Guess Who's Coming Home: Black Fighting Men Recorded Live in Vietnam.* The title played off the 1967 Sidney Poitier movie, *Guess Who's Coming to Dinner.*

Motown's singers may have been Black, but the company was top-heavy with white executives in its marketing department, because Gordy sensed that radio stations and corporations would be more comfortable in dealing with whites than Blacks. The whites on the Motown staff began listening to Terry's recordings, and this opened their eyes wider. Motown's publicity note accompanying the album referred to the Black soldiers as Bloods: "And the Bloods rap about everything—racism in America, Lyndon Johnson and Richard Nixon, Black Power and Ho Chi Minh—and what they plan to do when they 'get back to the world.' In this recording you will discover a war within a war, a double battleground. Whites against Blacks. Racial slurs. Cross burnings. Confederate flags. Knifings. Fraggings. The humor, intensity and anguish in the Bloods rap will make you laugh, it may make you angry, and it may make you cry as you share their world at war." These liner notes were written by Julian Bond, a star of the SCLC and an antiwar activist. "This album is real," Bond wrote. "Every sweat. Every swear. Every plea. Every promise. It may make you angry. It may frighten you. It may make you cry. Black soldiers, trained in the violent arts of guerilla warfare as no Blacks before, are coming home, determined to bring the war with them if America doesn't change her racist ways and give them the democracy they were sent to defend."

Inasmuch as the recordings were made under very challenging conditions—even subterfuge—it seems a small miracle they survived. The front cover of the finished album is dominated by the photo of a helmeted Black soldier sitting in grass and smoking a cigarette. He looks outward, as if into the abyss. The album itself resembles a long rap session, a gabfest of young Black soldiers spilling their guts. A lot of the recordings were done in and around Da Nang. The first sounds one hears from the album are the rat-tat-tat of machine-gun fire; then what sound like grenade explosions in the background. Audio vérité? The voices and commentary start to rush together. It is all so feverish. The album lasts nearly sixty minutes, like some kind of never-before-heard audio documentary.

"I woke up over here, man . . . in bad muthfuckin' 'Nam . . . We've seen things that make you wanna freak . . . They're ready to start another war."

"We should clean up our own home. Here is the black man fighting the yellow man for the white man."

"What do I think about the Black Panthers? Well, I'm gonna join them soon as I get home."

Sometimes there is nervous laughter. There's often war noise in the background.

It continues:

"We got put in a brig. And what they did when they caught a brother with the Afro? They just took him down to the brig and cut all his hair off and [threw] him in jail. And here it is, all these BS motherfuckers walking around here looking like goddamn girls, and we can't have hair motherfucking three inches long."

"Do you think the Black man belong over here?" a soldier asks rhetorically. "Well, for one reason, I think he do. The Black man has to prove himself equal in every field . . . He got to be able to prove himself that he can do what the white man can do . . . We got a bigger wall back home . . . But, you know, you got to sacrifice to get anything. Yeah."

"Either they say, Hell no, we won't go, or, Yeah, I've got to go and I'm here, but I'm not going to take no licks on me. I'm not going to come twelve thousand miles from home to be shit on by some girl in the club who's been hanging around with a bunch of Southerners. She doesn't know me and I don't know her, but she calls me a nigger like somebody taught her . . . because they are the ones who represent a new train of thought."

"I think we need the Black Panthers as an equalizer . . . It would give white people something to fear. They had the KKK put fear into us."

Sometimes it sounds as if Godfrey Cambridge and Richard Pryor and Flip Wilson—three rising 1960s Black comedians back in America—had taken over a hut in the jungles of Vietnam.

"We need more Black Marine officers. Not no Negroes, but some real Black brothers!"

"I used to sit in the mess hall and just rap and . . . everybody heard me, you know? Next thing I know, this man is talking treason. That's what he said to me. Why should I have to go to jail?"

There is no admission on the recordings of the presence of alcohol or drugs during the taping sessions. But the military admitted, to their frustration, that the use of drugs in the war zone was growing, and that they were unable to stem it.

"This is between integration and having the same privileges just like the master."

"Why should I fight . . . for prejudice in America?"

"I'm doing what my grandfather couldn't do. They got a riot, I'm gonna get involved. If I get killed, fuck it."

"The day after Martin Luther King, Jr., was killed, Confederate flags were flying here."

—

Berry Gordy and his publicity team were no longer going to shy away from the revolution. They would still produce their sugary hits with Diana Ross—gone solo now—and Stevie Wonder and the Four Tops and all the other acts under their tent. But they wanted the world to know they were dealing, in their own way, with reality. Motown issued a statement:

> T. S. Eliot once said that the world cannot stand too much reality. We think that the world cannot stand much more FANTASY. Our youth are opting for reality. They seem better able to handle the pain of it than many of their elders. They are agreeing that you need to know where you are and who you are in order to know where you're going and what you can become. Motown is proud to communicate this message of humane profundity. That is why we put Black poets to music, off the printed page, and let them join our singers who are poets also—only in their own tradition, not in someone else's.

Well, no one, after listening to Motown and Wallace Terry's compendium of voices, would be prepared to call the Black soldiers of Vietnam anyone's poets. But they had voiced their feelings in raw language, albeit in a subversive and anonymous manner.

Would such an unprecedented album gain any traction? Not much, although it wasn't for lack of effort. On November 4, 1972, Terry made an appearance on *Soul Train.* The program, hosted by Don Cornelius and featuring top Black recording stars of the day, had been on air just over a year. Authors were certainly not routine guests. But Cornelius felt beholden to Motown, whose bevy of stars kept his show a must-watch on Saturday afternoons throughout Black communities. Terry stood with Don Cornelius, who was holding a copy of the just-released Vietnam album. Both author and host sported huge Afros. It was difficult to get the audience's undivided attention, given the backdrop and their eagerness to see that week's guest performers, but Cornelius tried, urging the sweating dancers to buy the album.

There were so many rumors swirling: That the war was about to end. That Nixon's national security adviser, Henry Kissinger, was off engaging in secret behind-the-scenes peace talks with the North Vietnamese. But President Nixon had been in office for years now—and the war was still going on, and still with American-led raids in-country.

A soldier talking to Wallace Terry in one of those interviews said, "The brothers are starting to talk to other brothers back home about what is really going on over here."

"America," another soldier said to Terry, "is doing a lot for Coca-Cola in Vietnam."

The rawer and more incendiary comments from the soldiers did not end up in the May 26, 1967, *Time* magazine cover story, "The Negro in Vietnam." Terry had hoarded a cache of notebooks from his Vietnam interviews and began telling friends he thought *Time* too hawkish in its coverage of much of the war. Finally, he decided he wanted to do what so many war correspondents aimed to do: write a book about the war they had covered. And because no one was writing about Blacks in the Vietnam War, he'd write that book. Another Nieman fellow at Harvard, Larry L. King—who had gone on to co-write the book for *The Best Little Whorehouse in Texas*—put Terry in touch with literary agents in New York City. Terry donned a suit and tie and made the rounds to various agencies, accompanied by Janice. "Everyone said they were not interested in a book about Black men who had weapons and could go out in the street and kill someone," Janice Terry recalls. The rejections surprised them, especially since white writers—both novelists and nonfiction writers—were getting contracts to write books about Vietnam. Wallace Terry just knew he had the makings of an interesting book about what went on with Black soldiering. "It was a traumatic experience," he recalled. "To be eighteen or nineteen, to be in the war, to get the news of King's death, then to watch your brothers in arms raise Confederate flags and burn crosses—it was a devastating experience for any human being." Not only months but years passed, as Wallace Terry's dream of getting someone to publish his book faded. He even went back to some publishers he had contacted earlier—"hoping the people I talked to the first time had left."

Just like the newspaper world, American book publishing was not a place where Black authors were easily welcomed. Editors were overwhelmingly white. And they were conditioned to publish only those Black authors who were extraordinarily gifted and already held in high praise by mainstream white society—James Baldwin, Ralph Ellison, Richard Wright, Toni Morrison. Blanche and Alfred Knopf had been outliers in this arena, having proudly published Black writers during the halcyon days of the Harlem Renaissance.

While Wallace Terry was shopping his book, and the years were rolling by, a trio of white writers had gotten contracts and published their books about Vietnam, both fiction and nonfiction. Frances Fitzgerald's *Fire in the Lake* came out in 1972; Philip Caputo's *A Rumor of War* in 1977; and Tim O'Brien's *Going After Cacciato* in 1978. Terry grew despondent. His wife implored him not to give up.

Through a series of starts and stops, Terry finally met Erroll McDonald, an editor at Random House, an Ivy Leaguer who was Black. Terry showed him his six-hundred-page nonfiction book. Something about it wasn't working for McDonald. He suggested a radical idea: that Terry ditch the narrative approach, take the most powerful voices, and turn the book into an oral history. Ever since Studs Terkel's 1970 book, *Hard Times: An Oral History of the Great Depression,* had been published, the term "oral history" had become more and more familiar to the reading public. "They were looking for a market," Terry recalled about the new idea for his book. "I couldn't say no to Random House. They're like E. F. Hutton: When they talk, you listen." There was something else. As 1982 came into view, there was talk of a Vietnam Memorial. Slowly, a nation seemed ready to at least start grappling with the lies and fallacies and myths of the war. Wallace Terry signed his book contract. He went off and culled all of his interviews down to twenty Black soldiers who were in Vietnam. His book, *Bloods: Black Veterans of the Vietnam War: An Oral History,* was published in 1984. The reviews were wonderful. Terry went around the country on a book tour, talking about the war. Colleges and universities kept asking him to come visit. By the 1980s, college students were a little more than a decade removed from Vietnam, but they kept hearing references to it, and their curiosity about the war was strong. Sometimes conversations ended awkwardly. "I lost 22 close friends in Vietnam," Wallace Terry would tell people, as if it would somehow, for a moment at least, bring a bit of them back to life.

More voices captured by Terry:

"Some of us . . . educated as we may be . . . came over here to fight and set an example for what the Negro was qualified to do . . . I consider myself a professional. I am a professional killer. No, I am a professional Marine. I am a professional. I love the children. That's my duty."

"We didn't ask to come over to America. No motherfucking way . . ."

"Wow. The Confederate flag. As a matter of fact, I think it ought to be some damn lawyer to fucking [come] outlaw them. Goddamn flags, man. Fucking Confederacy is gone, man. You know what the Confederacy did, man? He tried to rise up and fuck up the whole country, man."

The voices keep churning, veering from the insightful to, at times, the rather bizarre. They are Black young men—mere boys to some—who have been at war, who came out of ghettos back home, who are constantly wondering what they will have to go back to; who have gotten letters about dads disappearing, about factories either hiring or not hiring.

Another soldier ponders leaving Vietnam and returning to America—"to go back and find out nothing has changed."

"We will use the backbone of this revolution," another soldier said about the war.

Terry, as narrator, interjecting his own commentary: "Perhaps some of the anger, some of the rhetoric will fade as the brothers return. What is clear is that they are worse off now than when they left . . . the big cities. I see them walking the streets, still wearing their army jackets with nowhere to go and nothing to do."

"Well," said one soldier, "if I come back to the States, he's [the white man] got something to deal with. When I get back, I ain't coming back playing."

Chapter Thirteen

Requiem for Art Gregg

Art Gregg entered the military during its heyday of segregation, served in the Korean War, then went to Vietnam and orchestrated logistics and the shipping of supplies during that war. The old soldier—now ninety-four years old "and still counting," he allows—is sitting at a diner in rural Virginia. He still drives his own car. He still rises early every morning. His story is about endurance, timing, and a reckoning in America.

Born in Florence County, South Carolina, in 1928, young Art Gregg was cocooned from racial mistreatment because of his parents, who shielded him on their large farm. Nothing was more important to his parents than education. But when Art came of age to attend high school, there was a problem: the county's Black high school was ten miles away. It would be a daunting daily trek to the school and back, so the family came up with a plan: they'd send Art out of state, to Virginia, where an older brother lived, who pledged to house him so he could attend a high school there within easy distance of his home. At Huntington High in Newport News, young Art was a model student. Teachers were fond of him, as were the parents of his

Art Gregg joined a segregated Army and eventually landed in Vietnam as a chief logistics officer. He became the first Black lieutenant general in the Army.

fellow students. He graduated in 1945. "In my senior year, we had quite a few classmates drafted into the Army," he says.

Friends and neighbors were always wondering what career path Gregg might choose. He wasn't interested in the Army at the time, but was intrigued by medical technology, the work that took place inside laboratories. One Newport News parent suggested he inquire about the Chicago College of Medical Technology. He applied and was accepted, so he moved to Chicago, and stayed with some relatives who lived in the city. The school offered a six-month course to qualify as a medical technician. To pay for his schooling, he worked evenings in a factory, packaging and shipping light bulbs. Upon his successful completion of the course, Gregg was happy to be offered a job as a lab technician at Michael Reese Hospital. He was now a young man on the move, living on Chicago's South Side, surrounded by many Blacks who were either in the middle class or aspiring to get there.

Among his duties as a hospital lab technician was responsibility for drawing blood samples off-site and bringing them back to the lab. Things were going well. He dreamed of someday opening his own medical clinic. And then, one day, he was summoned to meet with a hospital superior. "I was told I couldn't visit white patients," he says. "So I abruptly quit."

His Chicago relatives worried about him. He would not go hungry, but he had put himself in limbo, and they knew it. Gregg certainly did not relish being yet another young unemployed Black man in Chicago, so he suddenly became interested in the United States Army. A segregated Army could be cold, and even dehumanizing, but friends had given him decent reports about their experiences in the armed forces. And the Black soldiers he saw around Chicago impressed him.

He joined the Army in January 1946, landing at Camp Crowder in Missouri. "It was an all-Black experience," he says of his entrée into the segregated military. "The only white person was a Lieutenant Roberts, a West Point grad and a very fine leader." Gregg hoped his six-month certificate from the Chicago College of Medical Technology might garner him work in some aspect of medical operations after he completed basic training. He was shipped out to Germany, where the wreckage of World War II and the Nazi horrors seemed to be everywhere. He started reminding military officials of his medical technology degree. "But no hospitals in Germany," he says, "would accept me as a medical laboratory technician." He was assigned to a variety of military jobs over the next three years—policeman and unit supply sergeant among them. The latter job intrigued him. In that position, he knew that moving supplies actually kept the military humming, and he was good at it: deciphering paperwork and orders, keeping things moving. In 1946, he got a promotion to corporal.

His family members back in South Carolina looked forward to having Art return home after his first couple of years of military service. Maybe he'd find work in one of those Black hospitals that dotted the landscape around the country. But Gregg saw too many stories of racial terror in the newspapers. He didn't see much opportunity back in America. And when President Truman desegregated the military in 1948, he felt optimistic that this would be a way to become a full American. He applied for Officer Candidate School and was accepted.

Art Gregg arrived in Kansas and reported directly to Fort Riley. He counted about a hundred cadets in his officer class, three other Blacks among them. "You had to demonstrate leadership and character. And there were the academics. But the academics were not that tough to me," he says of the course. Only two of the Blacks in his class graduated, Gregg one of them. He received his military commission, and the next stop was Fort Lee, Virginia, where he took the Quartermaster Basic Officer Course. Truman might have desegregated the military, but it didn't seem that way to Art Gregg at his new posting. He wasn't permitted into the officer's club. "Things were still segregated," he says.

In 1950, on the suggestion of a friend, Art Gregg went to Philadelphia to meet a young lady by the name of Charlene, who worked in public health. There were sparks, and they married that fall. "She was the best thing that happened to me in my life," he says. Charlene came to take easily to the gyrations and unpredictability of military life.

In 1953, Gregg found himself in the Korean War. He was assigned to the 443rd Quartermaster Depot. There were different units from different countries among the allied forces in Korea. "I supported those who charged the hills," he says, referring to equipment and machinery that he was tasked with ordering. He also worked in communications, giving briefings to soldiers about current world events. Newspapers and magazines were shipped in from Stateside; he devoured them, and also listened to a lot of radio. There were, as well, American college professors in Korea on military assignment who could teach courses, and Gregg availed himself of some of those courses. Even though most of the fighting in Korea had ended by the time he arrived, it was still a military operation. "We were still on high alert," Gregg says.

Working in the supply-and-services field, he found a rhythm to moving paperwork. He spent months ordering tents and clothing and setting up laundry facilities for the soldiers. He trekked through the mud—his .45 pistol strapped to his waist—doing what he could to make life tolerable for the troops, one of those who made the massive machinery of war run. He made sure parts were ordered quickly when things broke down, and there were schools and churches to help rebuild. It delighted him when loads of goods and materials arrived, the result of meticulous paperwork and foresight on his part. On his last day in Korea, as he was bidding farewell to friends, a French soldier walked up to First Lieutenant Art Gregg. America had not yet fully engaged in Vietnam; it wasn't in the American headlines yet. But "he said, 'I'll see you in Vietnam.'" Gregg was bewildered; he couldn't imagine what the French soldier meant.

Based in Washington with a desk job at the Pentagon, he heard all the rising anti–Vietnam War talk and saw the newsreel footage of the demonstrations. The increasing public outcry about the war meant nothing to him: "A soldier follows orders." At the beginning of 1966—by now he had acquired a college degree—his own orders arrived to go to Vietnam. His task there was the ordering and monitoring of supplies—"to get everything to the soldiers in order for them to fight the enemy," as he put it. He realized it was going to be a huge and very important job, equivalent to a corporate vice-president's position in the civilian world, except that Blacks weren't getting corporate vice-president jobs in 1960s America. "I knew my chances of advancement were better in the Army than out in the civilian world," he says.

When Art Gregg's 1966 deployment orders were being written up for Vietnam, they coincided with the Fulbright hearings taking place on Capitol Hill. The two events had nothing to do with each other, except, in a certain sense, they had everything to do with each other.

After his undergraduate studies in Arkansas, J. William Fulbright took an advanced degree at Oxford, in England. The world of English manners entranced him; he became an Anglophile. President Woodrow Wilson, a segregationist and one of Fulbright's political heroes, had also been an Anglophile. Fulbright took easily to politics and arrived in the U.S. Senate in 1945. The integration of the American military in 1948 unnerved Fulbright so much that in 1950 he cosponsored an amendment to give white soldiers the choice of serving, or not serving, in an integrated unit. The amendment failed. Two years later, Alaska applied for statehood. Fulbright blocked the legislation because he believed Alaska's representatives would become supporters of civil rights legislation. (Alaska did not achieve statehood until 1959.) In 1954, following the Supreme Court's *Brown v. Board of Education* desegregation decision, Southern senators began plotting to undermine it. Two years later, most Southern senators signed on to their so-called Southern Manifesto, a document in which they vowed to do everything they could to stop school integration. Fulbright's level of antipathy toward civil rights legislation continued apace: he opposed both the 1964 Civil Rights Act and the 1965 Voting Rights Act. The Black community of America considered him an enemy.

Fulbright, like his friend LBJ, rode the twin stallions of race and war with a certain kind of cockiness: He saw nothing wrong with Jim Crow laws, and he wanted to halt the drive of communism into South Vietnam by the North Vietnamese. But Fulbright found it difficult to lasso either stallion—race or war. The senator had risen to become chairman of the Senate Foreign Relations Committee. When he spoke, people on Capitol Hill listened. But a sense of foreboding about Vietnam began to appear, a realization that quicksand was gathering at the feet of so many in Washington. Reporters had been on the ground in Vietnam. Their eyes were not fooling them.

Fulbright received a letter from a reporter who was covering Vietnam in 1966: "The war is not going well," the reporter wrote to the senator. "The situation is worse than reported in the press and worse, I believe, than indicated in intelligence reports." The reporter relayed a chat he had had with a military officer who had told him: "If there is a God, and he is very kind to us, and given a million men, and five years, and a miracle in making the South Vietnamese like us, we stand an outside chance—of a stalemate." This was very worrisome to

Fulbright, inasmuch as he had been one of the cosponsors of the Gulf of Tonkin Resolution two years earlier, which jump-started the war.

Fulbright called for a series of hearings—to be televised—and invited several members of Johnson's war cabinet to testify. Those hearings began on the morning of February 4, the first of five days of testimonies. Among those who testified were former Ambassador George Kennan, Secretary of State Dean Rusk, and General Maxwell Taylor. Kennan held little back: "The first point I would like to make is that if we were not already involved as we are today in Vietnam, I would know of no reason why we should wish to become so involved, and I could think of several reasons why we would wish not to." Kennan said he did not want America zooming around the world like "an elephant frightened by a mouse." He cited John Quincy Adams and quoted him as having believed that America should "go not abroad in search of monsters to destroy." Fulbright told Kennan he was beginning to wonder if, even "with

Arkansas Senator J. William Fulbright eventually turned against the war, drawing the wrath of President Johnson, who began referring to him as "Senator Halfbright."

the best of wills," America could win in the end. "This is correct," Kennan said, "and I have fear that our thinking about this whole problem is still affected by some sort of illusions about invincibility on our part." Fulbright, the once-friendly hawkish ally to LBJ, now gave the impression of being a dovish inquisitor at the hearings. As a result, LBJ started calling him "Senator Halfbright." Years later, Fulbright, in speaking to an interviewer regarding the 1960s, LBJ, and the fog of all those wartime lies, said, "I was not only naïve, I was ignorant. You see, there was a time in my career, very late, when I felt governments told you the truth, too."

The Fulbright Hearings may not have packed the TV punch of the Senate's Army-McCarthy hearings in 1954, but they slowly began to have an effect. A month after the hearings, one poll showed that confidence in LBJ's stewardship of the war had declined from 63 percent to 49 percent. LBJ was hardly amused.

On June 8, 1966, Vice-President Hubert Humphrey addressed West Point's graduating seniors. Humphrey, in private, was concerned that the Johnson administration was reaching a point of no return in Vietnam, but in public he hewed to the administration's course. He told the graduates:

> We face a situation of external aggression and subversion against a postcolonial nation that has never had the breathing space to develop its policies or its economy. In South Vietnam, both defense and development—the war against the aggressor and the war against despair—are fused as never before. Vietnam challenges our military courage, our political ingenuity, and our ability to persevere. If we can succeed there—if we can help sustain an independent South Vietnam, free to determine its own future, then the prospects for free men throughout Asia will be bright indeed. We know this. Our friends and allies know it. And our adversaries know it. That is why one small country looms so large today on everyone's map of Asia.

One of the chilling deductions in the Pentagon Papers was that the United States, owing to its power, money, and worldwide clout, had helped *create* the Vietnam War.

There were 579 graduates in the West Point graduating class of 1966. Thirty of them would be killed in Vietnam, and more than a hundred of them would be wounded there.

Art Gregg's home when he arrived in Vietnam—and for half of the following year—was Cam Ranh Bay, a peninsula and deepwater port located on the central coast of South Vietnam. A rustic fishing village that the can-do American military had turned into a supply-entry station, it lay a little less than two hundred miles from Saigon. Piers were shipped in all the way from America. All branches of the military used the base for sea arrivals, the launching of air sorties (a ten-thousand-foot runway was built), and the planning of tactical operations. Gregg and his staff were tasked with ordering supplies and servicing everything soldiers in Vietnam needed. The American war machine for twelve months ran through Cam Ranh and Art Gregg. American companies received contracts from the Army to come to Vietnam and build equivalent machinery to aid in the production of what they produced in America—milk, dairy products, many foods. It was war on the fly, and the quicksand only deepened and deepened. Art Gregg needed some of those modern fancy computers, because the Army was modernizing, so he ordered lots and lots of them. It wasn't always easy to get them up and running, but the Army managed.

Not every soldier who landed in Vietnam engaged in battle. Not every soldier got lathered in the blood of a fellow soldier or an enemy soldier during a battle or a mine explosion. Those who worked in supply and service jobs were based at huge military bases such as Long Binh and Cam Ranh. No one complained about being at Cam Ranh. The place was huge, and the amenities were plentiful. Combat soldiers, however, had a habit of looking down upon those who held supply jobs. Second Lieutenant Vincent Okamoto, a combat soldier, put it this way: "These are the dudes that . . . never go out beyond the barbed wire of base camp. They sleep in a bed, with sheets. They have showers every day. They drink cold beer at night. Their only danger is every once in a while, they might be . . . hit with rockets or mortars. They're not humping the boonies every day in hundred degree weather, carrying a sixty-pound pack, thinking that if you don't get shot, you may die from heatstroke."

Those working in the rear were sometimes referred to as REMs—Rear Echelon Motherfuckers. The slander didn't bother Gregg. It was war, "and we ordered the weapons necessary to take the enemy down," he says. There was joy in getting C-rations, mail, notebooks to write on, uniforms—all the things and more that Gregg and company had to keep coming. Packages and supplies were sent out to units.

It didn't take Art Gregg long at all to recognize the large numbers of Black soldiers. He had been in Germany after World War II and Korea after that country's war, and in neither place had he seen such a large volume of Black faces. Gregg became alarmed by the sizable population of Black soldiers confined to the Long Binh Jail. "Historically, our criminal-justice system comes down hardest on African Americans. And the Army was no exception."

Lieutenant Colonel Art Gregg did not question the mission in Vietnam. But just a year before Gregg arrived in Vietnam, another lieutenant colonel, John Paul Vann, wrote a memo briefly analyzing what he thought the situation to be: "A popular political base for the Government of South Vietnam does not now exist . . . The existing government is oriented toward the exploitation of the rural and lower class urban populations. It is, in fact, a continuation of the French colonial system with the upper class (Catholic) Vietnamese replacing the French . . . The dissatisfaction of the agrarian population is expressed largely through alliance with the [National Liberation Front]." (Vann believed the war was unwinnable. The Army grew tired of his criticism. He had retired in 1963, but returned in 1966, having gotten a civilian development job. He died in Vietnam in a helicopter crash in 1972.)

The year that Gregg spent in Vietnam—from April 1966 to April 1967—was a year of racially ignited arrests and racial uprisings in Chicago; Waukegan, Illinois; Dayton, Ohio; San Francisco; and Benton Harbor, Michigan. Not all made national news, though many did. Gregg wrote to his wife, Charlene, and both worried about the safety of their relatives while walking the streets of America. It became difficult, while peering at TV screens, to differentiate war-zone images of Vietnam from the war zone–like images of America's inner cities.

Lieutenant Colonel Gregg and his battalion's troops—those Rear Echelon Motherfuckers—distinguished themselves enough in Vietnam to be awarded the Meritorious Unit Citation. Gregg personally was awarded the Legion of Merit as battalion commander. When he returned from Vietnam, he was mostly immune from the curse words and spittle that landed in the ears and faces of other soldiers in uniform, because he was assigned to the Army War College in Pennsylvania. Far enough away from the hippies and beatniks and Black radicals still marching around the nation's capital.

It took smarts to be at the forefront of logistics in the military, and the Army recognized such talent in Art Gregg. After his Vietnam assignment, other postings and promotions continued to mount. He became commander of the Nahbollenbach Army Depot in Germany in 1969; in 1971, he was at the Office of the Deputy Chief of Staff for Logistics, Department of the Army, in Washington. Another appointment saw him as director of troop support, supervising all manner of support needed by servicemen and servicewomen. In 1972, he received his first star and became a brigadier general. Then he was sent back to Germany as commander of the European Exchange System. In 1975, he was appointed deputy chief of staff for logistics, Headquarters, United States Army Europe and Seventh Army. Then came a promotion to major general—his second star—in 1976. In 1977, President Jimmy Carter appointed Gregg director for logistics, Office of the Joint Chiefs of Staff. He was responsible for coordinating logistics between all branches of the military. That same year, Gregg received his third star, becoming Lieutenant General Art Gregg, thereby making history as the nation's first Black three-star Army officer. He retired from the Army five years later. A tide of history lay behind him: the Black soldiers in the Civil War; in France during World War I; at San Juan Hill; the cold beaches at Normandy; the desolation he himself had seen in Korea; the body bags he had had to ship out of Cam Ranh.

The J. William Fulbrights and Robert E. Lees of America were never willing to respect the potential of Black soldiers. Fulbright spent his later years trying to convince people that his late-blooming anti–Vietnam War stance all but atoned for his dreadful record on civil rights. He did not find many believers. For his assault on the American government a century before the noise of Vietnam, General Robert E. Lee—the slaveholding West Point alum and leader of the Confederate Army—won acclaim throughout the South. His battle victories at Fredericksburg and Chancellorsville turned him into a kind of soldier-god. At Chancellorsville, Lee lost 13,460 of his men. The Union losses, however, were even more staggering: 17,304 dead. Lee couldn't quite imagine the contributions the Black soldier would come to make. Lincoln had ordered their enlistment; for freedom, they came in droves. In January 1865, Union troops, with Black troops among them, had surrounded North Carolina's Fort Fisher, a Confederate stronghold. Henry McNeal Turner, one of the Black troops, and a chaplain, was at the battle. "Indeed, the white troops told the rebels that if they did not surrender," Turner later recalled, "they would let the negroes loose on them."

The South had fallen, had lost, under the aegis of General Lee, and the reality of it deeply stung Southerners. But in due course, a resurrection began on Lee's behalf. There were seasons of hagiography: Laudatory books were written, portraying him as a heroic figure of the Lost Cause. Military installations, schools, and roads were named after him. His treason against the U.S. Constitution was ignored, and his advocacy of white supremacy dismissed. Behind the genteel myth of the South lay a brutishness rarely mentioned in school textbooks. The racial blood kept spilling across decades.

Art Gregg doesn't minimize Robert E. Lee's West Point education, but he laments that Lee joined the Confederacy and led a Southern insurrection against his nation.

The old soldier, many years removed from Vietnam, was sitting in the living room of his home in rural Virginia in 2020. There was something terrible looping on the television news. He leaned in to watch. The footage showed a policeman in Minneapolis, Minnesota, on the screen. A small crowd had gathered around him. It was made clear in the telecast that the event had actually happened on May 25, but only now was a video of it being released. In the video, the policeman was kneeling on someone, on the upper part of the man's back, near the neck area. And then came the reports that the man who had been on the ground, the unarmed Black man mostly shielded by the long leg of the white policeman—the unarmed Black man who had been crying out, "I can't breathe"—had died. The old soldier became incensed while watching this footage. And even more incensed when the whole sordid saga was written about in deeper detail: George Floyd, the man who had been facedown on the ground, had been arrested for purportedly trying to pass off a fake twenty-dollar bill. The white policeman who had crushed his spine and neck with the weight of his body had, in the immediate aftermath, filed misleading police reports, as did fellow officers who had been on the scene that day. The video had been taped by a young Black Minnesotan who refused to leave the scene. Darnella Frazier stared down the police officers in the area. "Thank goodness the young lady recorded it all," Art Gregg said.

Policing and soldiering had always had a distinct connection in the imposition of law and order throughout Black communities in America. Just as they had done after Korea, many of the soldiers in Vietnam—particularly white soldiers and officers—returned to America and took jobs in police departments. Those departments were already overwhelmingly white. (Federal decrees emanating from the Department of Justice caused some of the departments to integrate faster than others.) Police departments—during the times of these modern wars—routinely gave extra civil-service points to military veterans, making their entrée into a particular force easier. Derek Chauvin—tried, convicted, and sentenced to a long prison term for the killing of George Floyd—had served in the United States Army Reserve for eight years, and part of that time was spent as a military policeman.

The public killing of George Floyd shocked white America and re-energized Black America. It unleashed massive multiracial demonstrations, not just in America but around the world. The deaths of other Blacks—Sandra Bland in 2015 while in Texas police custody, the suspicious cause announced as suicide; Philando Castile shot by police in his car in Minnesota in 2016; Breonna Taylor shot by police in her Louisville, Kentucky, home in 2020—evoked memories of the past Black victims of police terror. For the world to see, the bones of slavery and Jim Crow were still rattling in the sweet land of liberty. The swearing-in of a Black president in 2008 had not vanquished the country's deep and painful history. The Floyd murder was so wrenching that institutions vowed to act against the slumber of their own inability to address racism. The American military actually began thinking of ways to deal with those Confederate statues that dotted the land.

Military bases had been named for "heroes" of the Confederate Army, the very Confederate Army that had fought across rivers and swamps with raised swords to keep Blacks chained and living in terror. Confederate symbols were not only in town squares, they were on college campuses, with nary a voice raised. All of that changed, however, in the aftermath of what happened on June 17, 2015, in Charleston, South Carolina, when Dylann Roof sauntered into the Emanuel African Methodist Episcopal Church. It was a Black church, though welcoming to anyone. A Bible-study class was in session. Some looked up and spotted Roof, a young white man, and offered smiles and then a seat. Roof nodded along as scriptures were read. Then, suddenly, he pulled out a Glock handgun and began shooting. He was a Confederate-loving white supremacist. The death total came to nine. Roof later received a federal death sentence. It was this murderous rampage that jump-started the military's movement against the Confederate symbols and statues.

Six years later, in 2021—with the murder of George Floyd ringing in its ears—the House of Representatives voted to have the Army do away with "names, symbols, displays, monuments and paraphernalia" associated with the Confederacy. It also created a Naming Commission, whose aim was to rename nine military installations that had been named for Confederates. In doing so, the American military finally set about distancing itself from the Confederacy and those who had attained enduring celebrity around their treasonous and criminal behavior, which for so long had been downplayed in books, plays, and motion pictures. The Naming Commission announced early on that it would pay particular attention to women and minorities who had served and been overlooked. The nominations came from all branches. More than thirty thousand submissions were received. Secretary of Defense Lloyd Austin gave the final approval of the nine names ultimately chosen.

Art Gregg was sitting in his Virginia home when the phone rang. It was Donald McEachin, U.S. representative from Virginia. He was calling to say that Fort Robert E. Lee—the very fort whose officers' club Gregg wasn't permitted to enter when he first became an officer—was being renamed Fort Gregg-Adams, in honor of both Gregg and Lieutenant Colonel Charity Adams. During World War II, Adams, who died in 2002, had headed a battalion of Black women in Europe responsible for mail distribution. By the end of the war, she was the highest-ranking Black woman in the armed forces. The renaming ceremony took place at the fort on April 27, 2023. When it concluded, the old soldier proudly walked into the officers' club and took a seat. He cut a suave figure as flashbulbs popped. He became the only living person in Army history to have a fort named after him. "This shows the Army has come a long way," he later said.

—

Those who asked Art Gregg to pinpoint the highlight of his long military career wondered: Was it during his stints at the Pentagon? Or maybe in Germany, with all its challenges? Or possibly in exotic Japan? He confided it was actually Cam Ranh Bay in Vietnam. "We built a great logistics base and developed close relationships," he said. "I still get calls from some of my people from that battalion. It was a great experience for me, I believe we performed extremely well, and I always look back on those days as the high point of my career."

Chapter Fourteen

Mr. Jellybean, in Twilight

It wasn't supposed to end this way for Lyndon Baines Johnson. He was the president whom so many Blacks had spoken of in Lincolnesque terms. He tried to finish what Lincoln had started, and often said as much. He had utilized his political genius to get three landmark civil rights bills passed, in 1964, 1965, 1968—integration, voting, housing. He had placed a Black in a cabinet position for the first time ever. He integrated the United States Supreme Court. So much good had been swirling. But, also, more than a few uncomfortable surprises. On January 18, 1968, Eartha Kitt strode into the White House, for what was billed as the 1968 Women Doers Luncheon. Ladybird was hosting. Kitt—a world-renowned chanteuse—was among the guests. She had previously testified before Congress about the need to address issues of juvenile justice. Among the groups represented were the Association of Colored Women's Club and the League of Women Voters. Polite conversation and salutations for those helping the cause of democracy were expected, but then, unprompted, Kitt spoke up, looking directly at Ladybird: "Boys I know across the nation feel it doesn't pay to be a good guy. They figure with a record they don't have to go to Vietnam." (By

LBJ meets with Martin Luther King, Jr., and other civil rights leaders. There was growing concern that funding for the Vietnam War was undercutting antipoverty programs across the nation.

"record" she meant a jail record. She obviously didn't know about Project 100,000.) There was some uncomfortable whispering. Kitt continued: "You send the best of this country off to be shot and maimed. They rebel in the streets. They will take pot, and they will get high. They don't want to go to school, 'cause they're going to be snatched off from their mothers to be shot in Vietnam. No wonder the kids rebel and take pot—and Mrs. Johnson, in case you don't understand the lingo, that's marijuana." The fallout from Kitt's outspokenness was immediate. The *New York Times* headline: "Eartha Kitt Denounces War Policy to Mrs. Johnson." Kitt's musical engagements started to dry up; she claimed the White House had been responsible for her blacklisting. The CIA began keeping a dossier on her.

But here was LBJ now, out of the White House, riding around on his three-hundred-acre Texas ranch, brooding about his enemies, how that damnable war had sullied what should have been his Lincolnesque legacy. There should have been medals, humanitarian awards. And honorary degrees from those elitist Ivy League schools on the East Coast—those very schools where the Kennedy holdovers and Ivy League grads who worked for him kept saying the war could be won. They had attended those schools because their families had deep pockets, unlike Johnson's own family. At least, when Lincoln's generals told him the Civil War was winnable, they knew what they were talking about. Maybe there would have been banquets and ceremonial dinners—if his political genius had stopped at the civil rights issue. That would have gotten his picture placed on mantelpieces in a hell of a lot of homes in the inner cities, just like so many Blacks had started to put up that picture of Jack, Bobby, and Martin. But he was the man who had steered the nation deeper and deeper into war. The glow of his civil rights accomplishments had dimmed. With Vietnam, he might as well have been swimming in blood. The tragedy of war kept tearing away at the galvanizing story of racial progress, of racial freedoms. And, of course, the bills he signed didn't make the racial problems vanish. Whites did not come easily to the notion of equality. The racial turbulence at home was as constant a media story as the war in Southeast Asia. So he said the hell with Washington and went home to Texas. Ladybird still loved him. Mary Davis, his Black cook, still loved him. At least, he imagined she did. His daughters still loved him.

Before he left the White House, Lyndon Johnson agreed to allow Walter Cronkite to come down to Texas and interview him. Johnson loathed the press, but Cronkite was Cronkite, respected far and wide. It was a three-part interview that aired on CBS. During the interviews, Cronkite asked questions about the Kennedy assassination, and Johnson expressed doubts about whether Lee Harvey Oswald had been the sole operative. When the program aired, Johnson was not happy; he felt that CBS had allowed Cronkite to rephrase some of the questions without alerting him. "Cronkite came down here all sweetness and light, telling me how he'd love to teach journalism at Texas someday, then he does this to me," Johnson would later say about the telecast.

He was only sixty years old, but men in his family had died young. Many of them had suffered heart problems. "I'm going to enjoy the time I've got left," Johnson said. He rode a horse around the ranch, looking over his cattle, yelling at cattlemen. Sometimes he told Ladybird to pack up and they were off to Mexico, where rich friends delighted in hosting him. There were fiestas, memories of his youth, when he had crossed the border for fun and parties. He didn't bother with the Hollywood crowd, and they didn't bother with him. There was the war, which anyone could see from the nightly news was still raging. The Republicans in Hollywood, for the most part, supported the war, but he wouldn't keep company with them. On the other hand, reporters wouldn't quite leave him alone. It was their job to plead for interviews, for time alone with the ex-president. They had so many questions. "I've served my time with that bunch and I give up on them," he said. "There's no objectivity left anymore. The new style is advocacy reporting—send some snotty-nosed reporter down here to act like a district attorney and ask me where I was on the night of the twenty-third. I'm always guilty unless I can prove otherwise. So the hell with it." Ladybird was happy on Christmas Eve, 1971, when he appeared dressed as Santa Claus—fake beard and all—riding around on a tractor, handing out toys to the children of ranch hands and other employees. On some Saturdays he was spotted in Austin, attending University of Texas football games. A lone Black kid was on the team now, the first time in school history. Julius Whittier broke the barrier, recruited to the school by Darrell Royal, the legendary coach. When Whittier arrived on the campus in 1969, freshmen were not allowed to play on the varsity, but he got enough playing time the following year to earn his varsity letter. When Whittier neared graduation, he was recruited to attend the University of Texas School of Public Affairs—by LBJ himself. Whittier also went on to get a law degree from the school. Call it the LBJ touch. The ex-president never lingered too long at the football games, though: The Vietnam protesters. They were everywhere.

Publishers—if not the public—have always clamored for the memoirs of former presidents. They are very much interested in behind-the-scenes details, any explanation of embarrassing scandals, blunt assessments of foreign leaders. The presidential memoir to emulate in modern times had always been Ulysses S. Grant's, published in 1885, not long after he died. Titled *Personal Memoirs of U.S. Grant,* the book was published in two volumes and drew raves for its style, content, and candor. Lyndon Johnson wanted to go the two-volume route, too: one volume covering the Great Society, and the second volume covering Vietnam. But his publishers nixed the idea and pushed for a single volume. Johnson never had an affection for writers; he didn't read many books. Memos and notes were fine, because he could swallow them like pills and go into action one way or another. The Harvard and Yale and Princeton boys read books, plenty of books, and all they did—especially when it came to Blacks and civil rights—was slow down action with their pontificating. "I took 4 million people out of poverty," Johnson reminded people, and he'd let them know he didn't do it by reading any damn books; he did it by cajoling and arm twisting and threatening, by stampeding, just like men with cattle in Texas sometimes had to do. He had a couple of his former speechwriters come down to the ranch and help him with the book, for which he was paid a whopping million-dollar advance, money that, he let people know, would go toward the building of his presidential library. "I make no pretense of having written a complete and definitive history of my Presidency," Johnson warned, months before the book's publication.

American presidents, long bewitched by race, for the most part avoided that topic in their memoirs. (President Grant had proved the exception: he seemed to take comfort in writing bluntly about the Ku Klux Klan and white supremacy in his memoirs. Lincoln, of course, tantalized historians, who wondered what might have been.) Being held hostage by those potent electoral votes across Southern states, modern presidents saw no upside in assailing white voters for their opposition to real freedom for Black Americans. Southern white voters have been hostile to civil rights in modern elections, throwing their electoral votes to conservative white candidates in national elections. Johnson's book, *The Vantage Point: Perspectives of the Presidency, 1963–1969,* arrived on bookstore shelves in 1971. His entire presidency had existed during the Vietnam War, as had the struggle for Black freedom. But that struggle came to take second place in the Johnson narrative. The book was dutiful, but seemed to have been pieced together in haste. Books about wars require distance; books about war *and* race require not only distance but a sense of American history. *The New York Times* assigned their former Vietnam correspondent David Halberstam—who had turned to writing books himself—to review *The Vantage Point.* Halberstam's assessment of the six hundred–plus pages would not have pleased LBJ, if he even read the review. "But where Lyndon Johnson was filled with human juices, this book is almost totally devoid of them," Halberstam wrote. "It is all tidied up, antiseptic, ordered, very calm; there are no villains, no personal opinions on people, no judgments, there is no anger, precious little intimacy." Halberstan did allow that Johnson "as a study in political psychopathology . . . is probably without peer." A review in the *Texas Monthly,* a respected publication from Johnson's backyard, said Johnson's book set down everything "except the man himself." *The Atlantic* called the book "a guarded, self-serving wax museum of a memoir."

His book came out the same year the dedication ceremony was held for his library. It was a huge library, larger than any other presidential library, spread out on the campus of the University of Texas in Austin. "History, with the bark off," he crowed about its contents on the day of the dedication in 1971. At that ceremony—in the distance, kept far enough away—there were about two thousand protesters, yelling and banging on things, making noise, talking about the blood spilled in Vietnam.

Blacks were not going to vilify him; they wouldn't come close to doing such a thing. And that warmed him. But all the civil rights battles he had fought and won, had drilled into existence, had spent political capital on, were being talked about less and less. It was the war, always the war, overshadowing the Black freedom march, how he had had to battle the likes of George Wallace, the John Birchers, and Barry Goldwater; how he'd cussed people out on the phone when they told him integration was upsetting a certain way of life in America. And he'd reminded them of Birmingham and Selma—and then abruptly hung up the phone.

As the weeks and months in Texas piled up, it sometimes seemed LBJ was living in a self-imposed exile. Now and then, he'd get intelligence reports from the Nixon White House, a courtesy long provided to ex-presidents. For the most part he didn't trust the contents of the reports. He believed the Nixon folks were up in Washington trying to make him look bad because he hadn't been able to end the war. He rolled his eyes across some of the pages. Henry Kissinger, Nixon's national security adviser, was even nervy enough to show up once at the ranch in person to deliver some papers, talking in that Eastern intellectual manner that Johnson was even more suspicious of since he had departed Washington.

Some nights, he had problems sleeping. He'd march into his study and get to dialing up folks. He didn't like the criticism *The Vantage Point* had received, so he began making plans to write another book, about the battle he had waged to get Thurgood Marshall onto the Supreme Court.

But the war wouldn't go away. Johnson told aides that Jack Kennedy, in the beginning, should have had more advisers in Vietnam. They would have seen the cliffs ahead, he thought. "Another mistake," he felt, "was not instituting censorship—not to cover up mistakes, but to prevent the other side from knowing what we were going to do next. My god, you can't fight a war by watching it every night on television."

There were times on the ranch when Ladybird couldn't find him. She'd be peering out windows, and then she'd spot the big white Lincoln Continental that he loved to zoom around in—with the Secret Service agents always trailing him, because the assassinations had proved there were murderous lunatics upon the land.

He hated the crew-cut look favored by H. R. Haldeman and the Nixon White House, so the ex-president let his hair grow long in the back. He looked like an aging hippie. Ladybird just chuckled. Doctors put him on nitroglycerin pills for his heart ailments.

Johnson had started talking to anyone who'd listen about

bigotry—about Eastern bigotry and Southern bigotry, and how the worst kind of bigotry was Eastern bigotry. He thought that the Eastern bigots were backstabbers, that they'd say one thing and do another when it came to race. He often failed to mention, however, that the Southern bigots often backed up their positions with bloody violence. Southern bigots walked in the ether of the Lost Cause with shotguns and pipe bombs.

The vast, open landscape surrounding the Johnson Texas ranch was such an incentive to think, to ponder. Sometimes Mary, the Black cook, would try to cheer him, would holler out to him that she was making a pecan pie, a favorite dessert of his. But Ladybird would see him out there, in the fields, sitting atop his tractor, the tractor not moving, just idle, and she knew he was brooding again. "How is it possible that all these people could be so ungrateful to me after I had given them so much?" he wondered after leaving the White House. "Take the Negroes. I fought for them from the first day I came into office. I tried to make it possible for every child of every color to grow up in a nice house, to eat a solid breakfast, to attend a decent school, and to get a good and lasting job. Just a little thanks. Just a little appreciation. But look what I got instead. Riots . . . looting. Burning. Shooting."

The truth of the matter was that the white way of life in America had been well funded, and for generations. But Blacks needed funding for schools and neighborhoods and housing, and it was now being cut. The money was being marked for Vietnam, and this seemed a gaping insult to the Black veterans returning home from the war. They wanted to know what was going on. Johnson wanted to know the same thing, but he was asking from a much different angle. Therein lay part of the conundrum of Lyndon Johnson. What he had given Blacks should have long ago been rightfully theirs; what he had given Blacks had come on the heels of generations of Black blood and sacrifice. Blacks, year in and year out, had had to squeeze liberty and justice from America. Most Blacks did not live in nice houses; too many Black children were still impoverished; schools were still defiantly segregated; police and fire departments in many cities and small towns had only begrudgingly considered Blacks for employment, and promotions were difficult to achieve. America had been fighting equality longer than it had been fighting the Vietnam War. It took money to fight a war, and it took money and consistent determination to fight poverty and systemic racism. A new generation of Blacks had come of age since his Senate years, and then another generation arose after he reached the White House. "Johnson felt particularly uncomfortable with this new group of poorer blacks from the inner cities of the North," said James Farmer, the director of CORE. "They were not like the poor blacks . . . that he had contact with down in Texas. These were different. They were raucous people, they were belligerent folk. They did not see Lyndon Johnson as a friend."

Ladybird knew what the ex-president wanted to do when he would start grabbing for the jellybeans. He wanted to go over to the Stonewall Elementary School, not far from the ranch. They had a Head Start program, one of those ambitious and grand War on Poverty programs he had engineered into existence. It provided nutrition to impoverished children and got them on an early start with education, with reading and writing. When he showed up, the kids would squeal and tug at his pant legs and hug him, and it meant the world to him. He'd start handing out the jellybeans—to white kids, Black kids, Hispanic kids. The children were between the ages of three and five, which were beautiful ages: they were too young to have racist thoughts and ideologies embedded in their minds. "Mr. Jellybean!" they began calling out to him upon seeing him. And the big wide LBJ grin would spread across his face. Heading back to the waiting car, he'd nearly be weeping from the joy the visits gave him.

Many of the beneficiaries—and lions—of the civil rights movement were invited to his presidential library on December 9, 1972, to honor him, to assess the unmistakable achievements he had enacted on behalf of Black Americans and their civil rights. It was billed as a two-day symposium to discuss civil rights. Among those in attendance were Chief Justice Earl Warren, architect of the galvanizing *Brown v. Board of Education* desegregation ruling; Clarence

Mitchell, the longtime NAACP lobbyist; and Barbara Jordan, just elected to Congress as the first Black woman U.S. representative from Texas, and the first Black woman elected from the South since 1898, who had also been the only woman in her graduating law class at Boston University's law school, and had been helped enormously in her congressional win by LBJ's prowess. There was Hubert Humphrey, who'd made his reputation battling the segregationists and their agenda. And, among many others, Julian Bond, the charismatic young Georgia politician. They filled the big auditorium. LBJ mentioned some successes in the fields of fighting discrimination and poverty: "We are on our way," he said, and there was wide applause. But he then swerved into more sobering territory, all the work still to do, all the evidence of inequality that still lay across the land. He admitted he hadn't always "seen this plight" of Black pain in America. He let the gathering know—as if to indicate his bona fides—that he had first met Thurgood Marshall back when Marshall came to Texas to file a lawsuit against the University of Texas School of Law because they had denied admission to Heman Sweatt, based on his race. Marshall and Sweatt sued the school. They eventually won the lawsuit, forcing the school to integrate. Though mental stress caused Sweatt to drop out, *Sweatt v. Painter* became a groundbreaking victory. Johnson told the gathering that on the second floor of the library was the original document of Lincoln's Emancipation Proclamation. "A decade ago, in the year 1963, we observed the 100th anniversary of that proclamation," he said, mentioning a speech he had given at Gettysburg at that time, when he was vice-president. "Black Americans are voting now, where they were not voting at all 10 years ago." It was impossible not to link him with Lincoln, even if Lincoln won the Civil War and he had lost Vietnam. The American habit of not voting worried LBJ, and he mentioned that only a little more than half of all American voters had voted in the most recent national election. He wanted something akin to compulsory voting. "I'm kind of ashamed of myself that I had six years and couldn't do more than I did," he said, and this made those in attendance even more proud that they were there to acknowledge what he had done. "Moreover, and we cannot obscure this one fact, the black problem remains what it has always been: the simple problem of being Black in a White society." He went on: "While the races may stand side-by-side, Whites stand on history's mountain and Blacks stand in history's hollow." White Americans, he said, had been listening far too long to "the language of evasion." Everyday employers, the government, colleges and universities, and "the military," he allowed, must do more in the fight for equality. When his remarks drew to a close, he got a standing ovation. "We shall overcome," he said, using those three sacred words that had become so prominent in the civil rights movement.

In time, they would be coming for him, and he knew it—the scholars and historians and opinionated writers. They were lining up. What to make of him? He himself understood the problems that lay ahead in terms of his role in history. "I knew from the start," he had said in 1970, "that I was bound to be crucified either way I moved. If I left the woman I really loved—the Great Society—in order to get involved with that bitch of a war on the other side of the world, then I would lose everything at home. All my programs. All my hopes to feed the hungry and shelter the homeless. All my dreams to provide education and medical care to the browns and the blacks and the lame and the poor. But if I left that war and let the Communists take over South Vietnam, then I would be seen as a coward and my nation would be seen as an appeaser and we would both find it impossible to accomplish anything for anybody anywhere on the entire globe."

He always believed he would have accomplished more in the realm of civil rights were it not for his critics. "Yet everything I know about history told me," he said, "that if I got out of Vietnam and let Ho Chi Minh run through the streets of Saigon, then I'd be doing exactly what [Neville] Chamberlain did in World War II. I'd be giving a big fat reward to aggression." His Black-and-white army in Vietnam was still fighting, but his Black-and-white army in America had frayed.

—

He died six weeks after his well-received Texas address, the last public address of his life. In the Black churches of America, prayers went out to him and his family.

The multiracial assemblage of kids at the Stonewall School looked for Mr. Jellybean. Their teachers broke the news to them as gently as they could that Mr. Jellybean would not be returning.

Chapter Fifteen

A Mirage and an Endgame

For the Black soldiers serving in the Vietnam War, 1969 was their first year serving under a Republican president. There was much curiosity about the new commander-in-chief. Since gyrations in the presidency always had a profound effect upon Black lives—for better or worse—most Blacks, in the military or not, were eager to learn about President Nixon. Among his campaign promises had been a vow to get America out of Vietnam and end the war.

Like most American presidents, Richard Milhous Nixon had had very little interaction with Blacks in his lifetime. Growing up in the small town of Whittier, California, did not enlarge his worldview. He served in World War II, but in a segregated military. After his entrée into the world of politics—the House, the Senate, the vice-presidency—a good many of the Blacks he saw were domestic workers or simply everyday Black Americans with whom he had little real contact. Since the days of Lincoln, the Republican Party, Lincoln's party, had counted on a working relationship with Black publishers. Republican advertising dollars, even if paltry compared with what they spent in the mainstream press, went a long way in helping to keep the Black press solvent, which was always a chal-

The Vietnam veteran John Kerry was among the first white veterans to discuss racial inequality in the military openly. He later became a United States senator and presidential candidate.

lenge. Those publishers got invited to the White House to talk about what Republicans could do for Black businesses.

When he had been running for the presidency against Jack Kennedy in 1960, Nixon had refused to make a phone call to Coretta Scott King on behalf of her husband, who had been arrested in Georgia. The Nixon camp in time realized what a boneheaded move it had been and couldn't help but wonder how many Black votes it had cost them in that very close election. In his effort to defeat the Democratic nominee in 1968, Nixon aimed to be smarter. In November, *Jet* magazine published a special campaign issue. All the candidates were able to have their messages to Black America published. Candidate Nixon got a two-page spread. On the opening page was a man by the name of Homer Pitts, nattily dressed and holding books, giving him a studious appearance. The headline: "This Time Vote Like Homer Pitts' Whole World Depended on It." The accompanying text was Richard Nixon's pitch to Black America:

Black Americans accused President Nixon of "turning back the clock" in the arena of civil rights.

> He'll get his degree. Then what? . . . laborer, factory job . . . or his own business. A vote for Richard Nixon for President is a vote for a man who wants Homer to have the chance to own his own business. Richard Nixon believes strongly in black capitalism. Because black capitalism is black power in the best sense of the word. It's the road that leads to black economic influence and black pride. It's the key to the black man's fight for equality—for a piece of the action. And that's what the free enterprise system is all about. This time . . . Nixon.

The Nixon team also began putting together campaign film spots. During production of one ad, Nixon's advertising team allowed Joe McGinnis, a writer working on a book, to view how it was being made. In the commercial that McGinnis was watching, Nixon provided voiceover. There was a picture of a Black soldier, obviously in Vietnam. "They provide most of the soldiers who died to keep us free," comes the Nixon voice. When Leonard Garment, a Nixon adviser, looked at the segment, it bothered him. "We can't show a

Negro just as RN's [Nixon's] saying 'most of the soldiers who died to keep us free.' That's been one of their big claims all along—that the draft is unfair to them—and this could be interpreted in a way that would make us appear to be taking their side." The team agreed with Garment; the picture of the Black soldier disappeared, and a white soldier took his place.

Once in office, Richard Nixon surrounded himself with a coterie of white male aides. Charles Colson served as his legal counsel. Doug Hallett was one of Colson's aides. Hallett thought he had a good bead on what liberals really thought of Richard Nixon: "Nixon is a low-brow, not very thoughtful, low-quality, mid-1930s Depression-influenced, out of date man-on-the-make" is how he summarized it. "Poor boy made good, he reflects all the worst aspects of American conservatism—a bigoted, reactionary, unfeeling, unhumanistic make-it-or-else philosophy."

It did not take very long for the Black community to catch on to the political philosophy of President Nixon.

It was thought and hoped—especially by Blacks—that President Johnson had set a precedent when, in 1966, he named Robert Weaver as secretary of housing and urban development. It was powerful symbolism to have Weaver, a gifted Black man whose government service stretched back to the days of Franklin Roosevelt, named to the cabinet. Weaver had been director of the Negro Manpower Service during the latter stages of World War II. With Weaver as a benchmark, it was hoped by many that the days of all-white cabinets were history. But under President Nixon they were not. Nixon not only had no Black cabinet members, he had no women, either. In the late summer of 1969, Nixon—who had promised to name "strict constructionists" to the Supreme Court if the opportunity presented itself—nominated Clement Haynsworth, a South Carolina federal judge, for a seat on the court. Haynsworth's judicial record favored segregationists, and enough Blacks and liberal Republicans coalesced to doom the nomination. In January 1970, Nixon nominated Georgia Judge G. Harrold Carswell to the high court. It was revealed that Carswell had bellowed in a 1948 speech about his allegiance and support for white supremacy. His nomination was also doomed.

On the campaign trail, Nixon had been unapologetic in the promises he made to white America, the constituency he talked most directly to. He referred to them as the Silent Majority—code words for whites who were not at all thrilled about the legal energy behind integration. They wanted integration slowed down; they wanted integration on their terms. And some wanted integration to be all but a crushed dream. Nixon favored the implementation of "law and order" policies to stifle the urban rebellions across the land. And he let it be known that he was no admirer of LBJ's Great Society program and would find ways to dismantle as many of the programs under its umbrella as he could. Richard Nixon had his mind set on a Southern strategy whereby he would rally the whites of the South to his brand of politics. That Model Cities Program that was so popular under President Johnson and that brought Blacks jobs in city halls? Its funding was slashed. Those beloved school-lunch programs that served poor children of all backgrounds? Their funding dwindled. The Nixon administration had a civil rights enforcement team, but they did not get good marks at all. In 1974, a report was issued, conducted by the U.S. Commission on Civil Rights, that analyzed the degree of enforcement of the 1968 Fair Housing Act. Among its findings: "Present programs often are administered so as to continue rather than reduce racial segregation." The report further stated that minority neighborhoods were being decimated by zoning rules, and that Black home buyers were routinely being steered to Black areas as opposed to white areas. Yet another 1974 report, issued by the Center for National Policy Review, released findings about school desegregation enforcement under Nixon. This 117-page report, titled *Justice Delayed and Denied,* showed that actions directing federal enforcement went from sixteen corrective actions taken in 1969 to zero in 1974. The lack of enforcement activity was alarming, given that school segregation remained prevalent in many parts of the nation, as shown by the NAACP Legal Defense Fund, which had been filing lawsuits for years. In 1973, a federal judge had become so incensed by the Nixon administration's inaction on school desegregation enforcement that he began instituting enforcement proceedings against seventy-four Southern school districts. The National Policy Review concluded, "There is little question that the Nixon administration's negative policy declarations have impaired enforcement action and demoralized the HEW civil rights staff." Nixon bemoaned school busing, calling it "forced integration." He believed those who "want instant integration and those who want segregation forever" were little more than extremists, just at opposite ends of the conversation. In 1969, Nixon appointed Warren Burger as new chief justice of the United States Supreme Court. Two years later, the Burger court issued a stinging defeat for Nixon's Department of Justice when it came to school busing, believing they had moved too slowly to enact years-old integration court decisions. "All things being equal, with no history of discrimination, it might well be desirable to assign pupils to schools nearest their homes," the chief justice himself wrote in the opinion. "But all things are not equal in a system that has been deliberately constructed and maintained to enforce racial segregation."

The Black military veteran returning home from the war might well have begun to sense that the Johnson administration had stopped short in providing ample funding for the civil rights and antipoverty movements. And that the Nixon administration didn't truly care for those programs at all. Tom Wicker, the *New York Times* columnist, penned a column outlining what he thought had been the attitude of the white Nixon voter and follower of the George Wallace caravan: "He is fed up with a war that is not being won, but shocked at the notion of an American defeat. And he is inclined to agree with J. Edgar Hoover that justice is only incidental to the maintenance of order."

For Black veterans home from Vietnam and looking around at early-1970s America, it was a somber reality to see so much pain and sadness. There was the proliferation of drug addicts in the urban ghettos. There were mental-health woes exacerbated by living in low-income areas. Many of the Black vets loudly badmouthed the war. Nixon's aides told him he was clearly losing the PR battle when it came to the war.

The 1972 Republican National Convention was scheduled to get under way on August 21. But even before that, Nixon's presidency had already set the stage for its own demise. On June 17, some misfit burglars broke into the Democratic National Committee headquarters in Washington. Frank Wills, a Black security guard, had discovered a piece of tape used to keep a door propped ajar to allow the burglars to get in. Wills called the local police. Few outside Washington had ever heard of the Watergate complex, site of Democratic headquarters.

The Nixon White House believed that the reporting on Watergate would die down soon enough, that the nation didn't care about it. "Now, everybody around here is all mortified by it," Nixon told his aides. "It's a horrible thing to rebut. And the answer, of course, is that most people around the country think this is routine, that everybody's trying to bug everybody else. It's politics. That's my view. The purists probably won't agree with that, but I don't think they're going to see a great uproar in the country about the Republican committee trying to bug the Democratic headquarters."

Nixon was already wrong. The Watergate Hearings, which began on May 17, 1973, represented the earth-crashing residue of the break-in at Democratic headquarters. The hearings were televised, and a nation sat riveted. Barbara Jordan, the Black congresswoman from LBJ's Texas, took a starring role, her rhythmic voice landing in living rooms with the weight of a spoken-word album with the volume turned high. "My faith in the Constitution is whole, it is complete, it is total, and I am not going to sit here and be an idle spectator to the diminution, the subversion, the destruction, of the Constitution."

The snake was loose now. And the months ahead would reveal there were no more hiding places. Watergate hissed louder and louder.

—

The timeline of the Vietnam War grew more and more confusing to the American public. Nixon announced a cease-fire, but it was a lie. He announced he would start bringing ground troops home. That was the truth, but the air bombings continued. Nixon was as spooked by communism—and China—as LBJ had been. "I would rather be a one-term president than be a two-term president at the cost of seeing America become a second-rate power," Nixon said.

The antiwar movement that had coalesced with the Martin Luther King, Jr.–led civil rights movement had an indomitable momentum. And the political patience with the endless war was eroding faster than ever. In 1973, Congress said no to Nixon's request for more war funding. But it was mostly a symbolic vote. It carried no weight in the Senate. Senate Majority Leader Mike Mansfield reminded folks that Congress "can't end the war . . . it's really up to the President. We shouldn't fool ourselves in that respect." War had a habit of molding tyrannical behavior in men; LBJ was a victim of this, and now so was Nixon. No matter how hard he tried to slip offscreen from the steadily unfolding Watergate drama, Nixon found it an impossible task. *The Washington Post* had kept up their reporting, and other publications launched their own investigations. The American public was introduced to a cadre of unsavory characters who were embroiled in the episode: G. Gordon Liddy, E. Howard Hunt, Jeb Magruder, Bebe Rebozo, H. R. Haldeman. "Every president needs a son-of-a-bitch and I'm Nixon's," Haldeman wrote in a diary he kept. Nixon grew defiant. "People have got to know whether or not their President is a crook," Nixon said to a gathering of managing editors from the Associated Press in Florida. "Well, I'm not a crook. I've earned everything I've got."

One thing that proved consistent in the long duration of the Vietnam War connected Jack Kennedy with Lyndon Johnson, and Johnson with Richard Nixon: none of them had a Black voice in his ear, someone who might have looked at the war through a different lens, who might have prevented it from being viewed, as Kennedy feared, as "a white man's war."

—

The 1970s would be the first decade in the nation's history begun with real evidence of freedom under the American flag for Black Americans. But terrible vestiges of the war remained. "In the past four or five months," a physician in Vietnam confided to *The New York Times* in late 1970, "there appears to have been a four- or five-fold increase in multiple amputees. I hope this is all incredible someday. Right now, it's all too credible."

By 1972, enough veterans had returned from the war to noticeably increase the numbers in the Vietnam Veterans Against the War (VVAW). A multiracial group, they had held meetings in early 1971 to hear from veterans. In April 1971, they descended upon Washington, a city with a large Black population—and plenty of Black veterans. More than two thousand VVAW members came, long-haired, bearded, dressed in hippie-ish clothing. Nixon loathed them and had been telling aides that only "30 percent" of the group were really veterans. This was another lie, of many lies to come, following the many lies that had already been told. "Only 30 percent of us believe Nixon is president," one vet cracked after hearing what Nixon had said about them. It was chilly in Washington when the vets arrived that week. A lot of them slept on the mall the first night. A lady who didn't agree with the protesting crossed paths with some of them.

"I don't think what you're doing is good for the troops," she told one of the vets.

"Lady," came the reply, "we *are* the troops."

The veterans had chosen John Kerry as one of their leaders and spokesmen. He was soon to testify on Capitol Hill. Kerry was a Yale man and former Navy officer who had served in Vietnam and was awarded medals for bravery and injuries. His congressional testimony got under way on April 22. His hearing—part of the Fulbright hearings—was standing room only. Kerry was not dressed in the usual attire for those about to give congressional testimony: a bland suit and tie. Instead, he wore a green shirt, the kind a soldier might have worn in the jungle. His military insignias were attached to his shirt. Kerry shared what he had heard from various Vietnam vets, many of whom had been at earlier meetings, in Detroit:

> They told the stories of times that they had personally raped, cut off ears, cut off heads, taped wires from portable telephones to human genitals and turned up the power, cut off limbs, blown up bodies, randomly shot at civilians, razed villages in a fashion reminiscent of Genghis Khan, shot cattle and dogs for fun, poisoned food stocks, and generally ravaged the countryside of South Vietnam in addition to the normal ravages of war and the normal and very particular ravaging which is done by the applied bombing power of this country.

This was not the type of military testimony American politicians were accustomed to hearing. The gasping was at a low volume, but it was heard. Kerry went on to talk about the perilous position the people of Vietnam were put in:

> They only wanted to work in rice paddies without helicopters strafing them and bombs with napalm burning their villages and tearing their country apart. They wanted everything to do with the war, particularly with this foreign presence of the United States of America, to leave them alone in peace, and they practiced the art of survival by siding with whichever military force was present at a particular time, be it Viet Cong, North Vietnamese or American.

Then John Kerry said this:

> We found also that all too often American men were dying in those rice paddies for want of support from their allies. We saw first hand how monies from American taxes were used for a corrupt political regime. We saw that many people in this country had a one-sided idea of who was kept free by the flag, and blacks provided the highest percentage of casualties.

Shivers of appreciation swept through the Black vets in the room and in the hallways. Kerry had spoken to a nationwide audience—

since the hearings were televised—and he had spoken of their unique sacrifice and losses. For those whites who had tired of hearing about civil rights and the historical anger of Blacks, Kerry had put the war in searing perspective on behalf of Blacks and their patriotism. When he rose from his chair, John Kerry had become an instant villain to some—and an instant hero to others. The following day, a group of veterans rolled over to the grounds of the U.S. Capitol, intending to deliver their wartime medals in a bag to members of Congress as an antiwar statement. But they were greeted by a wire fence that had been erected on Nixon's orders to keep them out. That really tore at them: however misguided the war may have been, they had shown up; they hadn't lied and dodged the draft; they hadn't hidden behind privilege and family connections. So they threw their medals—Silver Stars, Bronze Stars, discharge papers, Distinguished Flying Crosses—on the Capitol steps.

The geopolitics of Vietnam continued to haunt the Nixon administration. Nixon fretted that North Vietnam was sustaining itself and the war on weaponry from the Soviet Union and China. He went to Moscow for a nuclear-arms summit with Leonid Brezhnev. Before the summit, Brezhnev had warned Nixon against more bombing in Vietnam. However: "We can lose the summit and still not lose the country," Nixon believed. "But we cannot lose this war without losing the country." This echoed the superpower mumbo-jumbo that had been voiced by both Kennedy and LBJ. The Paris Peace Accords, which Nixon signed on January 27, 1973, set in motion the beginning of the end of the war. Nixon himself exited the world stage on August 8, 1974, when he resigned the office of the presidency, strangled by the dangerous and calamitous machinations of the Watergate scandal.

When Spiro Agnew resigned the vice-presidency on October 10, 1973, having pled guilty to a charge of tax fraud dating to his days as governor of Maryland, Nixon had chosen Gerald Ford, speaker of the House, to take his place. Ford, raised in Grand Rapids, Michigan, was a hard-core Republican. Jerald terHorst, Ford's first press secretary in the White House, saw some contradictions in his boss: He'd give a poor kid "the shirt off his back," terHorst said of Ford. "Then he'd go right into the White House and veto a school-lunch bill." But Ford's eyes were not closed to racial perceptions. He named a Black man, William Coleman, as his secretary of transportation, integrating the president's cabinet once again. Coleman was a highly respected attorney who, in the 1950s, had fought alongside Thurgood Marshall in many civil rights battles for the NAACP Legal Defense Fund.

It had long worried Blacks that they were punished disproportionately more than whites for being draft offenders. Ford didn't like the racial imbalance of those decisions and ordered reviews. After the reviews were completed, four out of five of those who had requested them were recommended for pardons.

In early 1975, the American military, still in Vietnam but in dwindling numbers, began making plans for Operation Babylift. President Ford had given his approval. With the North Vietnamese advancing, the plan was for the American military to get as many orphans as they could out of South Vietnam. On April 4, on that very first day, disaster struck: a plane carrying many dozens of orphans and American personnel crashed, killing 138, among them 78 children. The heartbreaking horror seemed to focus the military even more on its completion of the mission. In the end, upward of three thousand orphans were rescued.

The struggle for Black freedom and an end to the Vietnam War came to be joined in the fabric of America. One became tethered to the other. The Black civilians, ministers, vets, farmworkers, sharecroppers, hosed-down children—joined in time by conscience-stricken white allies—began the revolution. The Vietnam War–era Black soldier, military-trained, vowed to finish it.

It took two years beyond 1973 for the war to really end. North Vietnamese troops began a brutal attack on Saigon on April 29, 1975. In a mad dash to save lives, the U.S. Embassy was evacuated. The American military and embassy officials had to scramble to get as many South Vietnamese civilians out of the city as they could. It was a hellish scene, one that even caught the CIA off guard.

The communists were back in charge.

—

The people of Suffolk, Virginia, were getting ready. Schoolchildren had been drawing posters. Veterans from other wars were reaching for their own medals and insignias to affix to their suit jackets. Fred Cherry, the longest-held Black POW in North Vietnam, was going to be fêted in a parade in downtown Suffolk. When the hour arrived, there he was, spotted sitting in the back of a white Caddy convertible, waving. His mangled arm hurt. The caravan stopped at Peanut Park, where Cherry took time to shake hands and kiss cheeks. There was a dinner for him that evening at the local National Guard armory. He stood before a microphone. "I am an American fighting man and I wear this uniform to protect you and your way of life," he said, talking without notes. "I would have given my life if necessary, proudly and honorably. I was tortured severely. I was severely ill, but they never broke me. They didn't because I had faith in God, in my country—and in you. If necessary, I will do the same thing again because I want America to be what you want it to be."

The Suffolk County area that Fred Cherry called home had waged one of the fiercest anti-integration efforts in the country. In 1966, while Cherry was being tortured in North Vietnam, Virginia Governor Mills E. Godwin was in office, having pronounced his views on segregation during his campaign. During the week of Fred Cherry's hero's welcome, one newspaper account took note that the area was "the home of conservative Governor Mills E. Godwin, Jr., whose known anti-black attitude . . . is an extension of the feelings held by most whites in this South Side Virginia city."

Fred Cherry wanted to fly again. The Air Force wouldn't allow him—it was the arm. Now and then, neighbors would spot a not-so-old man standing in his yard, staring at an Air Force jet flying overhead. Fred Cherry imagined that the pilots were waving to him, so he'd wave back.

CHAPTER SIXTEEN

SOME ARE ASKING: WHO THE HELL IS MAUDE DEVICTOR?

Across decades, even centuries, it was often difficult for America's soldiers to return home from wars. The public saluted their patriotism, but preferably from a distance. Up close, bean-counting politicians retreated to their offices and often shortchanged the patriotic veterans on benefits and attention to their postwar needs. This malady was even more pronounced when it came to Black veterans.

In the aftermath of the Revolutionary War, men—who had amassed debts while away fighting—were given paper slips they were told would be redeemable for currency in their states. Most of those paper slips, after a certain date, proved worthless. State governments were financially strapped; war had taken a toll. Anger among the military vets grew. In 1783, Major General Henry Knox warned of this brewing disenchantment: "Let the public," he said, "only comply with their own promises, and the army will return to their respective homes the lambs and bees of the community. But if they should be disbanded previous to a settlement without knowing who to look to for an adjustment of accounts and a responsibility of payment, they will be so deeply stung by the injustice and ingratitude of their country so as to become its tigers and its wolves."

The chemical agent sprayed above the trees and fields in Vietnam was an American-produced defoliant that came to be known as Agent Orange. It caused severe illnesses and deformities among thousands.

Similar problems arose in the aftermath of the Civil War, in which Black soldiers—when finally allowed to fight—were paid less than white soldiers, and sometimes their payments were delayed. Colonel T. H. Barnett had sympathy for the Black soldiers and in January 1866 tried to mollify them. "Soldiers, I tell you, you can well afford to wait; for the time is coming, and is not far distant, when those who enslaved you, shall be forced to acknowledge, that to have been a colored soldier, is to be a citizen, and to have been an advocate of slavery, is but another name for traitor." Such words carried little power to make their anger subside. They were desperate men and faced uncertain futures. One Black corporal wrote to the secretary of war in 1867: "I am about to be mustered out without any bounty . . . I have no space to live. After serving the U.S.A. almost three years then to put me out without anything. I am sorry to know that." Whites soon grew tired of hearing about Black soldiers. They were actually tired of hearing about the general state of Black misery and all its attendant manifestations. A woman who wrote to President Andrew Johnson expressed her hopes that Congress would "for an hour drop the eternal Negro question and devote that time for the interest of the suffering soldiers"—a plea echoed by many other whites who held the same sentiment.

Future wars—World War I, Korea, and World War II—fortified the vehemence of soldiers who voiced their complaints about the way they were treated by their government after returning home. Complaints from whites were just as voluminous as those from Blacks, but the complaints from Black soldiers had a more urgent component: they often came on the heels of lynchings and racial uprisings, ignited when some white citizens found themselves displeased at the sight of Blacks in uniform. In 1945, Robert Watt held a position as an international representative of the American Federation of Labor, responsible for keeping expenses down. "If we give special status to veterans today," he felt, "we are faced with the problem of special consideration for minority groups tomorrow."

What peeved many Black veterans of the Vietnam War were the revelations that many of them had been punished unfairly during their service. From an administrative point of view, the Department of Defense was put on the spot because of these rising complaints—which were showing up especially in the Black press—and ordered a study. Released in 1972, the study revealed that Blacks received 34.3 percent of courts-martial, and 25.5 percent of punishments deemed to be nonjudicial (imposed by a commander for minor offenses). Military leaders vowed attention to the matter.

All of those concerns, however, were set aside for at least one day, the last day of March 1973, for a planned Times Square celebration to honor those who served in Vietnam.

Bagpipes and music from various bands were blaring as veterans from all branches of the military gathered on Broadway to be saluted for their service. The temperature hovered in the mid-sixties, which made it a fine day for a parade. At noon, Cardinal Terence Cooke led those gathered in prayer to honor the estimated fifty-five thousand who had died in the war. He encouraged everyone to pray with him "in a spirit of gratitude and reconciliation." The veterans ambled through Times Square, then made their way to Columbus Circle and on to Central Park West. No one, it seemed, wanted to give an estimate of the crowd size. Reporters finally went with an estimate of between 100,000 and 150,000, an anemic showing. On the same site, after World War II, on V-J Day, there were upward of two million. Politicians were in attendance, but not Nixon or his vice-president; Peter J. Brennan, Nixon's secretary of labor, came to represent the administration. New York Governor Nelson Rockefeller missed the festivities, sending representatives instead. New York City Mayor John Lindsay was vacationing in Colorado and also sent representatives. There was grousing among some of the veterans that the big names from Washington didn't bother to come, for fear there might be confrontations. "There were none of the blizzards of confetti that had greeted returning American servicemen in the great military parades of the past, such as those after both world wars," *The New York Times* ruefully noted. A contingent from the Vietnam Veterans Against the War was present, raising their voices as well as their placards. They came demanding better benefits, and amnesty for those who were drafted and refused to join the military, having fled into the wilderness—or up to Canada. Someone who had come to the parade held aloft a sign that urged "Jobs, Not Parades." Many were debating whether the war was really, truly, over. There were still American personnel in Vietnam. The most recent unemployment figures for Vietnam veterans from the Bureau of Labor Statistics showed the jobless rate at 8.6 percent; for Black vets it was 9.5 percent. In New York City itself, the jobless rate for Black vets jumped to 15 percent. Only a few "celebrations" of the Times Square kind were held across the nation.

A lack of jobs was hardly the only fallout from the war for Black Vietnam veterans. A scourge was ripping through many Black communities. Drugs, especially marijuana and heroin, seemed to be prevalent everywhere. Young men in rural towns as well as the inner cities were bending like pieces of licorice in alleyways, on the streets, and on living-room sofas from doses of heroin. The origin of a lot of the heroin showing up in Black communities was Vietnam itself.

In the latter stages of the never-ending Vietnam War, military officials in Saigon were reporting that at least 15 percent of soldiers were addicted to heroin. "When a man is in Vietnam he can be sure that no matter where he is, who he is with, or who he is talking to, there are probably drugs within twenty-five feet of him," one brigade officer reported.

In 1971, there were about 277,000 American military personnel in Vietnam. As many as 37,000 were identified as heroin users and faced some form of punishment. "Tens of thousands of soldiers are going back as time bombs," a military officer tasked with fighting the problem in Saigon told *The New York Times*—without offering his name, given the sensitive topic. "And the sad thing is that there is no real program under way, despite what my superiors say, to salvage these guys."

There was a particular area where the borders of Myanmar, Thailand, and Laos came together that was known for its wildly successful drug production. And a couple of Black American outlaws—having learned from Mafia connections in New York City—were orchestrating the introduction of those drugs, especially heroin, into American Black communities.

New York City law enforcement first encountered Frank Lucas in the early 1960s for a variety of criminal activities. He was in and out of prison. A native of rural North Carolina, Lucas had come under the tutelage of Bumpy Johnson, a notorious Black gangster. Lucas didn't stand out in Harlem just because he was an outlaw. He stood out because of his eclectic ways of making money. People on the streets of Manhattan in the late 1960s had gotten a whiff of high-grade, mostly pure heroin, but there wasn't enough of it around. Lucas found out that its origin was Southeast Asia, in the Golden Triangle area. Through his criminal associations, he contacted some former American military personnel still living in the region and told them his idea: he wanted to come to the area himself, confer with the Asian gangsters, barter for the heroin, and take it back to America. He was put in touch with a gang of Golden Triangle drug producers—some aligned with the South Vietnamese military—who were interested in hearing Frank Lucas's spiel on how to make money. There were meetings, discussions, plans set in motion. He was spotted wearing a military uniform. He started dapping with the Black soldiers. Lucas eventually got couriers to transport the drugs into America. He once claimed to have stashed some heroin in a false-bottomed coffin being returned home. When that story later got out, law enforcement called him a liar, but it was too good for the press not to print it.

Lucas and his workers started selling the heroin in Harlem and beyond. The drug trade made him rich enough to reside in a suite at the ritzy Regency Hotel. He drove a Rolls, and in the cold months wore a sable coat and matching sable hat. Tall and handsome with caramel-colored skin, he employed family members in his drug enterprise, and offered his brand of logic for doing so: "A country boy, you can give him any amount of money. His wife and kids might be hungry, and he'll never touch your stuff until he checks with you. City boys ain't like that. A city boy will take your last dime, look you in the face, and swear he ain't got it . . . You don't want a city boy—the sonofabitch is just no good." Lucas told an interviewer that he had turned to the drug business because of limited options in life. "Kind of sonofabitch I saw myself being, money I wanted to make, I'd have to be on Wall Street. On Wall Street, from the giddy-up. But I couldn't have even gotten a job being a fucking janitor on Wall Street." In the intoxicating world of Manhattan celebrity, Frank Lucas became a figure of curiosity. He held annual turkey giveaways during the holidays. He could be seen alighting from his Rolls, gliding past those bent men and women—some of them ex-military—on 125th Street who were zonked on his powerful drug.

Frank Lucas—eventually caught and sentenced to a long prison term—wasn't the only fanciful drug dealer operating in Harlem at the time. Nicky Barnes also made a fortune selling drugs to the young and all those home-from-war soldiers. Born in Harlem, Barnes had met some Italian gangsters during a prison stint when he was in his twenties. They impressed upon him the need to form an organization if he wanted to operate a muscular drug enterprise. Freed from prison, he organized a so-called council of seven operatives and made headway into the lucrative drug market. None of this would have been possible without the involvement of corrupt police officers. Because of the testimony of Frank Serpico, a police officer sickened by corruption in the department, Mayor John Lindsay formed the Knapp Commission in 1970 with a mission to identify and root out wrongdoing. The commission ultimately exposed instances in which police officers were involved in protecting narcotics traffickers, pimps, and those operating gambling dens. The commission demanded reforms. Many officers were miffed by the very existence of this commission. They considered Frank Serpico an enemy of the department. On February 3, 1971, Serpico and a few other officers were sent to an apartment in Brooklyn to monitor a drug transaction. During a confrontation with the heroin dealer, Serpico was shot in the face. He survived. The suspect who shot him was later caught and sent to prison. Serpico would forever feel that his fellow officers had set him up.

Nicky Barnes seemed to become invincible. He was confident enough to pose for the cover of a *New York Times Magazine* article about him. In his gray suit, blue shirt, and colorful tie, he looked like someone who might work on Wall Street. The headline: "Mister Untouchable." The subheadline: "This Is Nicky Barnes. The Police Say He May Be Harlem's Biggest Drug Dealer. But Can They Prove It?"

From the same story, reporting on Barnes's moves following his early prison stint: "He then proceeded to create his drug empire, police say, importing pure heroin, or heroin which had been cut only once—and is considered on the street to be pure—directly from what intelligence sources say were 'Italian suppliers.'" If the local police department couldn't stop the scourge of drugs flowing into Harlem, the parents who wailed at City Council meetings about the problem surely couldn't.

President Jimmy Carter was outraged at the magazine cover featuring Barnes. Not at the magazine itself. The article was just an example of what journalists did—find interesting stories and get them into print. Carter was incensed by Barnes's arrogance, the belligerence with which he seemed to be thumbing his nose at law enforcement. Carter ordered the Drug Enforcement Administration to intensify its investigation. They did, and when they convicted Barnes for operating a drug ring, to save himself from a lifetime of imprisonment, he turned federal informant.

The more the problems began to pile up for the Vietnam veterans, the more the Times Square celebration honoring them seemed premature indeed. Soldiers were still dying in Vietnam. Two years after that "celebration," the North Vietnamese push into Saigon became imminent. The NVA had started taking over large swaths of the country. There were still upward of five thousand American military personnel and diplomats in Saigon. U.S. Ambassador Graham Martin, aware that the North Vietnamese had bombed the Tan Son Nhut Air Base, ordered the U.S. Embassy evacuated. Over a course of two days, helicopters swooped in, in a dizzying military operation to evacuate as many Americans and South Vietnamese as they could. The Fall of Saigon had begun. There would be reports of uncommon bravery, of American pilots flying nonstop for more than fifteen hours.

After the war, Black soldiers who straggled into drug rehab centers in America had plenty of stories to tell, about the power of heroin and the grip it held on them, about having gone through detox in Vietnam courtesy of a makeshift rehab facility that would pop up now and then—usually an empty warehouse that had been commandeered by Black soldiers—and how those interventions had not really done them much good. Phil Bidler, a white combat veteran, had a bead on the white-Black dynamics of Vietnam: "We realized collectively we had nothing to fight for, that nobody cared about us, and we didn't give a shit about them. Our sense of motivation was a buddy system: 'We are in this and nobody cares, but at least we can care about each other.' Blacks had even another kind of microcosm—they cared for each other. I felt the whites were explicitly bigoted."

Late in his life, after the shame of Watergate and a prison stint, John Ehrlichman, a onetime domestic-policy adviser to Nixon, spoke to *Harper's Magazine* about Nixon's War on Drugs. "You want to know what this was really all about? The Nixon campaign in 1968, and the Nixon White House after that, had two enemies: the antiwar left and black people. You understand what I'm saying? We knew we couldn't make it illegal to be either against the war or black, but by getting the public to associate the hippies with marijuana and blacks with heroin, and then criminalizing both heavily, we could disrupt those communities. We could arrest their leaders, raid their homes, break up their meetings, and vilify them night after night on the evening news. Did we know we were lying about the drugs? Of course we did."

The woes for the returning veterans seemed to mount, month by month. Representative Olin Teague, a Texas Democrat, had accused the Nixon administration of using the Veterans Administration like a "dumping ground" for those who had worked for CREEP—the Committee to Re-Elect the President.

John Bivens, a Black Vietnam vet who had served in the Air Force, went to Alabama after the war and worked in civil rights. Bivens, who also had a law degree, concluded that the two events—civil rights and the war—had much in common, especially when it came to Black veterans: "The direct cause of black veterans not getting a fair shake," he said, "is because they are black. They got a fair shake when it comes to fighting Viet Cong, but when we got on the plane coming home, it was back to black versus white."

In 1970, Mayor Lindsay appointed Eleanor Holmes Norton as

chair of the New York City Human Rights Commission. A Black Yale graduate, Norton had worked in the South as an organizer for the Southern Christian Leadership Conference and had been arrested several times for protesting. In New York, military vets came knocking on her door, pleading for help. Holmes began an investigation of the government care that the four thousand Black and white vets in the New York City area had received and found that it was "seriously inadequate." She said the Defense Department seemed to have treated the POWs who first arrived home—many of them "high-ranking, well-educated white officers," as she put it—much better than the later-arriving soldiers, who were "far more numerous, low-ranking foot soldiers who are disproportionately poor, black or brown, and as ill-educated when they returned from the service as when they went in."

One of the many tools used by the American military in Vietnam was the spraying of the herbicide and defoliant Agent Orange, which contained a harmful contaminant called dioxin. It was used to clear forests of elephant grass and foliage that concealed enemy soldiers. The Air Force largely handled the task, spraying the landscape from helicopters and planes. American soldiers couldn't escape the herbicides. Some time would pass after their return, but the illnesses began, sometimes five, six, or seven years later. They began experiencing peculiar symptoms: sores that wouldn't heal, unsightly lumps on their skin, trouble breathing, weight loss, a change in eye color. The wives of some of them were giving birth to deformed babies, or experiencing a high degree of stillbirths.

Though vets came to realize the need for unity between white and Black vets against the powerful structure of the United States government and its many VA centers, many Black vets lacked trust in white VA administrators. J. C. Peckarsky—who had started working for the VA in 1946—was just the kind of white administrator Black vets began to loathe. He was director of the VA's Compensation and Pension Service, which meant he pretty much had the final say to grant or deny an Agent Orange application. Peckarsky didn't trust the science that told of the deleterious effects of dioxin. He also thought vets were trying to "game" the system—and get money they didn't deserve for their illnesses. He'd corner politicians and share his suspicious feelings with them. He became notorious for denying Agent Orange applications. "Part of my job is to say no" is how he put it in 1979. Little wonder many Black vets began looking for any Black VA employee who might be more understanding of their problems.

Maude DeVictor was another VA government employee, who spent hours shuffling paperwork and trying to help veterans with their many needs. She worked out of the Chicago office. A veteran herself, she was another of those Black Americans who had joined the military—the Navy in her case, back in 1959—figuring it would offer good training and a steady paycheck, things not always guaranteed in the civilian world. She was happy to go to work for the VA after her service, because she wanted to help others. And she was a good listener.

Ethel Owens had gotten to know Maude DeVictor at the Chicago VA because Ethel's husband, Charles, had served in Vietnam and in 1977 lay in a Chicago hospital. He had had no health problems before he landed in Vietnam. But now he had lung cancer, and had lost about seventy pounds. Ethel Owens told DeVictor that her husband had told her that "those chemicals in Vietnam" would be responsible for his death. DeVictor was concerned enough that she decided to send his files to higher-ups in Washington. They studied the Owens case and told her that there was no "true incident of significant exposure to herbicides recorded" in the records of Charles Owens. That didn't sit well with DeVictor. She began wondering about other veterans, and what effect herbicides were having on them. So, when they visited her, she began asking questions about any illnesses they had contracted since their service. A dozen or so vets mentioned rashes, swollen skin, trouble breathing, a loss of sexual energy, all of which they believed related to the spraying of herbicides while they were in Vietnam.

More vets came forward with similar complaints. DeVictor couldn't stop thinking about this strange phenomenon—chemical spraying. She wanted to know from the vets any problems they might have been having with vision, weight loss, sexual appetite. They practically jumped out of their chairs. They had been telling other counselors about those very symptoms.

It was not exactly in Maude DeVictor's purview, but she started making phone calls to chemical companies that had produced the chemicals in Agent Orange, among them Dow Chemical and Monsanto. Ignored, she kept calling, wanting to know exactly what was in the herbicide, Agent Orange, that had been sprayed in Vietnam. Sometimes her conversations were cut short, but she'd call back a day later, hoping to get someone else on the line, and when she did, they would start talking, until they also would get suspicious. But with each conversation, she was accumulating information. At home, she laid out maps, marking where Agent Orange had been sprayed and connecting the dots of soldiers and their platoons. It was like some kind of big jigsaw puzzle. She heard a name mentioned, Air Force Captain Victor Young, who someone had told her had a lot to do with Agent Orange. He became a crucial part of her coming-together puzzle: Young had designed the nozzles that sprayed Agent Orange from the helicopters and planes in Vietnam. Young confessed to her that he believed the military was staying abreast of the news about Agent Orange "with extreme concern, in the event that favorable decisions . . . should open the way to possible litigation." DeVictor found out that during the course of the Vietnam War the military had sprayed twenty million gallons of the chemicals that made up Agent Orange.

This deskbound Black woman, Maude DeVictor, a government worker-bee for so many years, began to feel alive in more profound ways than ever before. Black and white veterans—and vets of other races, too—were hurting, and they were dying, and she knew it. She kept files; she started asking veterans who came to see her about where they had been stationed in Vietnam, then whether they had Agent Orange symptoms, and if they said they did, she'd go to her maps and connect them to the vicinity of the spraying data she had accumulated. She tracked down biologists, then she tracked down chemists. Her notes were later said to have been meticulous. She turned herself into an investigator. Though she was helping all vets, she noticed something: how the Black vets practically fell into her arms, because they had rarely felt so cared about before, certainly not so intently. Many of them had been second-guessed before going to Vietnam, were second-guessed once in Vietnam, and now, back in America, and sickly, they were being second-guessed again. The illness of course knew no color, but Maude DeVictor understood their accumulated agony. She began wondering if she was on to some kind of strange and bizarre conspiracy, some kind of cover-up. Just how many veterans were in pain, were having nightmares, were having marital problems? How many had grown afraid and weary of VA doctors? It was now much easier to believe in government wrongdoing, because of the Watergate scandal.

It didn't take long for word to start spreading beyond the halls of the Chicago VA office about this imposing Black woman who was asking all sorts of questions about Agent Orange, asking people all over the country, including many not even in the military. Some, obviously nervous, would ask her to call back on a different phone line at another time. Managers and administrators in various VA offices around the country started wondering: Who the hell is this Maude DeVictor? They contacted her bosses and complained about her. In the spring of 1978, DeVictor's bosses marched into her office and started grilling her about her so-called and unauthorized investigations. She was told to cease all inquiry about Agent Orange, told that it was something she should not be concerned with at all. And she was warned that she was putting her job in jeopardy.

Come evenings, in the comfort of her home, Maude DeVictor fairly boiled over with rage. Those interactions with her bosses summoned old feelings about being disrespected by those in power, being second-guessed, especially by white men. It was a curse that Black women bore stoically, and she was tired of it. She wouldn't—couldn't—just stop what she was doing.

However, she realized she needed help, someone outside the VA who would understand her mission. Maude DeVictor picked up the telephone.

Bill Kurtis was an investigative reporter for a local CBS station in Chicago. Since his father had been a Marine brigadier general, Maude DeVictor figured he'd be interested in her Agent Orange stories. He was more than a little interested. "She had accumulated some names of veterans," Kurtis recalls of his meeting with her. "They all had sort of the same tale. They were all telling her, 'Well, the doctors can't help me.'" DeVictor handed over her names and contacts to Kurtis. At about the same time, Kurtis's boss slapped a mysterious large yellow envelope down on his desk. Inside was more information about Agent Orange and soldiers' complaints. Kurtis wondered if it had come into his office in a roundabout way from DeVictor. He began reading the contents. "And I said, 'Oh, God,' because I could immediately see this was a violation of chemical warfare—against our own soldiers. I could see this was a big story."

Kurtis and his team went to work. "All I had was names. I knew that I was going to have to go out and interview these people." The first person he met was Ethel Owens, the lady who had found a friend in Maude DeVictor. Even though Charles Owens had died—just thirty days before Kurtis knocked on his widow's front door—Ethel Owens said something to Kurtis that stilled him: "She said her husband told her that there was a mist in the air in Vietnam that looked like fog in Los Angeles." Driving away, Kurtis held on to that image: mist, fog. He pulled up to a house in Madison, Illinois, the home of another soldier from DeVictor's list of names. The soldier invited Curtis inside. He had served in Pleiku. "That happened to have been an area that was sprayed," Kurtis says. The soldier, thin, frail, was seated on a sofa. "He said, 'We saw it dripping on trees,'" and the "it" was what the man thought was Agent Orange. "But the real killer was that, as we were talking," Kurtis adds, "the man's little son comes out from a back room. He puts his hand on his father's knee. The tip of the kid's finger was hanging from the finger by a bit of skin. It was very dramatic. My cameraman was already zooming in on the picture of it. It was a deformity. It proved to me it was a congenital deformity. We came away with the kernel of the whole story." On another occasion, Bill Kurtis found himself sitting in a low-income housing-project apartment. A poverty-stricken Vietnam helicopter crewman was telling him about the suffering he had been enduring from Agent Orange. "This man, a helicopter gunner, a Black man, went to Vietnam," Kurtis says, recalling the encounter, "fought for his country, and had to come back to this."

Bill Kurtis had to piece the story together between other assignments, but he kept at it. He talked to Barry Commoner, a renowned environmentalist. "Commoner turned out to be a real star in this," Kurtis says. "He had been working for Monsanto. He said that it could be that these vets were exposed to the chemical and it was lodged in their fatty tissue. And then, years later, it could be released into their systems, and it could do its damage." Aside from those working on the story with him, Kurtis kept things quiet from others inside the network. "No one," he says, "knew the story until it aired, because we didn't want the chemical companies coming after us and threatening us." Maude DeVictor told Kurtis it would be best to conceal her name.

Just before the air date of March 23, 1978, the TV station began airing promos for "Agent Orange—Vietnam's Deadly Fog." Maude DeVictor saw that promo, and something changed within her: this was going to be seen by millions; it was the kind of publicity needed for those who were suffering from the effects of Agent Orange. "She told me I could use her name after all," Kurtis says.

The televised promo spot immediately caused a buzz and caught the attention of Chicago's Vietnam Veterans Against the War. A small group of VVAW members were renting a house in Chicago, sharing not only for camaraderie, but also to save expenses. They called the house "the Barracks." Just hours before the program's March 23 airing, there was a knock at their door. "You've got to watch channel 2 this evening, this is earthshaking—this is the next movement," said an excited Bill Shunas, a friend of theirs.

Later that evening, the vets all gathered around the TV. The Agent

Orange telecast began with footage of Vietnam and airplanes spraying above treetops. The deep voice of Bill Kurtis was heard against the footage:

> A chemical defoliant that was spread over ten million acres of jungle to take the leaves off the jungle and expose the enemy . . . Everyone thought it was harmless. It was a mixture of herbicide that had been used for thirty years . . . They took no precaution in mixing it . . . Dioxin is a contaminant that is the most dangerous made by man . . . The Vietnamese complained that it was causing birth defects. Two years ago, Maude DeVictor, on her own, categorized the symptoms of the veterans and came to us . . . There were blood deaths and spontaneous abortions . . . The dioxin was not expected to stay in the body ten to twelve years.

During the program, Kurtis revealed that upward of twenty million gallons of the herbicide had been sprayed over Vietnam, ingested by Americans and Vietnamese alike. Kurtis had sat with both Black and white vets in their homes, men whose fear about what was coursing through their bodies could be read on their faces. All throughout Chicago and the surrounding areas, veterans stayed glued to their sets. They started calling other veterans.

After the show's airings—"it received the highest of ratings," Kurtis remembers—the Chicago VVAW group got in touch with other chapters and started distributing literature about the TV program. Abner Mikva, congressman from Chicago in the U.S. House of Representatives, arranged for a showing of the documentary program to the House Committee on Veterans' Affairs. "He was a big help in getting word out about Agent Orange," Kurtis says.

As for Maude DeVictor, the woman who started it all, she became an honored guest at many of the subsequent VVAW meetings. She bravely spoke her mind to the press as well. "The VA doesn't even have any rating criteria for chemical disabilities," she told a news outlet. "They're not doing anything on these cases because they don't have any standards for evaluation. Each case is either denied outright or 'diaried'—that is, placed in a computer where it's programmed to pop up every sixty days for review."

The Veterans Administration assailed the Chicago program. "All VA personnel should avoid premature commitment to any diagnosis of defoliant poisoning," came the official statement from the VA. Max Cleland, President Carter's veterans administrator, announced, "To date there is no demonstrated association between exposure and disease." The vets found such statements abhorrent.

Maude DeVictor imagined that it was only a matter of time before she lost her job at the VA, but she survived inside the bureaucracy longer than she imagined she would: she didn't lose her job until 1985. "She literally became a hero," Barry Romo recalled. A Vietnam vet staying at the Barracks, he had reached out to her after watching the documentary, and they became friends. "When they fired her, she had no money and a family. But they could no longer tie her down. She would go to places across the country."

The VVAW had filed a class action lawsuit against the chemical companies, which was finally settled in 1984 for the amount of $180 million. That number would inch up over the years. The average payout to each veteran, or their families if the veterans had died from exposure to Agent Orange, was thirty-eight hundred dollars. The veterans considered the amount paltry, but they had to take what was given.

Even though she no longer worked for the Veterans Administration, Maude DeVictor continued helping various VVAW chapters. She'd bound into their meetings wearing an AGENT ORANGE KILLS T-shirt, imploring their members to help elect Harold Washington as Chicago's first Black mayor. (Two years after Washington's election, a young man arrived in the city. He was inspired by Washington's victory and the multiracial coalition he had formed. His name was Barack Obama. And he would become very interested in politics.)

DeVictor had promised the vets Washington would be on their side and he was. As mayor, he became a fierce advocate for veterans, having served in the segregated Army during World War II. He also appointed Maude DeVictor as head of the Vets Human Rights

Commission, and devised a new jobs program for vets. "I'm pretty sure VVAW member Dave Curry and Maude wrote it," Romo said of the jobs program. In this program, Washington stipulated that vets would get extra points on exams to qualify for the police and fire departments for having served in Vietnam and would receive free training and tutoring for those exams. Chicagoans received a shock on November 25, 1987, when Washington died of a heart attack while in a meeting at City Hall.

In 1992, some VVAW members hopped a train to go to New York City to celebrate the twenty-fifth anniversary of their organization. Maude DeVictor was low on funds, so they paid all her expenses to attend. She later relocated to California and became involved with a variety of causes—election ballot reform, antipoverty issues, literacy for schoolchildren, homelessness. Her role in the exposure of Agent Orange sometimes came up. "I knew something was there but I didn't know how much," she told the *Los Angeles Times,* "like when you see lipstick on your husband's shirt."

Maude DeVictor died in 2019.

"We loved her," said Romo. "She was a woman activist, Black activist, vet activist and an international activist as well."

Before she died, the American Legion gave Maude DeVictor their "Unsung Heroine Award."

Chapter Seventeen

Flashback: 105 Degrees and Rising

Those still in Vietnam at the beginning of 1975 were wondering why there had been a Vietnam Home with Honor Parade in Times Square two years earlier. Yes, the last of the American POWs were back home. But nine months after they had been released, President Thieu of South Vietnam told his countrymen that the war was on again, evidence that the strange, byzantine world of South Vietnamese politics had hardly abated. And in April, when the worrying signs became downright dangerous, when North Vietnamese tanks were spotted rolling in the direction of Highway 1—which led straight to Saigon—when the U.S. Embassy realized it was time to shred paperwork and get out, the war's coda had truly come for all disbelievers: America would have no kind of victory, Pyrrhic or otherwise. In the weeks and months—and years—to come, many would replay those last days in and around Saigon and mull about how it had all come undone so quickly. The planning and thinking that all went awry would keep churning like a very bad dream.

On March 29, 1975, a throng of North Vietnamese soldiers marched into Da Nang. That city, the country's second largest after

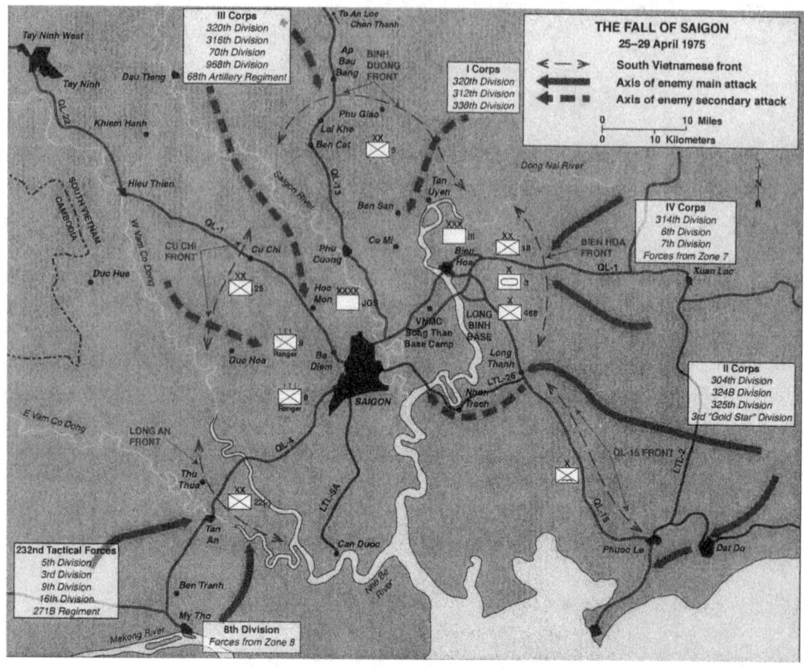

The Fall of Saigon, on April 30, 1975, was an unscripted collage of horrors.

Saigon, lay five hundred miles from Saigon. A battle was expected, but there was no battle. Instead, large numbers of the South Vietnamese Army fled. An American Boeing 727 arrived in Da Nang to evacuate Americans. Paul Vogle, a UPI reporter, was among those who clambered on board the plane. He was stunned to see members of the Hac Bao, a feared military unit of the South Vietnamese Army, aboard. If the toughest of the tough had given up, as Vogle could painfully see, this was a bad sign. The soldiers' weapons were gathered up once they were on the plane. "They didn't need them anymore . . . They had gone from humans to animals and now they were vegetables," Vogle concluded. Many in the villages surrounding Da Nang now wanted to flee to Saigon, where they thought there would be more security. It was nearly impossible to find transportation for such a long trek on such short notice. Colonel Ho Huu Lan of the North Vietnamese Army became excited by the scenes in Da Nang. "We would look at the map every day and see how the ARVN [the Army of the Republic of Vietnam, the South Vietnamese Army] had retreated," he recalled. "It was amazing. We were making more progress in a day than we made in years. One day was like twenty-five years of progress."

Frank Snepp, a CIA analyst on the ground in South Vietnam, immediately realized that the collapse in Da Nang meant trouble. He wired a cable to Washington, outlining the gravity of the situation, revealing that eight provinces in three weeks had now been claimed by North Vietnam insurgents. "The entire complexion of the Vietnam war has altered and the government is in imminent danger of decisive military defeat," Snepp warned. No one had imagined that the entire northern tier of South Vietnam could fall so quickly. Graham Martin, the newly appointed American ambassador, told Snepp he was wrong, his intel was faulty. Martin, who had worked in various American government positions since the 1940s, announced that he had not been named ambassador to "give Vietnam away to communists."

Philip Caputo had fought in the war. He went home and got a job as a reporter with the *Chicago Tribune,* and the newspaper decided to send him back to Vietnam. "The ambassador couldn't believe this was all ending the way it was ending," Caputo recalled of the unraveling. "They would come out with these statements to the effect that the South Vietnamese are going to pull back and turn Saigon into another Stalingrad or that the North Vietnamese were going to negotiate."

There were ghastly scenes unfolding at Cam Ranh Bay, where crowds surged to get onto ships in hope of being ferried to Saigon. Fights broke out; people were trampled. Up and down the coastline, other cities began to fall—Quy Nhon, Tam Ky, Quang Ngai. The North Vietnamese were clearly aiming for Saigon. American military officials realized that contingency plans needed to be mapped and Saigon had to be evacuated. General Frederick Weyand had advice for the White House: "For reasons of prudence, the United States should plan now for a mass evacuation of some six thousand U.S. citizens and tens of thousands of South Vietnamese . . . nationals to whom we have incurred an obligation [of] protection."

What had become of the cease-fire? Of the peace treaty? Of all the backroom dealing by Henry Kissinger—now the secretary of state—and his team? No one could answer. "The one ending no one could have imagined in Vietnam, an outright battlefield victory for one side or the other, now seems not only possible but perhaps inevitable," wrote Arnold R. Isaacs, a *Baltimore Sun* reporter.

Throughout large sections of South Vietnam, wild and chaotic roadside scenes began appearing, of fleeing families, mothers carrying infant children like footballs cradled in their arms. Families carrying potato sacks filled with their possessions raced toward helicopters and boat piers. Ambassador Martin was claiming to be in consultation with the French—who knew all about losing to the Vietnamese. He was going behind the scenes to broker a power-sharing agreement between the North and the South Vietnamese. "He desperately wanted to believe there was a chance for South Vietnam to survive," Snepp felt.

By April 8, it had become clear that North Vietnamese troops were trying to capture Xuan Loc. If they did so, they would have nearly a clear road to Saigon. General Le Minh Dao, a South Vietnamese Army commander, was intent on holding important territory. "I vow to hold Xuan Loc. I don't care how many divisions the other side sends against me. I will knock them down." Back in America, President Ford was pleading with Congress for emergency aid to South Vietnam, reminding them that North Vietnam had violated the 1973 peace agreement. He told them that all the remaining Americans, and the South Vietnamese who had aided the American military through the years, needed rescuing.

The U.S. Marines were already landing in Phnom Penh, Cambodia, to evacuate Americans from the embassy there.

Congress rebuffed Ford's plea, deciding not to give any more military aid for Vietnam, but they did agree to provide evacuation funds. Politicians in South Vietnam felt betrayed that more military aid would not be forthcoming. Bui Diem was South Vietnam's ambassador-at-large with a versatile portfolio. He saw no need to conceal his rising anger. "The U.S. spent billions and billions in Vietnam," he said. "But at the last minute the Congress washed their hands. I didn't think that was good for a big nation like the U.S.

to behave like that. Because by that time we weren't asking for the blood of American soldiers."

Politicians in Washington, of course, thought Vietnam was all but over. The bloodshed and protests in their own country had exhausted them. "I will give you large sums for evacuation, but not one nickel for military aid" is what New York Senator Jacob Javits told President Ford.

It was now a seesawing battle of words and secret plans, back and forth between America and Vietnam, while the North Vietnamese tanks rolled in the direction of Saigon. President Ford's secretary of defense, James Schlesinger, warned Congress that more than two hundred thousand Vietnamese would be slaughtered if they were trapped in Saigon when the North Vietnamese arrived.

Frank Snepp kept at it, meeting with officials and trying to get Ambassador Martin to prepare for the worse. "I briefed American civilians, I briefed American journalists and businessmen, and I briefed Marines who were showing up to assist with the evolving evacuation planning," Snepp would recall. "They were astounded because Ambassador Martin had convinced . . . them and convinced himself that the communists would allow for a ceasefire, a coalition government, and a peaceful transition." Snepp also consulted with Master Sergeant Juan Valdez, the Marine responsible for the security guards at the U.S. Embassy. Valdez was a second-generation Mexican immigrant, living in Texas, another Marine who had joined the Corps right out of high school. Valdez was on his second tour of Vietnam. He listened closely to Snepp's warning. Intel wasn't always solid, but Valdez figured that if anyone knew anything substantive it would be the CIA. "The situation didn't sound good," Valdez recalled. "We started doing more training, going out to the rifle range and doing more firing. But when you're on embassy duty you really don't have much of any support weapons. You have shotguns, revolvers, and tear gas. That's about the extent of it. You can't face a big force coming at you with that type of weapons."

A quite ominous addition into the conflict came with the participation of the Khmer Rouge, who had joined forces with the North Vietnamese. A ragtag army out of Cambodia, they possessed a lethal and unforgiving mindset. Their soldiers were partial to wearing red bandannas. Their loyalty to North Vietnam could be traced to the fact that parts of Cambodia had once been taken by the South Vietnamese. But President Thieu of South Vietnam remained steadfast, not fearing the Khmer Rouge, and vowing to fight "to the last bullet and the last grain of rice."

On April 20, worried citizens began a run on Saigon's banks, sensing collapse. A day later, Highway 1 was without defenses and considered wide open. Bands of South Vietnamese soldiers were seen there, without their weapons—tantamount to a show of surrender. April 20 also brought more headline-making political news: President Thieu abruptly resigned, though not before castigating America: "You Americans with your 500,000 soldiers . . . were not defeated, you ran away." Vice-President Tran Van Huong assumed the South Vietnamese presidency. Huong was an aging man, known to be in bad health. The American military was already ordering C-130 and C-141 transport planes to leave air bases in Guam and the Philippines and get to Saigon. Those who had helped the American cause, who had risked their own lives throughout the war, wanted desperately to get out, but found it nearly impossible to get visas. Frank Snepp, the American spy, was determined to work through the unfolding chaos and help people leave. "We began going to Vietnamese friends and smuggling them out on cargo aircraft that were leaving with their cargo bays empty," he said. "We began mounting basically a black airlift around the ambassador's orders without his knowing it."

Over in Soul Alley, the scene had not been hopping for the past couple of years. Soul-food menus had disappeared. And those Black AWOL deserters who had taken refuge there had absconded for destinations unknown.

No one could understand the reticence of Ambassador Graham Martin to start evacuations. He kept repeating that it would cause panic, but panic had already set in. On April 24, a U.S. naval attaché estimated that thirty thousand evacuees could be boarded onto ships and suggested that Martin authorize it. Martin nixed the idea: his reasoning, yet again, a perceived onslaught of panic. Intelligence reports were showing that one hundred thousand North Vietnamese troops were heading for Saigon, maiming and killing along the way.

Finally, some good news came from America: the House and Senate had approved an immediate evacuation-aid package for South Vietnam in the amount of $327 million. Not a nickel of that was for military aid. "The string had run out for the United States," General Jack Cushman offered. "The public was just not going to support that. You couldn't ask them to do that. By that time they had been convinced they were striking a match on a bar of soap."

Rockets had not been fired upon Saigon in at least five years. But in the early morning of April 27, they dropped on the city. Homes were engulfed in fire and smoke and reduced to rubble. The crazy war was back! A North Vietnamese commander said the goal was to attack Saigon "like a hurricane." Ambassador Martin, sick with pneumonia, still held fast to the possibility of peace negotiations. Some thought he had become mentally unhinged. "He was terribly enfeebled," Snepp concluded. The sinking political life of South Vietnam took another turn on April 28, when General Duong Van Minh was sworn in as the new president and found himself welcomed with news that the North Vietnamese had hijacked aircraft from South Vietnamese pilots, and were now dropping bombs around South Vietnam. The runways of the Saigon airport were littered with debris, and Americans realized that flying in and out any longer would be more than risky. When Ambassador Martin traveled out to the airport to see for himself, he realized it would be impossible to land more planes on the airport's cratered grounds.

April 29 came to be remembered as the official beginning of the Fall of Saigon. Marine Lieutenant Colonel Fred Jones waited offshore with other Marines and naval personnel in a flotilla of ships to help rescue American citizens and the Vietnamese who had worked alongside Americans during the war.

—

Fred Jones was raised by a single mother on the south side of Oroville, California; they were one of the few Black families in this city. He got a football scholarship to Oregon State University. One of his football coaches was a Marine Reserve captain. During his senior year at the university, a Marine recruiter—doubtless encouraged by the football coach—paid Jones a visit. "He was a little bit on the arrogant side," Jones recalled. "And I'd never seen a black Marine." When Jones expressed a growing interest in the Marines, friends tried to convince him to steer clear of that particular military branch. They talked about racism and what they perceived would be a lack of opportunity. Jones let them know that, with his college degree, he'd be entering the Marines as a future officer. He went through two officer-candidate classes—the only Black in either class. He got his commission in late 1964. That same year, Jones found himself at a Marine base party. He was told he was now one of fewer than forty Black Marine officers, out of a total of about twenty-three thousand Marine officers. One major told Jones he looked like a career Marine officer. "I said, 'Major, there is absolutely no way in the world that I could stay in an organization like this, when I look around and there is nobody that looks like me.' "

During an early assignment at Quantico, Virginia, Jones became good friends with his fellow Marine George Lancaster, who was white. Lancaster went to Vietnam, and when Jones heard he had been badly injured—though he survived—he felt guilty; he felt he should be in Vietnam instead of spending time playing on the Marine football team.

Jones landed in Vietnam in 1967. His wife, Shirley, worried night and day while he was away. By the end of his tour, he had completed his Marine commitment and was ready to go out into the civilian world. One higher-up Marine officer gave him a warning: "Do you think it's going to be any easier for you in the private sector than in the Marine Corps? How many black faces do you think you're going to see in the boardroom at Mobil today?" The conversation struck a deep chord with Jones. He thought it all over—a gamble with the white world of civilian life in 1960s America, or a gamble with race and the United States Marines? He had more faith in the Marines. "I enjoyed—frankly, on a personal, ego basis—I probably enjoyed being one of 'the few.' "

By the spring of 1975, he was Lieutenant Colonel Fred Jones, commanding officer of the Logistic Support Unit, 3rd Battalion, 9th Marine Regiment, aboard the USS *Mobile,* which sat just off the coast of a battered Saigon and a besieged U.S. Embassy, to which thousands continued rushing. "My people and the infantry group were on the boat," Jones recalled about waiting in the flotilla of thirty American warships with fellow Marines and Navy personnel. "We had Mike-8 boats. The Vietnamese are small people." The Mike-8 boats were large enough to fit about 150 people on them. The plan was to pick up refugees in the boats and ferry them to nearby cargo ships. But Jones began worrying when they did not receive the orders. "The ambassador kept delaying the operation," he said. In the early-morning hours of April 29, two Marines—Lance Corporal Darwin Judge, from Marshalltown, Iowa, and Corporal Charles McMahon, Jr., from Woburn, Massachusetts—were killed in a rocket attack near the U.S. Embassy. "It was a direct hit," Juan Valdez, a fellow Marine, recalled. "I was very upset and very mad. I still blame the ambassador for that. This shouldn't have happened. If the ambassador had taken action and gotten people out of there instead of trying to think that he was going to negotiate with the North Vietnamese, this would have never happened."

The horrors kept mounting. South Vietnamese soldiers were not only retreating—many had begun rioting, and those who were not rioting were clambering over the walls of the embassy. Ambassador Martin finally authorized release of the code signal over the radio airwaves: "The temperature in Saigon is one hundred and five degrees and rising." Those who heard those words knew what the signal meant: they were to get to assigned evacuation points immediately. The courtyard of the embassy was a major evacuation area. Embassy staff quickly realized there was a problem—the huge tamarind tree that stood in the courtyard. "We had to get chain saws," recalled Juan Valdez. "It was See Bees [*sic*], mostly, with a couple of Marines, and they had to chop this big tree down, cut it in pieces, tow it away. And then they had to get the fire department to wash off all the debris and everything so when the choppers landed they wouldn't suck up all that debris into the engines." Improvisation was a signature feature of war.

The ground forces got a lot of miscommunication from Martin at the embassy—as well as decision makers back in Washington. It was finally decided that there had been too many delays, and they had to nix the boat evacuation plans, although some South Vietnamese jerry-rigged boats on their own and took to the water. The rescue helicopters launched their mission and began flying back and forth from the site of the embassy and various other locations. "We finally realized the Mike-8 boats were not going," recalls Commander Fred Jones. "We're gonna do it all by helicopter. We start taking in the refugees by helicopter. We vigorously screened for weapons [when they boarded]." There were still rescue boats in the vicinity. Jones and his Marines were now tasked with processing and helping board those who had been rescued. "There were women and children, from infants to grandparents," Jones recalls. The mission went on all day and all night, April 29 to 30. "It was the longest day of my life," Jones says.

Waves washed over the fleeing Vietnamese who had climbed aboard small boats, hoping to get out to the American flotilla. Some of them simply vanished.

Philip Caputo, the former soldier turned *Chicago Tribune* reporter, now back in Saigon for the evacuation, was one of those hustling toward a helicopter to get out. "There were a lot of Vietnamese on board," Caputo remembers. "Vietnamese who had worked for us. One woman managed, small as she was, to run on there with a good-sized carry bag of gold bars. The chopper took off, and we're flying toward the coast. And you could look down and all you could see all around Saigon, all around the airfield, were plumes of smoke from burning buildings and exploding artillery shells. And then, finally, we crossed over the coastline. And I'll never forget seeing the entire Seventh Fleet and all of these merchant ships that had been press-ganged into naval service, dozens of them."

The CIA's Frank Snepp was in a secure location, listening to desperate pleas via radio. "Some Americans had left their billets so rapidly that morning they'd left their radios behind. So their Vietnamese friends were on the radios begging to be rescued. 'I'm Han the driver.' 'I'm Mr. Ngoc, your translator.' And I stood there wondering how in the world we could reach them. It's one of the most horrible memories of that day, because I could hear them on the radio and I knew that we couldn't get to them." James Fenton, a British journalist—and also a respected poet—was in Saigon in time to witness the evacuation: "There was no way of disguising this evacuation by sleight-of-hand, or, it appeared, of getting it over quickly. The noise of the vast helicopters, as they corkscrewed out of the sky, was a fearful incentive to panic. The weather turned bad. It began to rain. And as the evening grew darker, it seemed as if the helicopters themselves were blotting out the light." Just as others were doing, Fenton was musing about the war's epitaph: "The accumulated weight of the years of propaganda came crashing down upon a terrified city."

On the grounds of the embassy lay all matter of debris and confetti from shredded documents. A picture frame was spotted on the ground, with a quote from T. H. Lawrence of Arabia inside of it: "Better to let them do it imperfectly than to do it perfectly yourself, for it is their country, their way and your time is short."

Out at sea empty helicopters were being shoved from ships' decks into the water and junked to make room for other helicopters that had to land. There was no more room for them after the mission was completed.

Late on the afternoon of April 30, Ambassador Graham Martin was rushed to the rooftop of the embassy and hustled onto a helicopter. He held the embassy's American flag with him.

President Minh of South Vietnam announced surrender.

Three years later, the reconfigured Vietnamese military was back in the world's news, having invaded Cambodia and stopped the genocidal rampage undertaken by the Khmer Rouge, in which upward of two million people were believed to have died from murder, torture, and disease. Pol Pot, who ruled the Khmer Rouge, took his place in the pantheon of history's madmen.

A good many Black soldiers who had traipsed over to Soul Alley for cultural sustenance in Saigon were confronted with American versions of Soul Alleys when they returned home. The urban uprisings in the 1960s had left many Black neighborhoods scarred. Whites found it far easier to get federal home loans than Blacks, and fled to the suburbs. Many had imagined the 1968 Fair Housing Act would expose and remedy housing discrimination. But it certainly did not. The reason became obvious: the enforcement was, more often than not, quite lax. In 1974, the Equal Credit Opportunity Act had to be created to confront discriminatory practices when it came to mortgage lending.

Black vets came home to a nation still unsure how much it really wanted to invest in the cause of racial equality. One of those Black soldiers was Army Specialist Robert Holcomb, a native of New York City who had been an armorer in Vietnam. He returned Stateside in late 1970. Before his induction, Holcomb had actually tried to dodge the draft. The FBI caught up with him and hauled him to the induction station, where he was forced to take his induction oath wearing manacles. His parents were ashamed of him. "When South Vietnam started to fall, it was a drag," he said. "Watching the [South Vietnamese Army] run to the sea on television . . . I kept saying, these cats want what we want. To be able to express yourself. They know the Communist thing doesn't work. But they were fleeing." His first week home, Holcomb went to spend the holidays with his parents. "They told me that I was right in protesting the war and that they felt bad telling me to go. Then they made a bed for me upstairs in my old room. But I didn't really feel comfortable sleeping aboveground in a bed. So I moved down into a corner of the basement and put everything around my bed. Gun here. Stereo here. All your pot right here. Just like in the war. Then I could go to sleep."

CHAPTER EIGHTEEN

THE LONG WAY HOME FROM A LONG WAR

Black Americans emerging from the Vietnam War returned home with their own unique perspectives and interpretations about the war. Of the key characters in this narrative—Elbert Nelson, George Forrest, Joe Anderson, Wallace Terry, Dorothy Harris, Fred Cherry, Henry Reed, Art Gregg, Philippa Schuyler—only Schuyler didn't make it back home.

After she died, on May 9, 1967, in the helicopter that crashed shortly after takeoff, carrying orphans away from the war in South Vietnam, her name receded from public view. Schuyler had come to the civil rights battles late—inspired by the Black soldiers she met in Vietnam—and, for years, had no champions in the Black community. Her biracial pedigree confused many. But things began to change in the 1980s. A school—the Philippa Schuyler Middle School for the Gifted and Talented—was named for her in Brooklyn, New York. It's a magnet school, and its enrollment is made up largely of minority students. The school proudly promotes its namesake in its literature, describing Schuyler as "a child prodigy born in August of 1931, who was able to read and write at the age of two and a half, a pianist at four, and a composer by five. Philippa was

Dan Bullock was fourteen years old when he lied about his age to enlist in the Marines. A year later, now fifteen, the young Black soldier was killed in the Highlands of Vietnam by enemy fire. He became the youngest soldier killed in the long, hard war.

often compared to Mozart." Kathryn Talalay's biography appeared in 1995. Every now and then, a notice will appear in the press announcing that a composer somewhere—often a Black composer—will be playing some of the music of Philippa Schuyler at a recital. Philippa is remembered.

George Forrest couldn't shake the different receptions he got when he came home from Vietnam on his first and second tours. Like many soldiers, he had to quickly analyze the political landscape depending on which airport he was in. In liberal antiwar parts of the country, he'd change into civilian clothes before gliding through the airports. In conservative parts of the country, which were more pro-war, he'd leave his uniform on.

Forrest quickly realized that he didn't want to talk about the war. He had lost seventeen men on the battlefield; they were still haunting his dreams. He wondered about their families, the pain they must be enduring. He took a job as defensive coordinator and assistant head football coach at Morgan State University, his alma mater. He liked talking to the players about leadership on the field, about teamwork. After years in that job, he moved back to his hometown of Leonardtown, Maryland, and spent years teaching at a high school. In 2002, he was appointed county administrator of St. Mary's County, a job equivalent to the position of mayor. "The irony of that job is that when I was growing up," he says, "you couldn't go in the front door of the county administration building if you were Black. Now, as county administrator, I had the keys to the building."

In 1992, a book about the Battle of Ia Drang was published, titled *We Were Soldiers Once . . . and Young.* It was written by Hal Moore, the Army officer who became legendary from that battle, and Joe Galloway, a reporter who had been present during part of it. Ten years after the book's publication, a movie adapted from it arrived in theaters. But before he saw the movie, George Forrest began getting calls from some of the soldiers who served under him in Vietnam. They were irate, wanting to know why Forrest and his heroics were not portrayed in the film. When Forrest finally saw the movie, he realized that it only portrayed one of the two battles fought at Ia Drang. It did not include the Albany battle, in which he had distinguished himself. He calmed his men down. "Maybe the sequel," Forrest says.

When Maryland Governor Larry Hogan began hosting anniversary events for the state's Vietnam vets—he called them Welcome Home Vietnam Veterans Day—George Forrest was grateful. He would get dressed and go to these annual events, and it made him feel good. "I was at a reunion once, and a kid came up to me—about sixteen or seventeen. And he said to me, 'Thank you.' And I said, 'What are you thanking me for?' He said, 'My father was in your company during the battle, and he survived. I am here because of what you did to help him survive.' And you don't know what that did to beat off some of the demons." Sometimes area schools will ask George Forrest to come talk to the young students. He tells them that the Army gave much to his life, that he was proud to have served. But he doesn't shy away from talking about racial issues. "When I have to tell my story of how to survive as a Black man in a country I fought for, well, it breaks my heart."

After the nurse Dorothy Harris left Vietnam in September 1968, she was asked to extend her military commitment a few extra months and go to work at a VA hospital in San Francisco. She moved back to the Midwest after that, and got jobs as an industrial nurse, first for the Ford Motor Company, and then for General Electric. She also got a bachelor's degree and a master's degree. The GI Bill helped immensely with her education costs. When she finally tired of moving around, she settled back in her hometown of Cincinnati. Never one to sit still, she started doing volunteer work for a community program helping low-income people navigate the court system. But as the 1980s approached, Dorothy Harris was finding it harder and harder to get a good night's sleep. Things from her past started bothering her. She came to realize she had no one to talk to about her Vietnam experiences. Some days, she wondered if she might be having a sort of nervous breakdown. Finally, she joined the Vietnam Veterans of America. She didn't join the Vietnam Veterans Against the War (VVAW), because she thought they were a bit radical. It wasn't that she had loved the war; she just loved the people who gave to the cause, who were with her in Cu Chi. The VA diagnosed her with PTSD, a rather common stress ailment for those who had served in war zones.

One day, Dorothy Harris decided she needed to take a trip. She had to go see Leroy Pitts. She had loved Pitts. Not in a romantic way—she knew he was married when they met—but in a platonic way, a big-sister, little-brother kind of way. Leroy Pitts, of course, was dead. But she felt a calling to visit his gravesite. Though friends and relatives began fretting when she told them she was going to drive to Oklahoma by herself, she was not afraid of being out on the road as a Black woman all alone. "I was fearless!" she says, all these years later. She drove through parts of Indiana, over into Illinois, made her way on into Missouri, and finally to Oklahoma. She didn't have anyone's phone number, had never even met any of the Pitts family, but she knew he was from Fallis, Oklahoma, and that's where she pulled up. "I asked people for the cemetery where Leroy was buried," she says. They told her he was actually buried over in Spencer, about twenty-five miles away. In the small towns in that part of Oklahoma, everyone knew of Leroy Pitts. He was a war hero, had earned the biggest medal of them all, the Medal of Honor. She drove over to Spencer and found the burial site, took some pictures, and said a little prayer. Another idea came to her: she decided she needed to find Eula Pitts, Leroy's widow. When she began asking around, someone told her that Mrs. Leroy Pitts lived over in Oklahoma City, about ten miles from Spencer. She climbed back into her car.

Dorothy Harris stepped up onto the very same porch as the Army officers back in 1967, when they arrived to deliver the grim news that Army Captain Leroy Pitts had been killed in action. Eula Pitts welcomed Dorothy into her home, and it didn't take the two women long to start sharing stories about Leroy—his love of family, his joy in military life, his determination to get battlefield experience. Eula talked about the White House Medal of Honor ceremony, and how warm LBJ had been with the little Pitts children. Dorothy herself couldn't stop talking about Leroy's smile and the Coca-Colas he always brought to the nurses. About how so many of the nurses just couldn't ignore his handsome looks. Eula pulled out some photographs, and they summoned more memories. She had never remarried. When Dorothy got ready to leave, she promised Eula she'd stay in touch, and they have done so, through the years. Dorothy stopped at a gas station before exiting Oklahoma to fill up and prepare for the long journey back to Ohio. She loaded some Coca-Colas into the car. Then she rolled north, toward home.

Any military death causes a ripple. The edges of photos of lost ones are rubbed, touched, and looked over endlessly. The framed photos take up hallowed places on mantels inside thousands and thousands of homes. No one comes back from the dead. And yet, the voice of Leroy Pitts—the Medal of Honor winner—did. In 2020, his widow, Eula Pitts, was sitting in her Oklahoma City home watching a Muhammad Ali documentary made by Ken Burns. On her TV screen was a portion of the documentary where Ali talks about racism and the Vietnam War. An ABC crew was in the field around the same time talking to Black soldiers about Ali and his stance. They were supportive of his refusal to join the military because of his religious beliefs. At first it was just a flash, a Black officer in the background. But Eula Pitts knew what she had seen in that flash: her husband, Leroy; it was his voice. Even wearing his helmet, she knew it was him! So she picked up the phone and called her son, Mark, in Tampa. She told Mark she had just seen his father on a documentary, and she insisted he do some research because she wanted to see more of him. Mark couldn't quite get excited because he didn't quite believe it. "But you know how mothers are," he said. He knew some people who had some PBS contacts. There were fits and starts to his inquiry. It took four years, but in the summer of 2025 ABC archivists found the decades-old footage of Captain Riley "Leroy" Pitts, who had been the first Black *officer* awarded the Medal of Honor. The network flew correspondent Byron Pitts (no relation to the Pitts family) out to Oklahoma to visit Eula Pitts and talk about the stunning discovery. It was an emotional gathering for the family. Looking over photos of their captain, their dad, the Coca-Cola man. When it aired, the segment got quite a lot of attention. "You feel good about it," Eula Pitts told me after the news segment aired. "But the Medal of Honor of course doesn't help you raise your children. We wanted him back. Not the medals."

As I watched the Pitts segment on TV, it dawned on me that this is what it must have been like in my neighborhood of Columbus, Ohio, for all those mothers who fretted for their sons gone off to Vietnam—a war behind them, a war in front of them, and a war awaiting them. Leroy Pitts's two children, Mark and Stacie, were so small when he went off to Vietnam that they barely could remember his voice. Then one day there he was, in 'Nam, on the doggone TV. It was like a miracle. Sometimes war produces miracles.

Not everyone had nightmares. Not everyone woke up in cold sweats, wondering about Agent Orange and psychological wounds from Vietnam. Art Gregg had a corporate-type job in Vietnam—ordering uniforms, food, writing paper, pens, pencils, soaps, shampoo, materials to make hooches, air conditioners, refrigerators. When he returned home from Vietnam and, in 1981, retired from the military, he found himself being recruited by corporate headhunters. When he originally enlisted in the military, there were no headhunters looking for Black talent. He realized how much the world had changed. One of the headhunters connected him to Cox Enterprises, and he went to work for them in New Orleans as vice-president and general manager of Cox Cable. He held that job for a few years, then became vice-president of a steel tech manufacturing company. He closed out his nine-to-five workaday life as president of James Martin Government Intelligence, an information technology company. He later served on several corporate boards. There was money in the bank. He made national news when a military fort was co-named in his honor. In 2024, his daughter finally convinced him to move into an assisted living facility, though he remained spry and active. He kept receiving invitations to military events, and attended as many as he could. Soldiers fussed over him. He was sitting in his elegantly furnished home surrounded by framed medals and awards, by books and photographs of him and various dignitaries. There were pictures of him and Charlene. "My late wife is buried at Arlington," he said. "Of course, I will join her there someday. Chappie is three graves over." Chappie is Daniel James, Jr., the first Black four-star general in the military. Chappie was a friend. There was one thing Art Gregg lamented about the Vietnam War: "We did not have a victory celebration in the traditional sense," he says, remembering the World War II Times Square celebrations of 1945 quite vividly. Back then, Art Gregg thought the American military was invincible. On the day of our interview, he still felt that way.

Art Gregg died in a Richmond, Virginia, hospital on August 22, 2024. He was ninety-six.

When Henry Reed left the Marines, he still wanted to be around the military. He and his wife, Brenda, settled in the Baltimore area, and Henry became a ROTC instructor at Chesapeake High School in Essex, Maryland. He did not tolerate foolishness; he was a Marine. The kids were drawn to him. He stayed in the job for five years, then took a job helping disabled young adults. The young Reed nieces and nephews were in awe of him, looking at pictures of him in his snow-white Marine uniform, which he had donned for special occasions during his career. Occasionally, he was invited to military reunions, but he always declined, except when it came to the Montford Point Marines, those early Black Marines who had suffered all manner of indignities in their effort to fight for America. "He would go to their reunions because they paved the way," says Brenda Reed, now his widow. He saw his daughter, LaVonda, his only child, graduate from college, then law school, and become a law professor. Her success filled him with great joy. (In 2024 she was named Dean of the University of Baltimore School of Law.) Brenda wanted to talk to him about his ailments, to push him to go visit the doctor. "But he wouldn't go," she says. "And he wouldn't go to the VA, either." Whatever was causing his ailments—body pain, difficulty breathing—Henry wouldn't talk to anyone about it. "I'm sure he suffered from Agent Orange," Brenda Reed says. There was also the lawsuit against Camp Lejeune by those who, like the Reeds, had lived there when Henry was in the military. The water was found to have been toxic.

In 2013, the United States Marines published *Pathbreakers,* a book chronicling the exploits of a handful of history-making Black Marines. Henry Reed was one of those featured. He died two years later, on December 16, 2015. There is a picture of Reed in the *Pathbreakers* book. He is in South Vietnam. He is at war. Standing next to a jeep, he is wearing fatigues and a floppy hat. He is strapped with all manner of small weaponry, and there is a canteen on his belt loop and a cigar in his mouth. He'd soon be off and up into the jungle, hunting the enemy. According to his fighting buddies, he was happy loping off into the jungle, searching for combatants.

Wallace Terry was very honest when looking back over his time in Vietnam, admitting that he was "scared every moment I was there." After the publication of his oral-history book, *Bloods,* he had an admirable career, teaching and lecturing at various universities. That he had been one of the few Black journalists to have covered the civil rights movement *and* Vietnam gave him a certain cachet in journalism circles. Newsrooms lacked diversity, and in the 1980s and 1990s, he began recommending bright students to newspaper editors whom he knew around the country, helping several of the students get interviews and land jobs. Young Black journalists looked up to him as a role model. He became a contributor to *USA Today* and *Parade* magazine. He told audiences that Vietnam was the first place where he had seen Black and white Americans form tight bonds. "These men learned that an enemy bullet does not discriminate," he said.

Years passed, but the Vietnam War wouldn't let Wallace Terry go. In 2000, he coordinated a symposium—Rendezvous with War: Veterans, Correspondents, Historians, and Film Makers Reflect on the Vietnam War 25 Years Later—at which he helped bring together many of the most admired print journalists who had covered the war, along with some of the military officers who had been stationed there. It took place at the College of William & Mary, whose president at the time was Timothy Sullivan, who had served in the Army Signal Corps in Vietnam. Participants at the symposium included Peter Arnett, Stanley Karnow, Phil Caputo, Hal Moore (of Ia Drang fame), and Everett Alvarez, the first American aviator taken as a POW in Vietnam. It was a telling commentary on American journalism that Terry was the only Black reporter with a major role in the event. Friends of Wallace Terry's would see him around Washington, D.C., engaged in street conversations with people who, minutes earlier, had been strangers to him. He'd be talking about Vietnam, and sharing his feelings that the nation was still not grappling with the aftereffects of the war. Three years after the William & Mary symposium, Wallace Terry died of a rare vascular disease. Appalled by the election of Donald Trump in 2016, Janice Terry, who had been so important to her husband's work, who had traveled in and out of Saigon when he was stationed there, gave up on America and moved to Berlin, Germany, with her son David. She felt America was playing a dangerous game with its democracy.

—

Whatever dreams Fred Cherry had as a prisoner of war in North Vietnam, he certainly knew they were just that—dreams. Seven years is an interminably long time to be away from a wife and kids, to be away from home. While Cherry had been imprisoned, Shirley Cherry took up with another man and invited him to move into her home. She also had her husband declared dead, so she could reap insurance benefits. The move outraged Fred Cherry's siblings. His children were quite confused. "The four of us were raising ourselves," his daughter Cynthia declared. Shirley Cherry had a baby with her boyfriend, a man whom she lavished with expensive gifts with the money coming from Fred Cherry's combat paychecks, which the Air Force was still sending to her. So Fred Cherry returned to an American nightmare. His accumulated pay while he was in captivity was $147,184. When he came home, the account had dwindled to less than five thousand dollars. In addition to the challenges of returning home as a POW, the domestic wreckage around Cherry was numbing. He couldn't understand why the Air Force continued to send his wife his checks when she clearly had abandoned their marriage, and was forced to sue the Air Force to get his back pay, or at least some of it. The case went through a slow-moving court system. The stories in the press—especially the Black press, always hungry for revenue—had a tawdry aspect: the ex-POW's wife who remarried while he was away and spent his money. A court of claims finally ruled that Cherry wasn't entitled to all of the money, because the children had needed support while he was away. He was awarded fifty thousand dollars. After lawyer's fees, he took home a check in the amount of thirty-five thousand. That came out to the sum of five thousand dollars for each year of his captivity and torture.

In the 1980s and 1990s, there were more calls to recognize Black accomplishments historically in all branches of the American military. The Air Force wanted Fred Cherry to speak at events, and he did so, until he died of cardiac arrest on February 16, 2016, at the age of eighty-seven. He had lived long enough to see an oil painting of him—looking glorious in his flight uniform, with a white scarf around his neck—unveiled at the Pentagon, where it now hangs.

—

When he was growing up in segregated Georgia, Elbert Nelson found it strange that the USO (United Service Organization) clubs for Black and white veterans were so different. "The USO club for Blacks was like a three-room shack," he says. "For whites it was just like a country club, with a swimming pool." When he returned home from Vietnam, Nelson, a doctor, didn't want to join any veteran organizations, because of those childhood memories of the USO. "I sort of stayed away from the military community," he says. He still had medical residency requirements to complete at home, and after accomplishing them, he joined the faculty of the University of Cincinnati College of Medicine, in the Department of Obstetrics and Gynecology—one of the first Blacks to join that department. He earned some distinguished-teaching awards, and there were stories about him in local magazines. Sometimes these mentioned his Vietnam War service. His children were very proud of him, and all was good.

Every now and then since his retirement, Elbert Nelson will open his file cabinets and look at papers, maps, and items from the war. He thinks of all the young Black soldiers who came under his medical care; so many of them felt a cultural kinship with him. He had tried to counsel them and caution against doing the kinds of things that would scar their military records. These were mostly the young Blacks who had arrived, like he did, in 1969, a time when the anti–Vietnam War anger in America was boiling. "They just did not want to be there," he says of those soldiers.

But Elbert Nelson, in his Cincinnati home, couldn't outrun medical realities. As a doctor, he sensed what was happening to his body. The symptoms began. "I lived in an area in Vietnam where Agent Orange was sprayed." He has had to make visits to the VA hospital, and has engaged there with the Vietnam veteran community, the very community he had shied from. But these days he finds comfort in the camaraderie.

—

After his Vietnam tours, Joe Anderson remained in the military until 1978, determined to utilize his West Point education and war experience to the best of his abilities. Once in a while, he was asked about the Oscar-winning French film *The Anderson Platoon,* and was happy to talk about it. *The Anderson Platoon* aside, the fact remains that very few of the Hollywood films about the Vietnam War—which began appearing in the 1970s and 1980s—have featured Blacks in leading roles. He considered himself mentally healthy after his wartime experiences—he had no demons to chase—and chalked that up to West Point: he'd been ready for war when he got to Vietnam. He was selected as a White House Fellow, and taught at West Point. He picked up a graduate degree at UCLA. General Motors wanted him under its roof, and he worked for more than a decade as an executive there. His GM unit had business revenue of more than a billion dollars. Inside GM, he was a star. But what Joe Anderson really wanted to do was introduce Blacks to finance, to money management, show them ways of making money. He became an investor, and founder and chairman of TAG (The Anderson Group) Holdings. Through the years, he has made plenty of money as an investor. He possesses a streak of generosity, and has spread some of his wealth around, and mentored people. "I'm all about creating wealth in the Black community," he says. "There are seven African American men that own their own companies that have worked for me." He adds: "I want my legacy to be about wealth."

It has long been a concern to Black vets that members of their race have been ignored when it came time to recognize battlefield heroism. They would hear about "lost paperwork" and other excuses, but it was clear that there was a racial component. No Blacks received Medal of Honor recognition during World War I or World War II. In the 1940s, a bespectacled Black scholar, Lawrence Reddick, sought to investigate why.

Reddick received two degrees from Fisk University and a doctorate from the University of Chicago, and in 1939 became a curator at the Schomburg Center in Harlem. (In 1972, the building would be renamed the Schomburg Center for Research in Black Culture.) Reddick launched an investigation into the lack of recognition of Blacks for wartime valor, beginning by putting ads in the Black press urging soldiers who had served in the world wars to write to him. For two years, 1944 to 1946, he amassed letters and memorabilia and began interviewing soldiers. His research resulted in an exhibit, "The Negro Warrior: His Record and His Future," which opened at the Harlem Branch of the New York Public Library in 1947, highlighting examples of bravery by Black soldiers during both world wars. The white mainstream press ignored the exhibit and its revelations, and the stories remained lost to history.

But then, in 1991, President George H. W. Bush addressed Lawrence Reddick's seven-decades-long concerns. Bush posthumously bestowed the Medal of Honor upon World War I Corporal Freddie Stowers, who joined the French Army to be able to fight for his native country, America. On September 28, 1918, Stowers and his men came under attack by Germans in France. Part of the Stowers citation: "While crawling forward and urging his men to continue the attack on a second trench line, [Stowers] was gravely injured by machine-gun fire. Although Cpl. Stowers was mortally wounded, he pressed forward, urging on the members of his squad, until he died."

The Army, not long after the Stowers honor was bestowed, initiated an investigation into whether "racial disparity" played a role in the manner in which Medals of Honor were given. The answer was yes. Congress then stepped in and passed a waiver, giving then President Bill Clinton an opportunity to award medals despite the passage of time. Seven Black soldiers were identified for their heroism in World War II and received the Medal of Honor. Vernon Baker was the only one of the seven alive in 1997 to come to the White House, but was joined by family members of the deceased. "To those that are not here with me . . . thank you, fellas; well done, and I will always remember you."

Some years later, in the early spring of 2023, another Black soldier found himself on the front pages of American newspapers for a delayed recognition of his bravery.

In the summer of 1965, Paris Davis, an Army Special Forces

Green Beret, led his men on an attack mission inside Binh Dinh Province in South Vietnam. They were outnumbered. Though Davis was shot, he kept charging, swerving only to check on his men. He dragged as many as he could to safety, but then took another bullet. And shrapnel. A helicopter came. His men begged the bleeding Davis to board the chopper. He would not, instead remaining with his men to continue the assault. His men later told Davis's superiors that his battlefield bravery was worthy of the Medal of Honor. "And although"—as President Joe Biden said at the White House—"the men who were with him on that June day immediately nominated Captain Davis to receive the Medal of Honor, somehow the paper—the paperwork—was never processed, not just once, but twice." On March 3, 2023, when Paris Davis received the Medal of Honor from President Biden, he was eighty-three years old. He uttered not a single word of bitterness. Instead, he praised his men; he praised America.

Epilogue: The Secretary

Lloyd Austin III, confirmed as secretary of defense on January 22, 2021, still held that position when he welcomed me into his spacious, elegantly decorated Pentagon office.

Afternoon sunlight was streaming in through the windows. A tall and barrel-chested man, he is said to be equally comfortable on a battlefield and in a corporate boardroom. There have been notable figures holding the title Austin held at the time of our meeting—James Forrestal, George C. Marshall, Robert McNamara, and William Cohen among them. Austin, however, was the first Black American appointed to the position. It is a job, of course, charged with keeping America—and, when necessary, the world—safe.

There were various pictures of soldiers, past and present, arrayed around the secretary's office. One large framed picture was of Henry O. Flipper, the first Black graduate of West Point, who had endured all manner of racial indignities before his graduation in 1877. The writing beneath Flipper's photo: "He became the first non-white officer to lead the Buffalo Soldiers of the 10th Cavalry. He also served on frontier duty in the southwest which included scouting, post engineering surveyor, construction supervisor, acting assistant,

In 2021, Lloyd Austin, a celebrated general and onetime commander of United States Forces–Iraq, became America's first Black secretary of defense, nominated to the position by President Biden. His historic appointment caused many to look back over the long arc of Black patriotism and sacrifice.

post quartermaster, commissary officer." Austin, standing, gazed at Flipper: "He's from Thomasville, Georgia, and I'm from Thomasville," Austin said. "I often think of what all he went through. He graduated. He went on to do great things. I put myself in his shoes when I think about him."

As a four-star general, Secretary Austin sat in rare air; as a Black four-star, the air is even rarer. Just like his inspiration, Henry Flipper, Austin also graduated from West Point, Class of 1975. Months before Austin entered the academy in 1971, a group of Black cadets became aware that President Nixon, during a visit, had implored the school's superintendent, Major General William Knowlton, to erect a monument to Confederate soldiers on the post. Knowlton discussed the matter with Percy Squire, the most senior Black cadet at the time. Percy gathered all the Black cadets. They wrote up a "Manifesto," a letter to the academy, stating that they came to West Point with great expectations but had experienced "blatant racism." Among the demands in their manifesto, they wanted to be able to grow Afros. They wanted Black speakers to be invited to campus—not just Black military officers, but political and cultural figures. And they especially wanted the idea of that Confederate monument nixed. Superintendent Knowlton came to side with the Black cadets on their demands.

Lloyd Austin came about his interest in the military while he was growing up in a Southern landscape that was only a few years removed from de facto segregation, and an area surrounded by military bases. When he was a teenager, he said, "it was uncles and cousins who served in Vietnam who inspired me. My father's brother served in Vietnam as a Green Beret. I spent time talking to him about Vietnam. The fact that he was a Green Beret was really neat." As painful a war as Vietnam had been, Austin came to realize that it had created a new narrative about how America viewed the Black soldier. "Vietnam was the first time this country had witnessed troops led by African Americans," he said. "Vietnam was really the beginning."

By the time Austin graduated from West Point, the Vietnam War had wound down. But he came to find his wars: in the spring of 2003, he directed the 2nd Brigade Combat Team's assault on Baghdad. "Austin was the brains behind the assault on Baghdad" is how a senior military commander put it years later. "He was always pushing. Pushing, pushing, pushing. He was one of the finest combat commanders I've ever seen." In 2010, Austin was heading U.S. Forces–Iraq in the battle to defeat ISIS. His battlefield lore caught the attention of then Vice-President Biden, who, as president, came to nominate him as secretary of defense.

For all of America's political and cultural upheavals, both among its civilians and in the military, the Secretary was still an optimist regarding the military. He sensed that the military—pushed by the Black activism that erupted inside its ranks during the Vietnam War—was managing to do what the larger society has not been able to do: "It feels like a meritocracy," he said of the military, calling it an institution where talent is justly rewarded, which, in his mind, only raises performance levels.

In the late summer of 2022, Michael E. Langley—son of an Air

Force veteran—was confirmed as the first Black four-star general in the United States Marines. The nomination and confirmation were big news throughout military circles, inasmuch as the Marines had been noted for being the military branch that had fought integration efforts the most aggressively.

The nation at large, however, can be another matter when it comes to equality. There has been an alarming rise in hate crimes against Blacks, Jews, and other minorities around the country, and headline-making marches staged by white supremacists. The January 6, 2021, insurrection at the U.S. Capitol saw the appearance of Confederate flags and Nazi symbols on TV screens. No attack of such magnitude had happened at the Capitol since the War of 1812, when British troops attacked. "But think of what could have happened if we weren't helping to defend this democracy," Austin said of the military. "It all had a chance to descend into something less than democracy. What this country is about is what we are. It's what we're fighting for. We recognize there will be challenges, and they go up and down when it comes to race relations. It's clear to the people in uniform that they see this democracy as worth defending. I don't see the military as anything other than protecting this democracy, this Constitution."

On September 20, 2023, a little more than a year after the Langley appointment, the U.S. Senate confirmed the appointment of Charles Q. Brown—also nominated by President Biden—to become chairman of the Joint Chiefs of Staff. Brown, a former Air Force pilot, commander of the 8th Fighter Wing, and chief of staff of the Air Force, is, like Langley and Austin, a highly decorated officer. Like Secretary Austin, Brown had a close relative who served in Vietnam: his father, Charles Brown, Sr., was an Army officer who served two tours in Vietnam.

On some days, Austin, Brown, and Langley were all in Washington at the same time. Those who caught sight of them and recognized them couldn't help but realize something: They were three of the most powerful military men in the world. They are also men risen from the smoke of Vietnam. Men giving credence to both the power of history and meritocracy.

POSTSCRIPT

It is little wonder why, during the early months of 1863, Frederick Douglass remained so worried. The Civil War had stretched into its second year. Cannon fire echoed through valleys and blood flowed across the land as a result of the South's insurrection. The nation was coming apart, and there seemed no resolution in sight.

Douglass, born a slave and now a fervent abolitionist, had been roaming the country, pleading with audiences about the wisdom of recruiting Black soldiers to help save the nation. The war, he felt, would not be won as long as the North refused "to employ the black man's arm in suppressing the rebels." There were those who agreed with him, but the ultimate decision had to come from President Lincoln. In Philadelphia, Douglass pushed on: "Once let the black man get upon his person the brass letters, U.S.; let him get an eagle on his button, and a musket on his shoulder, and bullets in his pocket and there is no power on the earth or under the earth which can deny that he has earned the right of citizenship in the United States. I say again, this is our chance, and woe betide us if we fail to embrace it."

Lincoln brooded, but he finally came around. "The colored population is the great available and yet unavailed of, force for restoring

Black Civil War soldiers, who volunteered to save a nation, no matter that they were threatened with death by the Confederacy if captured. This history cannot be diminished or scrubbed away.

the Union," the president wrote. "The bare sight of fifty thousand armed, and drilled black soldiers on the banks of the Mississippi, would end the rebellion at once."

Military leaders in slaveholding states announced that if Black soldiers were captured their fate would either be bondage—or death. Fighting under a death sentence, the Black soldiers remained defiant, rewarding the president's confidence in them. Lincoln was actually too optimistic when it came to his predictions of the war's timeline: it did not end until 1865. But when it did end, there was no doubt of the importance Black soldiers had played in the victory. Their medals for valor would be passed down through generations of family members. Before and beyond the Civil War, Black soldiers have certainly proven their patriotic duty and passion on behalf of America. The preceding pages have covered but one of those wars.

What has long been clear, in recent decades at least, is that American presidents, of both political parties, have expressed appreciation of Black patriotism, aware of the twin battles those soldiers have so often been forced to fight. That narrative, however, took an ominous turn in early 2025 as Secretary of Defense Pete Hegseth and President Donald Trump assailed a cadre of gifted Black military leaders, going so far as to fire Chairman Charles Q. Brown of the Joint Chiefs of Staff. As well, a website purge saw the erasure of many notable Black and female achievements in the military. Trump and Hegseth have shown a robust affinity for Confederate iconography. These racially charged Trump-Hegseth moves—which reeked of the attitudinal white supremacy that has stained America for so long—stunned military veterans of all backgrounds. Intense conversations began throughout many Black communities about whether their sons and daughters should rethink possible military careers. No one imagined this to be a positive development for the nation's defense. As *Time* magazine put it, Trump's firings were "part of a campaign led by his defense secretary to rid the military of leaders who support diversity and equity in the ranks." Not since the administration of President Woodrow Wilson—who was an avowed segregationist—has a White House expended so much energy in assailing Blacks and other marginalized groups in the military and federal workforce.

The year 2026 is America's 250th anniversary. The years ahead will tell if the Trump-induced rupture is an aberration on the way to a more perfect union, or if the nation has altered the course of its recent military dynamism and racial progress all at the behest of a malevolent political force.

ACKNOWLEDGMENTS

The existence of this book owes so very much to Peter Gethers, my editor at Knopf. The conversations and written communiqués we had about the Vietnam War—and the politics and racial environment related to that war—were always probing, meaningful, and insightful. I wonder if there is a better editor anywhere. Esther Newberg, my literary agent, felt passionate about the subject matter covered in this book—an era she knows quite a bit about—and I am the beneficiary of her boundless support. Tom Mulvoy, my onetime editor at *The Boston Globe,* sent me around the country in 1984 to interview World War II veterans for the newspaper's special report on the fortieth anniversary of that war's end. The assignment deepened my interest in writing about war, as did subsequent sojourns covering civil wars as a foreign correspondent in Somalia and Liberia for the newspaper.

Also at Knopf, I wish to thank Jordan Pavlin, Kathy Zuckerman, John Gall, Morgan Hamilton, Meredith Dros, Angela Rose West, Terry Zaroff-Evans, and Nicole Pedersen.

This book is dedicated to two individuals. From the moment I mentioned this project to Gregory P. Crawford, president of

Miami University in Oxford, Ohio—where I've held the Wiepking and Boadway professorships—his enthusiasm and curiosity about military history became very evident. As well, Miami University's involvement in annually honoring the 1964 Freedom Summer marchers who went to Mississippi (they had gathered at Western College for Women, directly across the road from Miami in Oxford) has certainly informed some of the personal poignancy of my journey while piecing together this saga. I myself arrived on the Miami campus as a freshman in 1972, eight years after Freedom Summer. Some years back, I was invited to the Redstone Arsenal military base in Huntsville, Alabama, to give a lecture. The invitation was at the behest of Dennis L. Via, at the time commanding general of the United States Army Materiel Command. It was a fortuitous invitation: When I started this book, the now-retired General Via was among the first people I contacted. He opened many doors for me in my search for veterans of the Vietnam War. This years-long research and writing project was aided immensely by the emotional support of both Crawford and Via.

Dorothy Huston, of Huntsville, Alabama, hosted unforgettable gatherings for me while I was in her city. Her aunt Catherine Willis was often by her side. Both cared about this book, and I am grateful for their friendship.

Writing is a solitary vocation, and the opportunity to engage with students and professors at Miami of Ohio has given me great pleasure. The following either are currently at Miami or have been affiliated with it across these past years, and they belong on my marquee of gratitude: Chris Makaroff, Bruce Drushel, Richard Campbell, Rick Momeyer, Ron Scott, Renate Crawford, Dawn Tsirelis, Kathy Squance, Patricia Makaroff, Jenny Presnell (especially for the *Bloods* album transcription!), Rosemary Pennington, M. Cristina Alcalde, Valerie Hodge, Elizabeth Mullenix, Ted Pickerill, David Hodge, Phyllis Callahan, Jim Callahan, Deb Scott, James Tobin, and Patti Newberry.

There were many others who rooted from the sidelines during this journey, and they also have my deep thanks: Steve Flannigan, Andrew Sheehan, Professor Serena Williams of Widener University Delaware Law School, Paul Hendrickson, Bob Miller, Marcus Barnes, Mary Jo Conte, Nick Saunders, Tony Stigger, Pamela Oas Williams, Diane Stigger, Abby Franzen-Sheehan, Ben Bradlee, Jr., Lynn Peterson, Larry James, Wonda Haygood, Greg Moore, Donna James, Tina Moody, Faness Haygood Neff, Lee Daniels, Ceil Hendrickson, and Linda Via.

I'm grateful that I could count on Jessica Goldstein and Dr. Emma K. McNamara and Bill Orrico for tech support.

Be it at their home, or their officers' clubs—or even on a houseboat idling in the Potomac—all of the veterans interviewed for this book were unfailingly receptive in discussing a war that remains complex in memory for so many. Their continued close bonds with other members of their respective military units left me in awe. The following veterans all have my deep thanks for taking the time to talk with me: Steve Collins, Joe Anderson, Arthur Gregg, Dorothy Harris, Elbert Nelson, Earl Wood (who accompanied me on a hot summer's day to the Vietnam Memorial), Rodney Coates, Anthony Zinni, George Johnson, Reynolds Peele, Johnny Wilson (who first told me about The Rocks, the name of a club formed by Black officers in the military to emotionally support one another), Larry Gillespie, Clara Adams-Ender, Jimmy Jones, Charles Bolden, Jeffrey Mims, Donald Jones, Leonard Powell, Charles Allen, Wally Arnold, Robert Marshall, George Forrest, Newman Jackson, Fred Jones, Dennis Wilson, Robert Stewart, Sr., and Andrew Perkins.

Additionally, Danny Bivens, Harry Haygood, and Bruce Eddins—all military veterans—have my gratitude.

Finally, a bountiful burst of thanks to Brenda Reed, Eula Pitts, Janice Terry, David Terry, LaVonda Reed, Neva Dunn, Celestine Bolden, Mark Pitts, Bill Kurtis, and Robert Harris, who shared memories of either a veteran or a family member connected to the war in some way.

Notes

Abbreviations cited in notes:

NYT (*The New York Times*)
Author int. (Author interview)

Epigraph

vii "We have seen": Heather Cox Richardson, *Letters from an American,* Aug. 6, 2022 (online column).
vii "Long, long before": *Cornell Daily Sun, Sunspots,* Oct. 10, 2018.
vii "Vietnam was the": Author int., Austin.

Introduction

xii "We were three percent": Author int., Collins.
xiii "It was because": Ibid.
xiv "looked like a needle puncture": *Columbus Evening Dispatch,* May 7, 1970.
xvii "the inadvertent victim": *Life,* July 28, 1967.
xviii "I'm known throughout Africa": Haygood, *King of the Cats,* 200.
xx "Now I want": Clayborne Carson et al., eds., *Reporting Civil Rights, Part Two,* 550–51.
xx "They think they can": Ibid.
xx "Negroes better than anyone else": Cagin and Dray, *We Are Not Afraid,* 438.

Chapter One: Doc Nelson Lands in the War Zone

4 “I knew, if I hadn’t”: Author int., Nelson.
5 “Watts changed everything”: Ibid.
6 “Negroes could be heard”: Branch, *Pillar of Fire,* 593.
6 “May we have a word”: Branch, *At Canaan’s Edge,* 50.
7 “Troopers, advance”: Ibid., 51.
7 “I’ve never seen”: Branch, *Pillar of Fire,* 53.
8 “EYEWITNESS ACCOUNT”: *Los Angeles Times,* Aug. 14, 1965.
8 “the most terrifying thing”: Ibid.
8 “the four ugliest days”: Branch, *At Canaan’s Edge,* 293.
9 “Let’s get busy”: Sugrue, *Sweet Land of Liberty,* 375.
9 “We’ve just got to find”: Ibid.
9 “sinister and evil”: Branch, *At Canaan’s Edge,* 294.
9 “All we want”: Ibid., 297.
10 “I’m here,” King told: Ibid.
10 “The federal government”: Author int., Nelson.
10 “race problem”: Simon Hall, “Fidel Castro Stayed in Harlem 60 Years Ago to Highlight Racial Injustice in the U.S.,” *Smithsonian,* Sept. 18, 2020.
11 “Castro will have to”: Ibid.
11 “by going to a Negro hotel”: Ibid.
12 “We still have twenty chances”: Dobbs, *Midnights,* 107.
13 “In control of the case”: White, *A Man Called White,* 130–31.
13 “All I was told”: Author int., Nelson.
14 “given a Geneva card”: Ibid.
14 “a different kind of war”: Ward and Burns, *Vietnam War,* 211.
14 “The American military”: Bailey, *Army Afire,* 8.
14 “The American people have for years”: *Indianapolis Recorder,* Oct. 19, 1968.
15 “Many black officers”: Ibid.
15 “a synonym for Uncle Tom”: Ibid.
15 “I have been a good nigger”: Ibid.
15 “Negro Major Charges”: Bailey, *Army Afire,* 8.
15 “Army Denounced by Negro Major”: Ibid.
16 “Although it hurts”: Ibid., 26.
16 “When I publicly accused”: Ibid.
16 “a true-blue American boy”: *Washington Post,* Feb. 1, 1998.
17 “like long silver bullets”: Author int., Nelson.
17 “We sit and watch”: Terry, *Bloods,* 67.
18 “There was nothing”: Author int., Nelson.
18 “The AK-47”: Ibid.
18 “I was interested”: Ibid.
18 “When the fight”: Ibid.
19 “What I can say”: Ibid.
19 “A lot of the Black kids”: Ibid.
20 “this ‘white man’s war’ ”: Ibid.
20 “Those young Black boys”: Ibid.

20 "If I had to line up": Ibid.
21 "there were rebel flags": Author int., Jackson.
21 "We weren't the only ones": Author int., Nelson.
21 "Colored GIs": Pamphlet in possession of author.
21 "Is it possible": Author int., Nelson.
22 "two souls, two thoughts": Du Bois, *The Souls of Black Folk,* xvi.
22 "There are several parallels": Roberts and Klibanoff, *Race Beat,* 361.
22 "their own particular incubus": Eldridge, *Chronicles of a Two-Front War,* 44.

Chapter Two: Refuge in Soul Alley

26 "The white man says": Parks, *Voices in the Mirror,* 287.
27 "If you want to train me": Eldridge, *Chronicles of a Two-Front War,* 49.
27 "The demeanor of many": Bailey, *Army Afire,* 154.
29 "I don't want to go back": *Time,* Dec. 14, 1970.
29 "Just after the 1 a.m. curfew": Ibid.
30 "Man, the Army's": UPI wire, April 25, 1971.
30 "Yeh, man": Ibid.
30 "I tell them no": Ibid.
31 "Man, we figured": Ibid.
31 "A white guy": Ibid.
32 "I was feeling good": Ward and Burns, *Vietnam War,* 302.
32 "In other words": Callahan, ed., *Collected Essays of Ralph Ellison,* 585–86.
33 "My dating opportunities": MacPherson, *Long Time Passing,* 553.
34 "President Johnson wanted": Ibid., 560.
34 "I don't know whether": *Time,* May 26, 1967.
35 "We are for you": Ward and Burns, *Vietnam War,* 251.

Chapter Three: Ia Drang Is More Than Unforgiving

38 "My mother later": Author int., Forrest.
39 "My friends, let us not forget": Branch, *Parting the Waters,* 880.
39 "immoral compromises": Ibid.
39 "We will not be satisfied": Ibid., 881–82.
39 "Tell 'em about the dream": Ibid., 880.
39 "I say to you today": Ibid., 882.
39 "I have a dream": Ibid.
39 "And when this happens": Ibid., 882–83.
40 "You were guaranteed": Author int., Forrest.
41 "Face the music": Litwack, *Trouble in Mind,* 79.
42 "Hal, I'm moving": Moore and Galloway, *We Were Soldiers,* 38.
42 "Here is your area": Ibid.
44 "By God": Sheehan, *Bright Shining Lie,* 573.
44 "I had a strong sense": Moore and Galloway, *We Were Soldiers,* 66.
45 "As we were advancing": Ibid., 73.
45 "Between one-thirty": Ibid., 80.

45 "I could see these streams": Ward and Burns, *Vietnam War,* 136.
46 "The enemy knew": Moore and Galloway, *We Were Soldiers,* 85.
46 "I got a call": Author int., Forrest.
47 "And so we walked": Ibid.
47 "For safety": Ibid.
47 "This was the": Moore and Galloway, *We Were Soldiers,* 223.
47 "McDade said we'd be": Ibid., 239.
48 "I'm going forward": Ibid., 246.
48 "I gave the order": Ibid., 249.
48 "I found stacks": Ibid., 253.
48 "It was clear": Ibid., 256.
49 "I knew we were surrounded": Author int., Forrest.
49 "The firing was coming": Ibid.
49 "Our company commander": Moore and Galloway, *We Were Soldiers,* 265.
50 "They found us": Author int., Forrest.
51 "The peasant soldiers": Ward and Burns, *Vietnam War,* 139.
51 "I call them national treasures": Author int., Forrest.
51 "I went into a shell": Ibid.
52 "We had been fighting guerrillas": Ibid.

Chapter Four: In the Dark-Green Jungle, a Star Is Born

53 "I have an intuitive feeling": *Time,* May 26, 1967.
55 "My brother would bring": Author int., Anderson.
55 "Negroes in the Navy": Haygood, *Showdown,* 66–67.
56 "pretty well balanced": Kluger, *Simple Justice,* 398.
56 "To separate [Black children]": *Brown v. Board of Education,* 347 U.S. 483 (1954).
57 "We got a lot of people": Author int., Anderson.
59 "Freeman, the only": Buckley, *American Patriots,* 123.
59 "There was no society": Ibid.
59 "There's the colored": Ibid.
60 "Welcome, Lieutenant [Anderson]": *West Point Center for Oral History,* 2015 (online).
60 "No," he replied: Ibid.
61 "As we continue": *Guardian,* Dec. 8, 1965.
61 "I am not happy": Ward and Burns, *Vietnam War,* 146.
62 "Headquarters wanted me": Terry, *Bloods,* 220.
62 "This is my": Ibid.
62 "I can't remember": Ibid.
62 "There may have": Ibid., 219.
62 "A bloody massacre": Ibid.
63 "I was gung-ho": Ibid., 221.
63 "I was an officer": Ibid.
63 "For many black men": Ibid.
65 "I've always dreamed": *NYT,* April 22, 2004.

66 "not knowing who they were": *West Point Oral History,* 2015.
67 "one significant area of conflict": Author int., Anderson.
68 "I was there to keep them alive": Ibid.
68 "They were trained": Terry, *Bloods,* 226.
69 "We blocked a northern route": Ibid., 222.
69 "Whenever we would go": Ibid., 223.
70 "I went back": *The Anderson Platoon,* film, CBS, 1967.
70 "It began on a Sunday": Ibid.
71 "The mere sight": "TV Reporting: Men at War: A French View," *Time,* Feb. 17, 1967.
71 "It took the country by storm": *West Point Oral History,* 2015.
71 "a many-sided experience": *NYT,* Dec. 18, 1967.
72 "the ultimate stress": Ibid.
72 "abashes the white man": Haygood, *Colorization,* 121.
72 "Let no smug": Ibid., 122
73 "above all because": Oscar telecast, April 10, 1968.
73 " 'The Green Berets' ": *NYT,* June 20, 1968.
73 "the phoniest, most laughable": *San Francisco Examiner,* June 27, 1968.
73 "Being featured in": Terry, *Bloods,* 227.
74 "I think we're": Ward and Burns, *Vietnam War,* 246.
74 "What was very clear": Terry, *Bloods,* 226.

Chapter Five: The Piano Player Caught in a Racial Quagmire

75 "These children are": Ward and Burns, *Vietnam War,* 566.
77 "rum and roistering": Gates and Higginbotham, eds., *African American Lives,* 750.
77 "I'm a son-of-a-bitch": Talalay, *Composition,* 67.
78 "slur, lampoon, damn": Gates and Higginbotham, eds., *African American Lives,* 750.
78 "They found that Negroes": White, *A Man Called White,* 81.
79 "Don't wait for the train": Ibid., 82.
80 "Something marvelous has happened": Talalay, *Composition,* 19.
80 "You, living with": Ibid., 22.
80 "You've always had": Ibid., 23.
80 "The Cogdells were all miserable": Ibid., 38.
81 "Prodigious at more": Ibid., 51.
82 "I often speculate": Ibid., 75.
82 "Most of her concerts": Ibid., 77.
83 "We have, as": Ibid., 110.
83 "[I] encountered vicious barriers": Ibid., 112.
85 "What on earth": Ibid., 210.
85 "NOWHERE in my forthcoming book": Ibid., 224.
85 "30 miserable years": Ibid.
86 "Imagine if we had a child": Ibid., 234.
86 "brainchildren of crackpots": Ibid., 263.

87 "I have visited": Ibid., 266.
88 "A disfigured girl": Ibid., 267.
88 "looking for a place to sleep": Ibid., 270.
89 "Concerning bravery": Ibid., 274.
90 "If you can convince her": Ibid., 4.
91 "I can't swim": Ibid., 5.
92 "passing for white": Bailey, *Army Afire,* 107.
93 "Philippa matured": Ibid., 275.

Chapter Six: Wallace Terry's Special Saigon Assignment

95 "The problem is urgent": "The 1968 Kerner Commission Got It Right, But Nobody Listened," *Smithsonian,* March 1, 2018.
96 "The journalistic profession": Cobb and Guariglia, eds., *Kerner Report,* 258.
96 "virtually no Negroes": Ibid.
97 "a gamble and an adventure": Michaeli, *Defender,* 427.
98 "I'm all for": Ibid., 428.
98 "We shouldn't have": Ibid., 429.
98 "immorality": Ibid.
98 "You're not from around here": *New Yorker,* Dec. 12, 2017.
98 "In Vietnam, a Negro": *Ebony,* Nov. 1965.
100 "I'd buy Smith": *Washington Post,* July 12, 1984.
101 "When he would say": *The Ringer,* June 11, 2020.
102 " 'They killed Medgar' ": Author int., Janice Terry.
104 "my old Harlem neighborhood": *Time,* May 26, 1967.
104 "The tank I rode": Ibid.
104 "*Time* had never done": Author int., Janice Terry.
104 "By channeling the energies": *Time,* May 26, 1967.
104 "I had a sense of fear": Author int., Janice Terry.
104 " 'another Philippa Schuyler?' ": Ibid.
105 "These travels were": *Time,* Sept. 19, 1969.
105 "a war within a war": *Chicago Tribune,* April 12, 1987.
105 "but I think": *Washington Post,* July 12, 1984.
105 "There's a certain honesty": William Hammond, "Who Were the Correspondents and Does It Matter," *Shorenstein Center Paper,* Spring 1999 (online).
106 "It was exciting": Author int., Janice Terry.
106 "The black soldier": *Washington Post,* July 12, 1984.
106 "The younger generation": Ibid.
107 "Some of us were restricted": Author int., Newman Jackson.
107 "A lot of the Vietnamese": Ibid.
109 "We are finally": Cynthia Tucker, "A Place at the Table," *Columbia Journalism Review,* May–June 2007.
110 "What changed was": *Washington Post,* July 12, 1984.
110 "Many times I have found": *Time,* May 26, 1967.
111 "Yet in a time": Ward and Burns, *Vietnam War,* 394–96.
111 "Hedley Donovan betrayed me": Halberstam, *Powers That Be,* 484.

111 "The young black soldiers": *Harvard Crimson,* Oct. 8, 1970.
112 "Would you call your mother?": *Washington Post,* July 12, 1984.
112 "I just couldn't": Ibid.
112 "She didn't ask": Ibid.
112 "Black soldiers schooled": *Harvard Crimson,* Oct. 9, 1970.
113 "A frightening number": Ibid.
113 "A fight between": Ibid.
113 "Percentage wise, I believe": Ibid.
113 "There was another guy": All soldier quotes here from *Washington Post,* July 12, 1984.
114 "He was mourned": *NYT,* June 13, 1969.
115 "split the sky": Ward and Burns, *Vietnam War,* 267.
115 "Your press is lying": Ibid., 277.

Chapter Seven: The Gambler, the Segregationist, and the Withering of a Dream

117 "We believe the system": "Russell Building an Injustice," *Roll Call,* Jan. 17, 2003.
118 "Dick, I love": Updegrove, *Indomitable Will,* 55.
118 "I am not": Caro, *Passage of Power,* 402.
119 "We have seen white men": Heather Cox Richardson, *Letters from an American,* Aug. 6, 2022 (online).
119 "Everything I had ever learned": Goodwin, *Johnson and the American Dream,* 178.
119 "Do you want": Zeitz, *Building the Great Society,* 183.
120 "a great gamble": Ibid.
121 "The house's been on fire": Eig, *Ali,* 228–29.
121 "The fact is": Ibid., 231.
122 "grave consequences": Ward and Burns, *Vietnam War,* 104.
122 "Aggression by terror": Ibid., 105.
122 "Grandma's nightshirt": Ibid., 106.
122 "The ability of the Viet-Cong": Halberstam, *Best and Brightest,* 562.
123 "deploy even greater forces": Ward and Burns, *Vietnam War,* 125.
123 "a bombshell": Ibid.
123 "Of the thousands": Ibid.
124 " 'We're landing the Marines' ": Ibid., 116.
124 "there's no way out": Ibid.
124 "The day's operation": Ibid., 127–28.
124 "Hello, Frank": Ibid., 128.
125 "fight in Vietnam": Years 1954–1975, *Amistad Digital Science,* sect. 13 (online).
126 "first two months of 1966": Hendrickson, *The Living and the Dead,* 265.
126 "Hundreds of bridges": Ibid., 284.
126 "subterranean poor": MacPherson, *Long Time Passing,* 558.
127 "Looks to me": Tamara K. Nopper, "Military Service as Liberal Policing: A Brief Racial History of Project 100,000," *The Abusable Past,* Sept. 2, 2020 (online).
128 "Warfare is steadily": Gregory, *McNamara's Folly,* 119.

129 "We're asking Negroes": Carson Clayborne et al., eds., *Reporting Civil Rights, Part Two,* 504.
130 "McNamara is trying": Ibid., 552.
130 "Negroes are dying": Ibid.
130 "my fifth kill, dad": Ibid., 561.
130 "They deserved every bit": Ibid.
131 "The people who support the war": Ibid.
131 "we fought 300 years": Ibid., 562.
131 "It was as though": *Detroit News,* July 26, 1967.
131 "I never thought": Halberstam, *Best and Brightest,* 769.
132 "We were poor": Author int., Robert Marshall.
132 "My mother went": Ibid.
132 "In Oakland, California": Ibid.
133 "I think McNamara": MacPherson, *Long Time Passing,* 561.
134 "I thought I would feel": Terry, *Bloods,* 117.

Chapter Eight: A Murdered Minister and a Prison Revolt

135 "President Johnson has a serious problem": Branch, *At Canaan's Edge,* 23.
136 "You don't think": Ibid., 265.
136 "Lyndon Johnson, in fact": Ibid., 228.
137 "I talked about": *Time,* May 17, 2023.
137 "not your friend": Branch, *At Canaan's Edge,* 505.
137 "direct his entire efforts": Eig, *King,* 517.
138 "because my conscience": Ibid., 519.
138 "As I have walked": "Martin Luther King, Jr.: Beyond Vietnam: A Time to Break Silence (Declaration Against the Vietnam War)," n.d., *American Rhetoric* (online).
139 "I came to have": Author int., Nelson.
140 "No one ran away": Currey, *Long Binh,* 19.
140 "We were the first ones": Author int., Wilson.
141 "I'll handcuff": Currey, *Long Binh,* 40.
141 "Either go into the military": Arnett, "The Forgotten History of a Prison Uprising in Vietnam," *NPR,* Aug. 29, 2018 (online).
142 "During that time": Ibid.
142 "Why am I even over here?": Ibid.
142 "We were hot": Ibid.
143 "damn near a joke": Author int., Powell.
143 "a little caucus meeting": Currey, *Long Binh,* 113.
143 "got a lot of tunnels": Ibid., 105.
144 "a white man's war": Ibid., 110.
144 "There was a group": Ibid., 112.
144 "approximately 1300 hours": Ibid., 114.
144 "The synchronization": Ibid.
144 "We saw guards": Ibid., 115.
145 "I was kicked": Ibid., 116.

145 "when the riot hopped off": Ibid.
145 "About 15 or 20": Ibid., 117.
145 "We went outside": Ibid.
145 "Both Negro and white": Ibid., 118.
145 "Childress, he helped": Ibid.
146 "Kill the chucks!": Ibid., 117.
146 "We saw the Negroes": Ibid., 119.
146 "He was nice": Ibid., 58.
146 "Kill the guards": Ibid., 121.
147 "He was bleeding": Ibid., 125.
147 "They wouldn't listen": Ibid., 126.
148 "Do you want": Ibid.
148 "the records room was burned down": Ibid., 127.
148 "We bayoneted a lot of them": Ibid., 129.
148 "After one day": Ibid., 132.
148 "Guys went back": Ibid.
149 "Those blacks turned native": Ibid.
149 "None of the prisoners": Ibid., 130.
149 "At any point": Arnett, "Forgotten History."
149 "I said, 'Now'": Currey, *Long Binh,* 134.
149 "We never had": Ibid.
150 "I figured the records": Arnett, "Forgotten History."
150 "After the riot": Ibid.
150 "planned and unbridled": Currey, *Long Binh,* 115.
151 "I'm still angry": Arnett, "Forgotten History."
151 "Well, I have had it": Andrew J. Birtlee and John R. Mass, "The Drawdown," *Center of Military History, U.S. Army,* 2019, p. 46 (online).
151 "In the past year": Ibid.
152 "The problem was": "Another Uprising That Made a Difference: Travis Air Force Base, 1971," *Convergence,* July 1, 2020 (online).
153 "This was an incident": Ibid.
153 "As things stand": *San Mateo Times,* Nov. 16, 1971.

Chapter Nine: Dorothy Harris Would Like Another Coca-Cola, Please

154 "I also had older brothers": Author int., Harris, and all subsequent Harris quotes this chapter.
155 "Your application to the Army Nurse Corps": "The Army's First Black Nurses Were Relegated to Caring for Nazi Prisoners of War," *Smithsonian,* May 15, 2018 (online).
156 "the worst insult": Ibid.
157 "And then," Okamoto recalled: Ward and Burns, *Vietnam War,* 324.
159 "Same! Same!": *Time,* May 26, 1967.
160 "He used to": Author int., Eula Pitts.
160 "We all said": Author int., Harris.
161 And then it ping-ponged: Ward and Burns, *Vietnam War,* 324.

162 "One of them was Black": Author int., Eula Pitts.
163 "go to heaven": Ibid.
163 "And my minister": Ibid.
163 "What this man did": White House citation, n.d., courtesy of Eula Pitts. For those interested in viewing the newly discovered ABC video footage of Captain Riley "Leroy" Pitts, see *Nightline,* presented by Juju Chang and Byron Pitts, originally aired May 26, 2025, on ABC. As of this writing available at "Newly Discovered ABC Footage Helps Family Hear Late War Father's Voice Again," posted May 27, 2025, by ABC News, YouTube, https://www.youtube.com/watch?v=Z9Klu51g4Jg.

Chapter Ten: Fred Cherry Parachutes into Hell

167 "All day long": Terry, *Bloods,* 266.
169 "We were flying": U.S. Air Force, "Tuskegee Airman Gives Account of 'Lucky' Day," *U.S. Air Force,* Feb. 8, 2012 (online).
172 "I can assure you": Korean War Legacy Foundation, "Charles Rangel," video transcript (online).
172 "First United States Victory": Buckley, *American Patriots,* 352.
172 "1,000-pound bombs": Terry, *Bloods,* 269.
173 "a well-dressed woman": Clayborne Carson et al., eds., *Reporting Civil Rights, Part One,* 134.
173 "That demand, I thought": Ibid., 135.
174 "I had no problems": Terry, *Bloods,* 269.
174 "It was fast": Ibid.
174 "On a normal flight": Ibid.
175 "We have to knock it out": Hirsch, *Two Souls,* 22.
175 "I had to keep the wingman": Terry, *Bloods,* 271.
175 "like an eel": Hirsch, *Two Souls,* 15.
175 "I consider Captain Cherry": Ibid.
176 "loaded to the teeth": Ibid., 24.
176 "I felt my aircraft": *Suffolk News-Herald,* Feb. 17, 2016.
176 "Let's get the F[uck]": Terry, *Bloods,* 270.
176 "Just blew up": Ibid.
178 "For days we played games": Ibid., 275.
178 "I was an invalid": Ibid., 277.
179 "Our country has no capability": Hirsch, *Two Souls,* 36.
180 "Now they want me": Terry, *Bloods,* 282.
180 "never got to home plate": Ibid.
180 "solidarity and support": Hirsch, *Two Souls,* 155.
181 "a colonialist war": Ibid.
181 "The V were demanding": Ibid., 162.
182 "He became a legend": Ibid.
182 "The Vietnamese are very democratic": Ibid., 200.
182 "My whole day": "Retired General Recalls Vietnam Deployment Was His First Trip Out of U.S.," *U.S. Department of Defense,* March 29, 2021 (online).

182 "You begin to calculate": Ibid.
183 "believin' I was comin' home": Terry, *Bloods,* 287.
183 "I know how": Hirsch, *Two Souls,* 156.

Chapter Eleven: Some Badass Marines Are Humping the Hills Around Da Nang

185 "No Negro, Mulatto": "African-Americans in the United States Marine Corps Timeline," *National Museum of the Marine Corps,* p. 2 (online).
186 "Because we lived": Allison and Wheeler, eds., *Pathbreakers,* 7.
187 "a definite loss of efficiency": *Fortitudine* 37, no. 2 (2012): 16.
188 "The white Marines": Ibid., 7.
188 "we were mistreated": Delmont, *Half American,* 247.
188 "Mortar shells were": *Fortitudine,* 19.
188 "I watched those Negro boys": Delmont, *Half American,* 247.
188 "When the battle of Saipan": Ibid., 248.
189 "organized grab-ass": *Boston Globe,* Nov. 2, 1989.
190 "Left column!": Ibid.
191 "I remember standing": Allison and Wheeler, eds., *Pathbreakers,* 49.
191 "most blacks are signing up": Ibid., 50.
191 "and they were": Ibid., 66.
192 "on the duties": Description of the Basic School, in *Mission: Marines: The Official Website of the United States Marine Corps* (online).
193 "The task is nothing less": Ward and Burns, *Vietnam War,* 122.
193 "If the Marines": Author int., Peele.
193 "They are leather-tough": Author int., Perkins.
194 "a bucket with a hole": Allison and Wheeler, eds., *Pathbreakers,* 99.
194 "calm, quiet fearlessness": Author int., Zinni.
194 "There were four": *WUNC, North Carolina Public Radio,* July 19, 2019 (online).
194 "The Marine Corps are returning": *NYT,* Aug. 10, 1969.
195 "Large secluded areas": Ibid.
195 "Most of them were on edge": *WUNC, North Carolina Public Radio,* July 19, 2019 (online).
195 "one thing about the Armed Forces": Ibid.
195 "marked low in loyalty": Allison and Wheeler, eds., *Pathbreakers,* 99.
196 "Walking tall!": Author int., Stewart, and all subsequent Stewart quotes this chapter.
200 "While struggling to": *Marine Times,* Oct. 8, 2020.
200 "Barely able to stand": Ibid.

Chapter Twelve: A Dancing Motown Comes to See the Blood on the Wall

205 "I don't know how many": *NYT,* May 26, 1971.
205 "No one who was there": Ibid.
205 "He was really close": Ibid.
206 "The brass wanted": Ibid.

207 "depression caused by": Ibid.
207 "Subject expressed doubts": Ibid.
207 "[Johnson] didn't confide": Ibid.
207 "This guy lives": Ibid.
208 "Congressional Medal of Honor Society": Ibid.
208 "He was exposed": *Washington Post,* March 21, 1977.
208 "was an effort": Ibid.
208 "Black Forum is a medium": Amar Patel, "The Sound of Struggle," *I Make Sense: Missives on Media, Marketing and More,* March 1, 2021 (online).
209 "I'm angry . . .": *Michigan Quarterly,* Fall 2010.
210 "taking things too far": Ibid.
210 "For months they wouldn't": Ibid.
211 "vast, melodically deft": William McKeen, ed., *Rock and Roll Is Here to Stay: An Anthology* (New York: Norton, 2000), 532.
213 "To see the conflict": *Time,* June 28, 1971.
214 "And the Bloods": Liner notes, *Guess Who's Coming Home: Black Fighting Men Recorded Live in Vietnam,* Motown, 1972.
215 "This album is real": Ibid.
215 "I woke up": From album recording.
217 "T. S. Eliot": White and Ales, *Motown,* 277.
218 "Everyone said": Author int., Janice Terry.
219 "hoping the people": *Washington Post,* May 18, 1986.
219 "They were looking": Ibid.
220 "I lost 22 close friends": Ibid., July 12, 1984.

Chapter Thirteen: Requiem for Art Gregg

222 "and still counting": Author int., Gregg, and all subsequent Gregg quotes this chapter, except where noted.
227 "The war is not going well": Vietnam Hearings, U.S. Senate, Jan. 24, 1966 (online).
228 "The first point": Ward and Burns, *Vietnam War,* 148.
229 "This is correct": Ibid., 148–49.
229 "I was not only naïve": Hendrickson, *The Living and the Dead,* 167.
229 "We face a situation": Ward and Burns, *Vietnam War,* 175.
230 "These are the dudes": Ibid.
231 "A popular political base": Evans et al., *American Century,* 532–33.
233 "Indeed, the white troops": Buckley, *American Patriots,* 107.
236 "names, symbols, displays": *NYT,* Aug. 10, 2022.
237 "I still get": Robert Philpot, "From No Electricity to Three Stars," *Xchange Newsroom,* Jan. 25, 2024 (online).

Chapter Fourteen: Mr. Jellybean, in Twilight

238 "Boys I know": *NYT,* Jan. 19, 1968.
240 "Cronkite came down": *The Atlantic,* July 1973.

240 "I'm going to enjoy": Ibid.
241 "I've served my time": Ibid.
242 "I took 4 million people": *NYT,* Oct. 31, 1971.
242 "I make no pretense": *NYT,* May 14, 1971.
243 "But where Lyndon": *NYT,* Oct. 31, 1971.
243 "as a study": Ibid.
243 "except the man himself": *Texas Monthly,* Jan. 1976.
243 "a guarded, self-serving": *The Atlantic,* Feb. 1, 1972.
243 "History, with the bark off": "History with the Bark Off: LBJ Presidential Library Celebrates 50 Years," *Texas Standard,* May 21, 2021 (online).
244 "Another mistake": *The Atlantic,* July 1973.
245 "How is it": Updegrove, *Indomitable Will,* 237–38.
246 "Johnson felt particularly": Ibid., 238.
247 "We are on our way": Lyndon Johnson, "Final Speech at a Civil Rights Symposium," *American Rhetoric,* Dec. 12, 1972 (online).
248 "I knew from the start": Goodwin, *Johnson and the American Dream,* 251–52.
248 "Yet everything I know": Ibid., 252.

Chapter Fifteen: A Mirage and an Endgame

252 "He'll get his degree": *Jet,* special ed., Nov. 7, 1968.
252 "They provide most": Buckley, *American Patriots,* 411.
252 "We can't show": Ibid.
253 "Nixon is a low-brow": Farrell, *Richard Nixon,* 476.
254 "Present programs often": Kluger, *Simple Justice,* 764.
255 "There is little question": Ibid., 765.
255 "want instant integration": Ibid., 766.
255 "All things being equal": *Time,* May 3, 1971.
255 "He is fed up": Farrell, *Richard Nixon,* 473.
256 "Now, everybody around here": Ibid., 477.
256 "My faith in": Evans et al., *American Century,* 598.
257 "I would rather": *Harvard Crimson,* June 6, 1995.
257 "can't end the war": "Vietnam Background: Congress and the War: Years of Support," *CQ Almanac* (online), 1975.
257 "Every president needs": Evans et al., *American Century,* 577.
257 "I'm not a crook": *Washington Post,* November 18, 1973.
258 "In the past four": Buckley, *American Patriots,* 425.
258 "Only 30 percent of us": Ward and Burns, *Vietnam War,* 479.
258 "I don't think": Ibid., 480.
258 "Lady," came the reply, "we *are*": Ibid.
259 "They told the stories": Ibid.
259 "They only wanted": John Kerry, speech before Senate Foreign Relations Committee, April 22, 1971, U.S. Oratory Project, *Voices of Democracy* (online).
259 "We found also": Ibid.
260 "We can lose the summit": Ward and Burns, *Vietnam War,* 500.
261 "the shirt off his back": Evans et al., *American Century,* 591.

262 "I am an American fighting man": Hirsch, *Two Souls,* 245.
262 "the home of": Ibid., 243.

Chapter Sixteen: Some Are Asking: Who the Hell Is Maude DeVictor?

263 "Let the public": Severo and Milford, *Wages of War,* 21.
264 "Soldiers, I tell you": Ibid., 160.
265 "I am about to be mustered": Ibid.
265 "for an hour": Ibid., 131.
265 "If we give special status": Ibid., 284.
266 "in a spirit of gratitude": *NYT,* April 1, 1973.
266 "There were none": Ibid.
267 "When a man": Ward and Burns, *Vietnam War,* 410.
267 "Tens of thousands": *NYT,* May 16, 1971.
268 "A country boy": *New York,* June 3, 2019.
268 "Kind of sonofabitch": Ibid.
269 "This Is Nicky": *NYT,* June 5, 1977.
269 "He then proceeded": Ibid.
271 "We realized collectively": MacPherson, *Long Time Passing,* 570.
271 "You want to": *Harper's Magazine,* April 2016.
271 "The direct cause": MacPherson, *Long Time Passing,* 571.
272 "seriously inadequate": Severo and Milford, *Wages of War,* 356.
273 "Part of my job": Ibid., 360.
273 "those chemicals in Vietnam": Ibid., 364.
273 "true incident of significant exposure": Ibid.
274 "with extreme concern": Ibid., 365.
276 "She had accumulated": Author int., Kurtis, and all subsequent Kurtis quotes this chapter.
277 "You've got to": *Veteran Newsletter,* VVAW, Fall 2019 (online).
278 "A chemical defoliant": "Agent Orange—Vietnam's Deadly Fog," aired March 23, 1978, *WBBM* (Chicago) (available online).
278 "The VA doesn't": *The Progressive,* Dec. 12, 2016.
279 "All VA personnel": Severo and Milford, *Wages of War,* 366.
279 "To date there is no": Ibid., 369.
279 "She literally became": Barry Romo, "Recollections of Maude DeVictor," *The Veteran,* Fall 2019 (online).
280 "I'm pretty sure": Ibid.
280 "lipstick on your husband's shirt": *Los Angeles Times,* March 31, 1985.
280 "We loved her": Romo, "Recollections."

Chapter Seventeen: Flashback: 105 Degrees and Rising

282 "They didn't need": Ward and Burns, *Vietnam War,* 535.
282 "We would look": Ibid., 536.
283 "The entire complexion": Ibid.
283 "give Vietnam away": Ibid., 538.

283 "The ambassador couldn't believe": Ibid.
283 "For reasons of prudence": Ibid., 540.
284 "The one ending": Ibid., 541.
284 "He desperately wanted": Ibid., 542.
284 "I vow to hold": Ibid.
284 "The U.S. spent billions": Ibid., 544.
285 "not one nickel for military aid": Ibid.
285 "I briefed American journalists": Ibid., 545.
285 "The situation didn't": Ibid.
286 "to the last bullet": Ibid., 546.
286 "You Americans with": Ibid.
286 "We began going": Ibid., 547.
287 "The string had run out": Ibid., 549.
287 "like a hurricane": Ibid.
287 "He was terribly enfeebled": Ibid., 551.
288 "on the arrogant side": Allison and Wheeler, eds., *Pathbreakers,* 44.
288 "I said, 'Major' ": Ibid., 46.
288 "Do you think": Ibid., 90.
289 "I enjoyed—frankly": Ibid., 91.
289 "My people and": Author int., Jones.
289 "The ambassador kept": Ibid.
289 "a direct hit": Ward and Burns, *Vietnam War,* 552.
289 "The temperature in Saigon": Ibid., 553.
289 "We had to get chain saws": Ibid.
290 "We finally realized": Author int., Jones.
290 "a lot of Vietnamese on board": Ward and Burns, *Vietnam War,* 555.
291 "Some Americans had left": Ibid., 557.
291 "The accumulated weight": Ibid.
291 "Better to let": Ibid., 559.
292 "When South Vietnam started to fall": Terry, *Bloods,* 213.
292 "They told me": Ibid.

Chapter Eighteen: The Long Way Home from a Long War

293 "a child prodigy": Description of the school, *Philippaschuyler383.org* (online).
295 "The irony of that job": Author int., Forrest, and all subsequent Forrest quotes this chapter.
296 "I was fearless!": Author int., Harris.
296 "I asked people": Ibid.
298 Captain Riley "Leroy" Pitts: "Newly Uncovered ABC Footage Helps Family Hear Late War Hero Father's Voice Again," *Nightline,* May 26, 2025 (available online).
299 "My late wife": Author int., Gregg.
299 "We did not have a victory": Ibid.
300 "He would go": Author int., Brenda Reed.
300 "But he wouldn't go": Ibid.

300 "suffered from Agent Orange": Ibid.
300 "scared every moment": *Washington Post,* June 1, 2003.
301 "These men learned": Ibid.
302 "The four of us": Hirsch, *Two Souls,* 217.
303 "The USO club for Blacks": Author int., Nelson.
303 "I sort of stayed away": Ibid.
303 "Agent Orange was sprayed": Ibid.
304 "all about creating wealth": Author int., Anderson.
304 "I want my legacy": Ibid.
305 "While crawling forward": Freddie Stowers citation, *Congressional Medal of Honor Society* (online).
305 "To those that are not": *Time,* Oct. 14, 2015.

Epilogue: The Secretary

308 "He's from Thomasville": Author int., Austin.
308 "blatant racism": Bailey, *Army Afire,* 270.
309 "it was uncles and cousins": Author int., Austin.
309 "Vietnam was the first time": Ibid.
309 "Austin was the brains": "Lloyd Austin Isn't Who You Think He Is," *Foreign Policy,* Dec. 16, 2020 (online).
309 "It feels like a meritocracy": Author int., Austin.
310 "But think of": Ibid.

Postscript

311 "to employ the black man's arm": Goodwin, *Team of Rivals,* 549.
311 "Once let the black man": Ibid., 550.
311 "The colored population": Ibid., 549.
313 "part of a campaign": *Time,* Feb. 22, 2025.

Bibliography

Allison, Fred H., and Col. Kurtis P. Wheeler, USMCR, eds. *Pathbreakers: U.S. Marine African American Officers in Their Own Words.* Washington, D.C.: History Division United States Marine Corps, 2013.

Bailey, Beth. *An Army Afire: How the US Army Confronted Its Racial Crisis in the Vietnam Era.* Chapel Hill: University of North Carolina Press, 2023.

Baldwin, James. *The Price of the Ticket: Collected Nonfiction, 1948–1985.* New York: St. Martin's/Marek, 1985.

Branch, Taylor. *At Canaan's Edge: America in the King Years, 1965–1968.* New York: Simon & Schuster, 2006.

———. *Parting the Waters: America in the King Years, 1954–1963.* New York: Simon & Schuster, 1988.

———. *Pillar of Fire: America in the King Years, 1963–1965.* New York: Simon & Schuster, 1998.

Buckley, Gail. *American Patriots: The Story of Blacks in the Military from the Revolution to Desert Storm.* New York: Random House, 2002.

Cagin, Seth, and Philip Dray. *We Are Not Afraid: The Story of Goodman, Schwerner, and Chaney and the Civil Rights Campaign for Mississippi.* New York: MacMillan, 1988.

Callahan, John F., ed. *The Collected Essays of Ralph Ellison.* New York: Modern Library, 1995.

Caro, Robert A. *The Years of Lyndon Johnson: Master of the Senate.* New York: Knopf, 2002.

———. *The Years of Lyndon Johnson: The Passage of Power.* New York: Knopf, 2012.

———. *The Years of Lyndon Johnson: The Path to Power.* New York: Knopf, 1982.

Clayborne, Carson, with David Garroway, Bill Kovach, Carol Polsgrove (Advisory

Board), eds. *Reporting Civil Rights, Part One: American Journalism, 1941–1963.* New York: Library of America, 2003.

———. *Reporting Civil Rights, Part Two: American Journalism, 1963–1973.* New York: Library of America, 2003.

Cobb, Jelani, with Matthew Guariglia, eds. *The Essential Kerner Commission Report.* New York: Liveright, 2021.

Currey, Cecil Barr. *Long Binh Jail: An Oral History of Vietnam's Notorious U.S. Military Prison.* Washington, D.C.: Brassey's, 1999.

Delmont, Matthew F. *Half American: The Epic Story of African Americans Fighting World War II at Home and Abroad.* New York: Viking, 2022.

Dobbs, Michael. *One Minute to Midnight.* New York: Knopf, 2008.

Du Bois, W.E.B. *The Souls of Black Folk.* New York: Modern Library, 2003.

Eig, Jonathan. *Ali: A Life.* New York: Houghton Mifflin Harcourt, 2017.

———. *King: A Life.* New York: Farrar, Straus and Giroux, 2023.

Eldridge, Lawrence Allen. *Chronicles of a Two-Front War: Civil Rights and Vietnam in the African American Press.* Columbia and London: University of Missouri Press, 2011.

Evans, Harold, with Gail Buckland and Kevin Baker. *The American Century.* New York: Knopf, 2000.

Farrell, John A. *Richard Nixon: The Life.* New York: Doubleday, 2017.

Faas, Horst, and Tim Page. *Requiem: By the Photographers Who Died in Vietnam and Indochina.* New York: Random House, 1997.

Fitzgerald, Frances. *Fire in the Lake: The Vietnamese and the Americans in Vietnam.* New York: Back Bay Books, 1972.

Gates, Henry Louis, Jr., and Evelyn Brooks Higginbotham, eds. *African American Lives.* Oxford, U.K., and New York: Oxford University Press, 2004.

Goodwin, Doris Kearns. *Lyndon Johnson and the American Dream.* New York: St. Martin's Press, 1976.

———. *Team of Rivals: The Political Genius of Abraham Lincoln.* New York: Simon & Schuster, 2005.

Gregory, Hamilton. *McNamara's Folly: The Use of Low-IQ Troops in the Vietnam War.* West Conshohocken, Pa.: Infinity, 2015.

Halberstam, David. *The Best and the Brightest.* New York: Penguin, 1983.

———. *The Powers That Be.* New York: Knopf, 1979.

Haygood, Wil. *In Black and White: The Life of Sammy Davis, Jr.* New York: Vintage, 2020.

———. *King of the Cats: The Life and Times of Adam Clayton Powell, Jr.* Boston: Houghton Mifflin, 1993.

———. *Showdown: Thurgood Marshall and the Supreme Court Nomination That Changed America.* New York: Knopf, 2015.

Hendrickson, Paul. *The Living and the Dead: Robert McNamara and Five Lives of a Lost War.* New York: Knopf, 1996.

Hirsch, James S. *Two Souls Indivisible.* Boston: Mariner, 2005.

Kluger, Richard. *Simple Justice: The History of Brown v. Board of Education and Black America's Struggle for Equality.* New York: Knopf, 1976.

Litwack, Leon F. *Trouble in Mind: Black Southerners in the Age of Jim Crow.* New York: Knopf, 1998.

MacPherson, Myra. *Long Time Passing: Vietnam and the Haunted Generation.* New York: Anchor, 1984.

Marable, Manning. *Malcolm X: A Life of Reinvention.* New York: Viking, 2011.

Maraniss, David. *They Marched into Sunlight.* New York: Simon & Schuster, 2003.

Michaeli, Ethan. *The Defender: How the Legendary Black Newspaper Changed America.* Boston and New York: Houghton Mifflin Harcourt, 2016.

Moore, Harold G., and Joseph L. Galloway. *We Were Soldiers Once . . . and Young: Ia Drang—the Battle That Changed the War in Vietnam.* New York: Ballantine, 1992.

Nguyen, Viet Thanh. *The Sympathizer.* New York: Grove Press, 2015.

Parks, Gordon. *Voices in the Mirror: An Autobiography.* New York: Doubleday, 1990.

Powell, Colin, with Joseph E. Persico. *My American Journey.* New York: Ballantine, 1995.

Roberts, Gene, and Hank Klibanoff. *The Race Beat: The Press, the Civil Rights Struggle, and the Awakening of America.* New York: Knopf, 2006.

Severo, Richard, and Lewis Milford. *The Wages of War: When America's Soldiers Came Home—from Valley Forge to Vietnam.* New York: Simon & Schuster, 1989.

Sheehan, Neil. *A Bright Shining Lie: John Paul Vann and America in Vietnam.* New York: Random House, 1988.

Sugrue, Thomas J. *Sweet Land of Liberty: The Forgotten Struggle for Civil Rights in the North.* New York: Random House, 2008.

Talalay, Kathryn. *Composition in Black and White: The Life of Philippa Schuyler.* Oxford, U.K., and New York: Oxford University Press, 1995.

Terry, Wallace. *Bloods: Black Veterans of the Vietnam War: An Oral History.* New York: Ballantine, 1984.

Updegrove, Mark K. *Indomitable Will: LBJ in the Presidency.* New York: Crown, 2012.

Ward, Geoffrey C., and Ken Burns. *The Vietnam War: An Intimate History.* New York, Knopf, 2017.

Weaver, Kendal. *Ten Stars: The African American Journey of Gary Cooper—Marine General, Diplomat, Businessman and Politician.* Montgomery, Ala.: NewSouth Books, 2016.

White, Adam, and Barney Ales. *Motown: The Sound of Young America.* New York: Thames & Hudson, 2016.

White, Walter. *A Man Called White.* New York: Viking, 1948.

Zeitz, Joshua. *Building the Great Society: Inside Lyndon Johnson's White House.* New York: Penguin, 2019.

INDEX

Page numbers in *italics* refer to illustrations.

IMAGE CREDITS

Page xii: Photo courtesy of Skip Dunn family
Page 4: Photo courtesy of Dr. Elbert Nelson family
Page 25: Photographer unknown
Page 37: Photo courtesy of George Forrest
Page 54: Photo courtesy of Joseph Anderson
Page 58: Photo courtesy of USMA Library Archives and Special Collections
Page 76: © Fred Palumbo, *World Telegram* staff photographer, public domain, via Wikimedia Commons
Page 95: © Alconte, CC BY-SA 3.0 <http://creativecommons.org/licenses/by-sa/3.0/>, via Wikimedia Commons
Page 117: Photo courtesy of U.S. Senate Historical Office
Page 136: © NARA photo 111-CCV-435-CC81143, public domain, via Wikimedia Commons
Page 155: Photo courtesy of Dorothy Harris family
Page 155: Photo courtesy of Leroy Pitts family
Page 168: © United States Air Force, public domain, via Wikimedia Commons
Page 186: Photo courtesy of Henry Reed family
Page 186: Photo courtesy of Robert Stewart
Page 202: © Jim Britt. Originally distributed by Motown Records, public domain, via Wikimedia Commons.
Page 203: © Walter P. Reuther Library, Archives of Labor and Urban Affairs, Wayne State University
Page 223: © Photo courtesy of Art Gregg

Page 228: Photo courtesy of U.S. Senate Historical Office

Page 239: © Lyndon Baines Johnson Library and Museum. Image Serial Number: W425-21. http://photolab.lbjlib.utexas.edu/detail.asp?id=9853

Page 251: © Warren K. Leffler, public domain, via Wikimedia Commons

Page 252: © Richard Nixon Presidential Library and Museum

Page 264: © USAF, public domain, via Wikimedia Commons

Page 282: © United States Navy—https://www.history.navy.mil/content/history/nhhc/research/publications/publications-by-subject/End-of-the-Saga.html, Public Domain, https://commons.wikimedia.org/w/index.php?curid=84235105

Page 294: © USMC, public domain, via Wikimedia Commons

Page 308: Public domain, no credit required, by SPC Kiyoshi Freeman, identified by DVIDS

Page 312: © Library of Congress, attribution, public domain, via Wikimedia Commons

A NOTE ABOUT THE AUTHOR

Wil Haygood has been recognized as one of America's foremost chroniclers of history where it intersects with the saga of race, investigation, memory, and truth. The author of ten books, he has received writing fellowships from the John Simon Guggenheim Memorial Foundation, the National Endowment for the Humanities, the Alicia Patterson Foundation, and the Starr Center for the Study of the American Experience at Washington College. His longtime journalism career—which took him around the world and into several war zones—was spent largely at *The Boston Globe,* where he was a Pulitzer Prize finalist, and *The Washington Post,* where he won numerous awards. He has written acclaimed biographies of Adam Clayton Powell, Jr., Sammy Davis, Jr., Sugar Ray Robinson, and Thurgood Marshall. Haygood wrote *The Butler: A Witness to History,* which was adapted into the award-winning film *The Butler,* directed by Lee Daniels and starring, among others, Forest Whitaker and Oprah Winfrey. His *Colorization: One Hundred Years of Black Films in a White World* was named a *New York Times* Critics' Top Book of the Year.

In 2022, Wil Haygood was awarded the Ambassador Richard C. Holbrooke Distinguished Achievement Award, an international prize bestowed by the Dayton Literary Peace Prize Foundation, whose recipients have included, among others, Margaret Atwood, John Irving, Colm Tóibín, and President Jimmy Carter.

A NOTE ON THE TYPE

This book was set in Adobe Garamond. Designed for the Adobe Corporation by Robert Slimbach, the fonts are based on types first cut by Claude Garamond (ca. 1480–1561). Garamond was a pupil of Geoffroy Tory's and is believed to have followed the Venetian models, although he introduced a number of important differences, and it is to him that we owe the letter we now know as "old style." He gave to his letters an elegance and feeling of movement that won him an immediate reputation and the patronage of Francis I of France.

Composed by North Market Street Graphics,
Lancaster, Pennsylvania

Designed by Michael Collica